I Once Was Lost

A True Story

By

FRED MOORE

ARTS
COUNCIL
WINSTON-SALEM FORSYTH COUNTY

JOMA

DEDICATION

This book is dedicated to the memory of my mother, Mrs. Florence Nekoda Sherard Moore, who lived an exemplary life, was a steady presence in the face of a hurricane, and who was the embodiment of compassion and forgiveness.

Also to my only sister Johnetta, for giving me the first words of inspiration while I was inside when she said, "Boy, you need to write a book!" To my brother, Johnny Boy (Moe), who encouraged me to take the manuscript out of its two-year entombment in my bottom drawer; to my two older brothers, Calvin and Winston, who provided crucial support when I needed it; to my very best friends, Jerry and Paula, for demonstrating unconditional friendship; and to Keith, for lifelong friendship, who came to see me more than once when I was inside.

ACKNOWLEDGMENTS

I want to thank all my family and friends who read the first rough draft and were helpful in pointing me in the right direction; to John and Shelley, who have been there as professional and social advocates from the beginning; to Pastor Mike, who extended fellowship from the inside to the outside; to my editor, Peg Robarchek, for her demand for excellence and her ability to make some sense out of a jumbled document; and to all those whose names have been changed, but are integral to the narrative of this book; and to artist Doug Brown, who designed the cover illustrations.

I also want to acknowledge the support of JOMA Arts & Consulting, LLC, which works on independent or collaborative efforts to create artistic productions or events.

I also want to acknowledge that this project was made possible by The Arts Council of Winston-Salem and Forsyth County and the North Carolina Arts Council, a division of the Department of Cultural Resources.

i

PROLOGUE

They were walking toward nowhere. Just another day trying to put something together to get a blast. Most of their days were spent this way, going from one place to another, by car or on foot, living from house to house, sleeping whenever and wherever they could because that's the way it was. Living this way came with the territory.

"Man, we got to get us a hustle somewhere!" one says.

"What kind of transport can we get?" asks the other. Each of them tired of walking, each of them tired of being broke.

"Well, I know a place where we can get a truck, but you gotta help."

"What you think I'm gonna do, just stand around? Where this place at? Can we walk there from here? Is it gonna take long?" The need, the urgency, the want, resonating in the timbre of their voices. Having been denied access to money, dope and a ride for as long as they had been, who wouldn't be on edge?

"Sure, we can walk there from here but, you know, it's best to wait til dark before we do anything. It'll give us, you know, a better chance of gettin' this done." The phrase "gettin' this done" being code for not getting caught, which is a consequence of high probability if you're found where you're not supposed to be, doing what you're not supposed to be doing. What if when you get there, the truck you had in mind is not there or what if the truck is there, but the exit is absolutely secure or what if everything is as it should be and things go as they should go, but you're spotted leaving the

1

place at three or four in the a.m.? Everybody know don't nobody come in or out of there until after seven.

What then?

03 80

Now, these two have the not-so-difficult task of idling a few hours away before they can begin their questionable affairs.

They are interested in this type of activity for an outcome they will pursue continually, endlessly: getting the goods or the money to exchange for crack. This is the always-has-been-and-always-will-be motivation for why they do what they do. "Man, I ain't have no money or nothing, so I went and did what I had to do so I could go get what I had to get. I had to get my 'medication'!"

And really, that's what it was. An elixir, a prescription, a real "Dr. Feel Good" that could be provided nowhere else by nobody else. It had to be had at any and all cost, at any and all risk. You wanna sell your soul, sell it. You wanna sell your children, sell 'em. You wanna sell your ass, sell it. It's all the same because this potion makes it all worthwhile. With the exception of eating, sleeping, pissing and shitting, getting dope is what life was all about. So, the answer to the question of what to do for now was a no-brainer.

One of them knows of a house that is unoccupied. The residents are either out of town or gone for an extended period of time. He knows this because he always scouts the locale, maybe two or three blocks around, certainly within walking distance, of wherever he's smoking so that when he runs out, he has an idea where a hustle could be made. This particular place was wide open. He knew this because he had asked a neighbor certain discreet questions earlier that day.

03 80

"Excuse me," he had said to the neighbor after knocking on the door, "I know that Will over there works on cars. I'm wondering if you can tell me where his shop is?" Of course, he already knew where the shop was; what he really needed was just one more bit of information.

"It's up on Patterson, just a couple of blocks over from here, up by the check cashing place. Why you ask?" the neighbor inquired,

2

demonstrating her community crime-watch instincts. What with strangers coming by and people being so mean, you never can be too careful, she was thinking.

"Well, he told me to stop by here today before he went to his shop. I been by twice already, but no one seems to be home. I called the shop and they said he was away, but didn't know for how long. Do you have any idea of his whereabouts?"

The neighbor paused for a moment. He seemed like a nice young man. "He'll be out of town for the next few days. I wouldn't check back by here 'til maybe the weekend or so. He ought to be back by then."

"Well, thanks so much. I 'preciate all your help. You take care and I'll check back by here next week, okay?"

"Okay, son, I'll tell him you asked about him."

We in there!

ᘓ ᘔ

"So, what we gonna do 'til it's time to check out this thing you talking about?" the other asks, a little annoyed. He was in the midst of crashing. That place where you can't go to sleep, but you really want to, when you're so tired, but you just can't rest, when you really don't want more dope, but you're under an irrational compulsion to get more dope. It's a place of intense irritability which can only be dissipated by making moves to get dope. It is a toxic, poisonous mental space no different from Satan's playground.

He thinks to himself, I ain't had a hit since this morning and now I gotta wait 'til later before I can make another move. Damn! I wish I could just let this shit go. This dude here says he's gonna help me get right, but what that's gonna cost? I been gone from the house since day before yesterday and I know everybody's wondering where the hell I'm at. Is he dead? Is he in jail? Is he hurt or what? And look at me, out here chasin' this shit like I ain't got no sense at all. I must ain't got none, 'cause I keep doing this same ol' dumb shit over and over and over.

"Actually," the first one replies, "I've got a little lick myself that I've been checkin' out and this just might be the time to see what's up with that. C'mon, let's take a walk."

And so it was that two relative strangers came to a common understanding.

CB BO

Will's house was a 10 minute walk from where they were. This was a local residence where crackheads got together and smoked. Some had jobs, many didn't. All of them were looking for a hustle, something, anything to get some dope when the money ran out. And it will run out.

As they approached the house, the other says, "Man, this street wide open. There ain't no place to hide or creep around in or nothin'. How we gonna do this in broad daylight? You know somebody always be lookin' out the window or somethin'."

The first one says, "There's a door that we can use on the side of the house next to those apartments. You see those little woods there?"

"Yeah."

"Well, we go through there, then behind the house next door an' there we are. Look, I'm a go unlock the door."

The other one waited in the parking lot of the apartments. At least he wasn't out in the street. He could keep some kind of discretion, maybe, by sitting on the steps or something. That dude sure is bold, he thought to himself.

What he didn't know was that dude had already been there earlier and had unlocked the door. He was inside going through the living room, through the kitchen, to the side door that they would use as though he lived there. It was a simple A-frame, two-bedroom cottage with a toilet in the short hallway between the bedrooms and the kitchen going right into the living room.

He came out of the side door, behind the house and through the little wooded area adjacent to the apartment complex, where he found the other one waiting. Maybe four or five minutes had passed.

"C'mon, man, it's all good!"

They return the way he came, entering the house through the side door and into the kitchen. Once they got inside, they were able to pick and choose which items would be of greatest value, but of little difficulty in carrying. "Maybe," he said to the other, "we can come back after we get the truck and get some of this other stuff. I mean, this TV looks real good, doncha think?"

"Yeah, but then we've got to worry about the neighbor since we'll have to go out front with it. But then, maybe not 'cause we could park the truck in the parking lot and tote this stuff back the way we came."

"Yeah, that's a idea. That'll probably work. We could get a bunch a this stuff then. I know folks that'll buy all a this shit."

"Me, too!" The cheery banter, the light-hearted camaraderie would belie the felonious nature of their presence as they made their way through the drawers, closets, and cabinets of this lonely, unoccupied place.

ONE

I was an inquisitive child, always had been. I was one of those kids that always asked "Why?" this and "Why?" that and was never satisfied when the answer was "I don't know."

One of my more memorable childhood experiences in finding out the answer to "Why?" involved Dad's cigarette lighter. I had overheard Mom talking about those fireproof trashcans and wastebaskets she had bought, so I experimented to see if they really were.

They weren't.

The bedroom wall where the wastebasket was located was headed to flames when Mom smelled smoke. When she came to investigate, she put out the "almost" fire, leaving a smoldering remnant of what was reputed to be a "fireproof" container. Little did I know that this particular kind of experimentation could be hazardous and especially so to a youngster's hind parts.

That's okay. It turned out that one of the results of this kind of curiosity is academic performance. I was a flower waiting to bloom, a fruit just beginning to ripen, who found the proper outlet for this curiosity in school. Now, this is not to say that I was academically gifted or that I was to be in accelerated courses, but I did have a thirst for knowledge and a real good memory, which made me an above-average student.

As the years passed, I found that I had a strong aptitude for the sciences. I could take a bit of information, store it and retrieve it accurately at a later time. This was probably just a part of the normal learning process, but as far as my family was concerned, it seemed like I was really bright.

Going to college was a rite of passage for young people of my generation and my parents took this as their sacred mission. Their solemn oath, repeated to me over and over, was hypnotic in its effect: "You will go to college, you will go to college." The mantra-like quality of this message was so powerful that, when I graduated from high school, it seemed like I had no choice. I may have thought about getting a job after high school, earning a living and having my own place or I may have thought about going into the Armed Forces for a couple of years to get some experience in the world outside of my hometown, but none of these ideas materialized. I had to go to college.

Fear of ostracism, fear of letting family down, fear of not knowing what to do next, all contributed to assurance that I was heading for a college education.

I went to a historically, predominantly Black school, known today as Hampton University, which played a fundamental role in the development of any character I may have.

Because I'd had some exposure to voice and piano lessons while in high school, I had vague notions of becoming a musician. So, in my application to Hampton, I indicated my desire to become a Music major. Interestingly, the independence in thinking that had eluded me prior to going to college showed up because I changed my major from Music to Biology.

"After all of those lessons, Ricky. After all of the promise you were showing, why would you want to do such a thing?" my mother lamented. "You sang so well in church, everybody talked about it and your piano playing is only getting better. What in the world are you going to do with Biology?"

"Well, Ma, I'm gonna be a doctor."

No hesitation, no second-guessing.

"I'm gonna go to med school no matter what it takes. I had a dream a few days ago, of me being in a hospital hallway with a stethoscope around my neck and a clipboard in my hand while I was talking to a nurse. It seemed so real, it's still so clear in my mind.

When I woke up the next morning, my whole focus had changed. I can't explain it and I'm not going to try, but I know I gotta do this. I ain't got no choice, Ma."

"Not 'ain't got', boy. 'I don't have a choice' is what you would say. How are you going to be a doctor talking like that?"

"Aw, Ma, that's just for around the house!"

 C3 80

Some events or circumstances can have irrevocable, life-changing effects on a person. The effect this dream had on me was enormous. There I was with my mind all made up to study Music and then, all of a sudden, right in mid-stream, I was compelled to change directions from something with which I had some familiarity and some experience to something with which I had no familiarity and no experience.

Not only was Mom perplexed by this seemingly impulsive, reckless and surely not well-thought-out decision, so was everyone else. My dad, my brothers, my sister all questioned my reasoning for doing this…but not me. In fact, I had no reason. I only had "The Dream."

C3 80

My mother was the kind of person who believed in thrift, dedicated work, sharing with others, and family. She was a saintly woman who was blessed with a gentle, forgiving nature, which was maintained by her membership at Mt. Zion Baptist Church. My father, by contrast, was a noisy, rude and, many times, ill-mannered man with a quick temper that was fueled by his chronic alcohol abuse. They were children raised on farms back in the first quarter of the 20th century and were introduced to the world by parents who had instilled the spirit of hard work in their offspring. My parents, in turn, did their best to instill that same work ethic in their offspring.

Mom was the fourth child of seven girls and three boys born on a farm in South Carolina. This piece of land had the good fortune of having the Savannah River as its southern-most border. Her parents loved each other and they loved their children. Though they were farmers and lived off the land, they knew the value of education and insisted that all of their children be educated, even go to college if they chose to.

Because her parents were just two generations out from the Emancipation, they knew that education was the only way to handle yourself in the white man's world. Her parents were not slaves, but I suspect her parents' parents were the offspring of freed slaves. So, she was raised in an environment of striving, improvement and determination to overcome the legacy of slavery, the hatred of white people and the inequality of Jim Crow.

Dad's history was not as clear as Mom's. Though we went to family reunions on his side and got to know his sister and brother, I was never sure who his parents were, what they did or how they came about. I do know that he got off that farm and joined the Army, which could be a possible explanation for his endless love affair with Seagram's Seven and his appetite for petty vengefulness and mean-spiritedness. This was tempered by small periods of clarity, peace of mind and harmony with family, which was more the exception than the rule.

He was having one of those rare moments, the curtain of alcohol-induced fogginess not having fully descended, when I talked with him about my decision to switch majors.

"Well, son," he said, "if this is what you want to do then, I'm all for it. I'm sure you'll be good at it, but I don't know how we're gonna pay for it. I guess we'll just have to see about that when the time comes."

To this day, I am sure that had he not given his blessings, I still would have pursued "The Dream."

ଔ ଓ

It was August of 1975 and there I was, a freshman at Hampton, being away from home and on my own for the first time in my 18 years. I was excited. Moving into James Dorm was the beginning of my settling-in process. I pictured Momma and my sister, Johnetta, dropping me and my belongings off in the front of the building, leaving me to wave at their dust as they sped back to Winston-Salem.

"Well, son, I want you to try not to forget to write, study hard and behave, okay?" Mom said.

"Okay Ma, but why y'all got to be leaving right now?" I said rather wistfully. "Y'all just gone drop me off and go? Dog!! Johnetta, why can't you and momma stay just a little bit longer?"

I'm sure it was humorous for them to see me there against the backdrop of those old buildings, making an attempt to hold it together, but failing miserably. They knew I would not whimper for long because, a few minutes later, I was smiling and waving good-bye to them amidst swirl of dust and car exhaust.

My room was on the third floor and we had to check in with the Resident Assistant, whose task it was to make sure all of these momma's boys were in the right room and, for some, to make sure they even had a room. No small undertaking.

"Where do you eat at around here?" I asked.

"Well, if you want to wait a little while, I'm going to Mickey D's. You can come if you want," he replied. "It'll be about 9:30 before I'm ready."

This gave me enough time to get some of my belongings in order and maybe meet my roommate who, as of yet, had not made his presence known. I put my clothes in the drawers, my luggage under the bed and 9:30 came quickly. I met the R.A. in the lobby.

"So, what are we riding in?" I didn't see a car anywhere, so I was mildly curious. He smiled at me, walked off and a minute later pulled up on a motorcycle. I had never been on a motorcycle and wasn't thrilled about getting on this one but, hey, I was hungry.

"Hop on!" he said, a gleam in his eye.

For sure, he sensed my unease. Reluctantly, I got on and we took off, the front wheel off the ground, with a roar peculiar to those vehicles.

This was not what I was used to and, after we got back, I was not anxious to do it again.

This was typical of my college years. Many of the experiences I had were brand-new, never-been-done-before situations for me. From having classes in a large auditorium with 70 or 80 students, the lectures going a mile-a-minute while I tried to take notes, to being around a great many females, all of whom were available...if I could only figure out how?

I came to this place holding no illusions of my ability—or lack of—to get a girl. Although in high school I had a girl here and there, for sure I was no Valentino and absolutely no Casanova.

So, I was quite taken when we'd go to the chow hall and grab a bite. Here, it was customary for everybody to mingle and socialize while eating. I mean, I had *never, ever* seen so many girls in one place at one time in my life! This place was way, way better than high school! Here, as long as I got my work done, I could make my moves on these cuties. I was gonna work it!

The top-shelf girls seemed to be out of my grasp, maybe even out of my league. Some of the other guys, who I thought were no better looking than me, were turning up with some really nice looking girls. I mean, for real, what's the deal?

Oh, don't get me wrong, I was getting some play, but it was what nobody else wanted.

Or so I thought.

And this idea that I was getting second-rate lasted throughout my college years. I did, finally, get a girl who was quite nice. She hadn't been around much and was real low-key. I could tell she was a virgin or close to it because things were kind of tight. I had done it before in high school and it usually went in kind of easy, but with her, the first time we got together, there was some fight-back and a bit of discomfort involved.

Subsequently though, our getting together became regular. It got easier and easier and better and better. I became quite proud of my little honey and thought I could see green looks of envy on the faces of some of the fellas I'd met. I'm sure they were wondering, "how did he pull that?"

Her name was Carmella and she was from Charlottesville, VA. She was majoring in Nursing. Since I wanted to become a doctor, much of our conversation was intertwined. We seemed fated to be together.

"Moe," she would begin, "when are we going camping?"

Even though everybody back home knew me as Ricky, I had begun calling myself "Moe" when I got to college. This was in the vain attempt to channel the spirit of the real Casanova I knew: Johnny Boy, my older brother, whom everybody called Moe.

Adopting this magic name must have worked since I now had this real nice girl in my territory.

"Camping?" I asked with some mystification. "Where we gonna camp at and what for?" What a silly idea.

"We can go to a local camping area and set up there. We can rent some equipment and everything. Besides, I just want to try it, being outside and all."

This is the cue I didn't pick up on even though she brought it up occasionally. By then, our sex life was tremendous. We really turned each other on. But, silly ol' me didn't hear what she was *really* saying. She wanted to get loose, she wanted to unwind, she wanted to fuck outside and I just didn't get it. I was down with that type of thing but she, being a polite girl and all, would never come right out and say it. To this day, I wish she had. Ol' silly me!

She was 3 or 4 inches shorter than I and was a real pecan brown. Her skin was flawless and her hair was thick and luxurious. I loved taking my hands full of it when we would be together. Her body was magnificent, though her propriety didn't allow her to think so. Not a scar, scratch or blemish anywhere. Just beautiful. Her hands were so delicate and her fingers, slim and nimble. Her nails were always cleaned and buffed, but never polished. The kind of girl you would take home to momma and, eventually, I did.

She was a little top-heavy, but with a narrow waist and wide, curvaceous hips. I mean, she was the complete package and just by looking at her, with her shy, coy demeanor, you'd never know the heat, the passion that smoldered beneath the surface. Whew! Our loving was volcanic. No, it was cataclysmic! Often, we would look at each other in awe and amazement, wondering how we survived yet another session with each other and lived to tell about it.

ଔ ଈ

So there I was, going through the process of post-high school education, learning about myself and integrating into the social scheme of living among people in my own age group, from my own racial and cultural background. This was very different from my local secondary educational experience, which had court-ordered integration. Simply put, I was in a healthy search for who I was.

I found that college was the perfect breeding ground for idealism, experimentation and challenge to the status quo. Dogma learned at home took a back seat. Very little of what I knew about "why things are" had come by direct experience; most of it was what I'd been taught. And at that age, when you found that issues were not as cut-and-dried as you'd been led to believe, the questions of "why *must* things be this way or that way?" arose. I was finding that the world was not as rigid as I had been led to believe.

Much of the dogma I fought with related to spiritual and religious matters. I'd been taught that there's only one God who became represented on the earth by His Son, Jesus. That you get to heaven by belief in Him and those that don't believe go to hell.

So, I started to question. Does this mean all of the Buddhists, all of the Muslims, all of the people who believe otherwise are going to hell? That God, in His Infinite Wisdom, would give a great portion of His creation to damnation? And what about death and dying? Why are we so afraid of the after-life if that's the reason why we're here in the first place, i.e., we live knowing we're going to die, so why are we afraid of it?

Without a doubt, these are concepts that can't be cleared up in a few years of school, but I decided early on to give these thoughts much attention in my daily living. Surely, there were principles nearby I had yet to perceive.

Ω Ω

My experimentation with drugs had been limited to weed and alcohol throughout college and it was actually more weed than alcohol. I had my first toke when I was maybe 15 or 16, Johnny Boy having taken care of those initiation rites of teenagedom as we were coming up.

My brother was a cool dude. He and I had always been buds, so it was sort of a Big Brother to Little Brother duty in his eyes for me to lose my weed virginity to him. Quite often, a family member provides introductions of this kind and my introduction was no different. He was a jock and a really nice guy. He played football all through junior and senior high school. Though he didn't get much appreciation on the field, he played with heart despite his diminutive size. The girls just flocked to him and I could never figure out why. Maybe, he had a "cool" that I could never have.

He was about 5'5", maybe 155-165 lbs. with a very athletic build. He had closely cut, dark brown, wavy hair and pretty, straight teeth.

A real Ultrabrite smile. Expressive eyes and a soft voice, combined with his other qualities (he had superb taste in clothes) suggested why the girls flocked to him. I was just too naïve to pick up on it at the time. He turned me on to the weed, but he wouldn't turn me on to the girls.

So, I got introduced to drugs in a safe and relaxed environment—home. Of course, when we did blaze, our momma and daddy weren't there, so we were able to keep things discreet. We maintained our grades, kept up our appearances and enthusiasm and continued to be "those Moore boys, aren't they something!" We were never suspected. For us, weed was just recreation.

I was never much of a drinker. I didn't catch my first drunk until I got to college, early in my sophomore year and I didn't like it. Not one bit. I didn't like the nausea or the bad-tasting mouth. I didn't like the spinning, with the rooms and ceilings going round and round. I didn't like the vomiting. No, I didn't like any of that. But, I did recognize that I could tolerate a certain amount of alcohol in my system. Whenever I'd get to that certain amount, I'd just stop drinking.

I learned that if you mixed a little alcohol with a little weed—a couple of beers or maybe a little Rum and Coke—you could end up with a perfect buzz, that just-right mixture of elements that puts you on a mellow, smooth plane of ease. Not stuporous and nauseating, like too much booze, nor numbing and conscious-deadening, like too much weed. This was the zenith of getting high.

In college, there was an unspoken, yet persistent, idea that went along with going to school and smoking weed: A buzz would help you concentrate and focus better. If you got high, your grades wouldn't go down but, more than likely, would go up.

"Hey, Moe, you gonna study with us for the test next week?" Mark asked. He was from Smithfield, a little town across the James River and he was just as average and ordinary as I was.

"Yeah, man. I was hoping we could do it at your place because the library is just too quiet. You know how we be talkin' and shit." I had learned, rather quickly, that most concepts were easier for me to understand when I explained it to someone else. This also helped relieve the tedium of individual study.

"You gonna bring something?" he inquired.

"I don't know. If I can find something, I will. Right now, I ain't got nothing."

"Well, don't sweat it. I got a little bit and it's pretty good. I think it'll do us right."

So, another night of study along with getting a buzz had been planned. Although smoking did not occur at all study sessions, it was present at a few. Since I was a B-average student, I felt that whatever gains I might have had in my grades without catching a buzz was worth the trade-off in how much fun I had in getting the grades that I got!

Throughout the campus, there was an underlying theme of sex and drugs. This symphony of primal impulses was like an unseen and unheard, yet deeply felt, rhythm that permeated campus life. It touched everybody. Course work and study time were add-ons, mere afterthoughts. You studied and showed up for class in your spare time, but things recreational trumped school. Sure, you went to class and participated in lectures, but this was done primarily as a way to catch some play. It turned out that there were social as well as academic incentives to having good grades—the girls admired a guy who had a party going on and kept his grades up.

I also found college to be an environment populated by people with whom I might have an intelligent conversation. Many occasions for discussion did present themselves and the topics of those discussions ranged far and wide, but there was a subject that seemed to rise above all others: girls.

"Man, what you doing?" I said to Martin. "I'm not even sure *you* know what you're doing."

He was a Biology major right along with me and we were recently getting to know one another. He and I had a crib in the same complex and we began to talk, having little chats about this and that.

"I never said I *knew* what I was doing, but that's the fun of it. You just step right up to her and say 'What's up?' and either she'll holla at you or she won't," he responded.

Martin was the kind of guy I'd never be—tall, confident and well-spoken with the looks to match. I mean, when a guy is so handsome that another guy has got to admit it, well, that's pretty handsome. He had dark skin and deep set eyes; a kind of narrow face and short hair that gave him a real chiseled look. He was nearly 6 feet tall, 190 lbs. and the girls would go out of their way to say hello to him. So, to him, this little game was easy. But not for me. What would I look like going up to some strange girl, fine as hell, talking about, "What's up?" Get real.

"I don't know, man," I said. "I mean, I kinda have to almost plan what I'm going to say to a girl ahead of time, before I go up to her and start trying to talk. I mean, rejection is a big issue for me and I have yet to figure out how to get through it."

"And I can relate," he said. "All the girls, at least the ones I want, don't just come flying at me like you think they do. I go through rejection just like anybody else and it ain't comfortable, but I've learned how to deal with it."

"How's that?" I asked as we walked into my apartment.

It was a neatly furnished place with a small sofa in green tweed fabric, a coffee table and a couple of bean bags in the living room. In the kitchen was a table with unmatched chairs and, in the bedrooms, mattresses on the floor. There was no standard wall-to-wall carpeting, but I was able to go out and find a rug with a nice, deep pile. The pale green curtains matched the rust-colored carpet and all of it together gave the place a young adult, I-don't-know-how-to-decorate atmosphere.

Martin shrugged. "You see, rejection is what, a sign that you don't appeal to somebody or are not attractive to that person. So, how you deal with that is what we're talking about. I mean, if you know what you're all about and have a good sense of self-esteem then, when you're told no, it doesn't have a lasting effect. In fact, as time goes on, it doesn't have any effect. You just accept it and move on."

"So, you're saying that a requirement for defense against the feelings of personal insecurity that come after being rejected is to think highly of yourself." As I moved into the kitchen for something to drink, I spoke a little louder. "Is that what you're saying?"

"Yeah, that's what I'm saying. I mean, I ain't got no scientific proof or no psychotherapeutic insight to base this on…"

"Psychotherapeutic? Hot damn, that boy sho' know his stuff don't he, grampa! Boy, you been really readin' that dictionary, ain't you."

"Well, to be honest, I try to do like you and put this so-called education into practice. But really though, I ain't got no way to say for sure that this is the answer. I just believe it is."

I came back into the living room, not having found anything worthwhile in the fridge. Typical.

"Well, that may be true for you and some others, but this guy still has problems steppin' up to a girl, knowing that he's exposing his most vulnerable side."

"Nigga, please! You ain't got no vulnerable side. That is a middle class cliché perpetrated on you by the devil white man, boy, and don't you forget it!"

We get a good laugh out of that…and this has become part of the bonding, the wordplay, that has happened over the short while we have come to know one another. Anytime we have a disagreement, point out inconsistencies or uncover double-standards in the other's logic, it's always due to "the myth perpetrated on us by the devil white man," one of the sayings we had heard during "The Readings of Malcolm X" series at the student union.

"Yeah, well, that particular perpetration has some validity to it. I'd like to think that I'm made of some kind of emotional steel, that nothing rattles my cage. But the truth of the matter is, my feelings do get hurt," I said.

Toward the end of my senior year, it was suggested that I go up to William and Mary, a small, prestigious, predominantly white school, just up the road in Williamsburg, and take a course in Biochem. Though I wanted to apply to med school right away I also wanted to be academically attractive. So, the advisors at Hampton recommended that a little more preparatory work would be beneficial, especially in that first, make-or-break year of school. Typically, students from minority schools fared less well than those from other schools. Why this is true is debatable, but it is true, nonetheless.

The wise decision was to beef up your weak areas and apply to as many schools as you could afford to. The application fee was

$30.00 per app at the time, so the number of schools a student applied to could become prohibitive. Obviously, this strategy offered a greater chance of admission to at least one school. Many M.D. wannabes applied to 10 or more schools to hedge against the competition for the few available spots. Not only are there spots for the academically gifted, there are also spots for those that are, simply, good.

The profession makes great effort to stress qualities other than academic ability as necessary to become a physician. So, it was quite reasonable, even expected, that a student from Hampton Institute or Virginia Union might get a spot while a student from William and Mary or University of Virginia might not.

"Well, are your feelings gonna be hurt if they don't let you in?" Martin asked.

I sensed a shift in the tenor and direction of our conversation. Martin knew I was adamant about how this should be done, but he had decided that he was going the traditional route by applying to a bunch of schools.

"Yo, homey, the way I got this figured, I can't be denied. My essay, my test scores, my interview, all of this, will put me in the let's-give-this-one-a-chance category, without a doubt. That's all I need!" I said confidently.

"On the real, what if these folks turn you down. Then what?"

"I've planned for the possibility of this whole thing backfiring. See, you don't know this and, to be honest, I didn't plan it this way, but I get a teaching certificate at the end of this semester when I pass my student teaching requirements, so I can always be a teacher."

"No shit! That's pretty good. I just thought that when you went to education as a minor, you wanted to avoid the foreign language requirements."

"I did."

He ponders this for less than a minute. "So, since you didn't plan it this way, what does that have to say about anything? You think you smart, don'tcha?"

"Who, me?"

TWO

Until college, I'd had no dealings with the guys in blue uniforms.

Though college encouraged you to sample a variety of experiences, to be open to multiple opportunities and to try new things, your personal judgment determined whether those experiences might be good ones or not so good.

My penchant for trying things different made me the likely aspirant to walk the thin line between doing what's right and doing what's not so right. Because I smoked a little weed and drank a little beer, the people I socialized with were likewise occupied. Sometimes, drugs more exotic than pot or booze would come on the horizon and who was I not to experiment? Microdot (a type of acid), crystal THC (the active ingredient in marijuana, crystalized) and powder cocaine were all legitimate candidates for consumption. I tried these new (to me) drugs in the company of those I hung out with. I also tried them by myself. I found that none of them had any long-lasting or substantial effect on me; I could take them or leave them.

Surrendering to a budding entrepreneurial spirit, I made attempts to enter the marketplace so that what I was using would pay for itself.

It seemed harmless enough. The people I knew were always, at one point or another, trying to get something. It only made sense that if I were to have some of what they were looking for, the best of both situations could be provided for. I mean, what could happen?

Getting caught was not even on the radar screen because everybody I knew and everybody they knew were all into the same thing. Wasn't nobody gonna just up and tell the police.

I mean, we're just trying to go to school and have some fun, right?

☙ ❧

Being unlearned in the ways of the world resulted in a see-no-wrong, do-no-wrong attitude. Little did I know that there will always be an element among us who, for their own reasons, would put anyone at risk. So, when Mike showed up at the apartment one day, unexpectedly and unannounced, I was a little surprised. He'd never visited before but hey, we're all students, right, and he was just trying to put his party together.

"What's up, man?" he said, after I opened the door. I'm sure my shock registered with him. "Just thought I'd stop by and see if anything's going on."

"Hey, what's up, Mike? We just in here talking. C'mon in."

Now, this guy was well-known around campus and I'm sure that was part of my surprise. I rationalized it by thinking my name was being heard in all of the right places.

"So, what brings you around? This a first," I said.

"Well, I'd heard that you might be doing something now and then, so I wanted to get a little sample, maybe ten bucks worth, just to see what you're working with. If it's straight, I'll be back for more."

So, I was right. My name was getting around.

"Well, just hang out in here for a minute. I'll be right back." I went into the kitchen where my neighbor Tonya was and took a bit from what we're using. I took this to Mike and was struck by a sense of extreme well-being, coming into my own as a businessman. "Well, what you think about this? This should be alright."

"It's good, man. I just 'preciate whatever you could do. I didn't have much money, you know, but I just felt like doing a line."

"Yeah man, I know what you mean. Well, holla back sometime if you want more, a'ight?"

"No doubt, man. I'll be back at you before too long."

That was a neat little transaction and I liked the sensibility of the exchange that went along with it. A couple more like that and I could go over to Eddie's and re-up without having touched any of my personal money. This is what it was all about. Free enterprise, supply-and-demand, and a marketplace economy.

God Bless America!

CB   BD

I guess I really didn't catch his drift or I was too green to think I could get into any major trouble because I was quite surprised a couple of days later when the police showed up at my place.

It was a regular evening, no different from any of the other evenings I'd had in Queen's Terrace Apartments. I parked in the space in front, got out and casually surveyed the surroundings then, put the key in and started inside. The weather was cool and dry; the skies were clear, not a cloud in sight. The windows were open, but the shades were down, the apartment catching the breeze of the soothing, salt-tinged air that is part of the Hampton Roads area.

One of the young ladies in the complex stopped me as I went inside. After a moment, we moved our conversation from the doorway to the kitchen.

"So, Moe, whatcha got?" she asked. Teresa had been a student at Hampton for a while and for reasons that are entirely unclear, she stopped attending. She was an attractive girl and I was told that it was her friendly and outgoing nature that caused her to leave school, a nature I wanted to become more familiar with.

"I just came back from across town, gettin' with my people over there. Let's see what the man done give us." I say with understated enthusiasm, attempting to include her in the "us" part of my conversation. Maybe this little bit of powder would grease the hinges on the door to that outgoing and friendly nature I'd heard so much about.

As we got settled at the kitchen table, there was a knock. I was so comfortable and secure, I didn't even ask "Who is it?" before opening the door. I had a girl with me that I've been trying to get to know and some interesting foreplay was gonna take place as I was going to try to get some of that juicy, so I knew that whoever it was on the other side of the door was not getting in there that night.

When I opened the door and the police were standing there, my astonishment was signified by a very audible, "Oh, shit!"

Teresa said, "Who is it, Moe?" As an officer stepped through the door, I heard her say, "What the fuck is this!"

"Mr. Moore," the plainclothes guy said, "we have a warrant to search this apartment."

There was no need of me saying "I've got company" or "Y'all come back in a minute," these guys were coming in anyway. As they came into the living room, I went to the back door, through the kitchen, and out there was another officer, this one sporting a 12-guage.

Shit!! This is serious, I said to myself.

"Mr. Moore, would you step back in here." All nice and polite. As I turned around, the other officers had made their way to where I was. He continued, "We have been informed that you possess and sell cocaine; consequently, we have been authorized to determine if this is true. Therefore, we will conduct a thorough search of these premises; however, we will ask, at this time, is there any contraband present? Should you wish to avoid some of the more unpleasant aspects of this type of search, you can come clean right now and we'll go easy on your place."

"This is all of it, sir." And there it was, right there, out in the open, on the kitchen table; what a pitiful amount to get in trouble for. Downright embarrassing. "There's no more in here regardless of how much you look."

He said, "Looks like this is where all the fun is. We need to be in here with you, don'tcha think fellas?" There was a low rumble of laughter among the three or four officers standing there. "Is there anymore lying around anywhere?" he asked, not challengingly nor aggressively, just rather humorously, as if he were saying to himself, "These college kids, they are so dumb!"

"No sir, there's no more." It's amazing how well-mannered you can be when your ass is in a sling. I never said "sir" to my daddy or my college professors.

So, they searched. The whole place. Upstairs, in both bedrooms; downstairs, in the kitchen and living room. They looked in the fridge, they looked in the stove and in all of the cabinets. Under the carpet and under the sofa cushions. They didn't find anything because there wasn't anything, but they didn't tear up the place either, so that was something to be thankful for.

After that, we all went downtown, me and my Hot Momma. In handcuffs. Wasn't her fault but, hey, she was there.

Needless to say, this wasn't going to go over well with mom and dad. I wasn't looking forward to making that phone call, but I didn't have a lot of choice. Either call home or stay in jail. That being my first time in confinement was enough to make me call right away. Wouldn't you know it though, Teresa had a guy friend who was sympathetic and was able to post her bond. Mine, too.

Still, I had to make that call.

CS BO

Parents, being the supportive, unselfish, unquestioning zealots that they are when it comes to their children, predictably will deny that their children could possibly be involved in anything against the law. My parents were of this stereotype. I could just hear them saying, "Not MY child!"

A sort of tunnel-vision sets in. An overpowering narrow-mindedness infects them as they rush to the aid of their stricken offspring. Such blind devotion is the cornerstone of the manipulation children can employ to further their own interests.

I was no exception. In fact, I found I was quite good at it.

Mom said, "Now Ricky, I know you're not involved with drugs are you?"

"No, Ma."

"Then, how could this have happened?"

"Ma, I just got caught up with some of the people from school and the police showed up."

"That's all! You act like this is no big thing. Well, it is a big thing, young man. Now, you're going to have a police record and how is that going to look trying to be a doctor? Nobody is going to let you in their school with a drug record, so explain that to me."

"Ma, I know it don't look good right now, but everything's going to be alright."

"Well, that's easy for you to say, but you don't really know. You've got so much promise. What went wrong?"

"Aw, c'mon, Ma…"

"Anyway, we'll be up there soon. I want to meet that nice young man that helped you to get out of jail."

 са   во

So, the family came, saw the lawyer, had a few words with him and, like magic, I was back in school like nothing had ever happened. No one knew of my brush with the law and I went on to classes as I waited for court. During this time, I met with the lawyer to find out what the real deal would be.

"Well, Mr. Moore, I can tell you this. Since this is your first time in trouble, you probably aren't facing any jail or prison time," said Mr. J. Ashford Gray, the type of guy you'd rather not deal with, but you have to because he is what the court has appointed. "But, there will be some type of probation with the usual fines, fees and court costs. I think we all can live with that, don't you?"

Mr. Gray was a fellow of undersized stature with a head full of silver-gray hair (just out of the beauty salon?). His eyes were behind blue-tinted bifocals (which went nicely with the hair, thank you very much) and he wore elevator-heeled shoes. A real greaseball.

"And since graduation is just around the corner, you really want to have smooth sailing, right?"

"Absolutely, sir. I don't want any problems."

са   во

As I approached the Big Day, I reflected on how I had been ceaselessly in pursuit of my dream. I had taken courses in the Sciences and in the Arts, and had done well. I had begun to put in my first applications to medical school and, because I was so sure of my destiny, only applied to three. I had my sights set on UNC-Chapel Hill, Wake Forest and UVA.

I got interviews at Wake Forest and Chapel Hill, but I didn't hear from UVA. That was cool, I wanted to be in North Carolina anyway. A part of my dream was to have a practice in Winston-Salem, right in East Winston, the low-income part of the city where I grew up. It seemed that the right and honorable choice to make for school would be a local school or, at least, one in the state.

My advisors had prepared me for the real possibility of being denied admission. Since medical school and the practice of medicine was such a tall intellectual, social and personal challenge, only the best of the best were chosen. However, some of the barriers had been lowered, making access to school available to students who may not have the best test scores or come from the best families. Consequently, when the letters of denial did come, I was neither swayed nor surprised.

It seemed to me that events in life, good or bad, occurred on their own, with little or no provocation from those of us attending this dramatic event called life. Things happened to folk because…things happened to folk. The idea that if you prayed every night, did good deeds and treated everyone by the Golden Rule that somehow you could avoid the more capricious, unpredictable and whimsical mishaps that life would toss your way, did not strike me as true.

As I moved through this time in my life, I fully recognized that just because I didn't say my prayers or treat everybody just right didn't mean that I would die and go to hell or that nothing would go my way and opportunities would pass me by. Quite the contrary. Along my travels, even though I had been on many occasions willfully disobedient, doors seemed to open for me anyway, almost magically. I looked at this and could see, without a doubt, that I was living on Divine Time.

I saw how blessed I had been to travel the highways and by-ways of North Carolina and Virginia without so much as a flat tire in over 4 years, at how I survived my brush with the law without any untoward consequences, at how my graduation came off flawlessly, how my family came and returned without incident and how I accommodated them all in the little apartment I got busted in. I saw how well my applications to medical school were being received and how I had signed up for and completed the course at William and Mary while working at the local psychiatric hospital. All of these events having occurred with such ease that I became completely secure in the rightness of my quest. I knew I would succeed though prayer and church were not an active part of my life.

Now, some would say that my apparent success was due to others who were praying for me, my safe movements and my accomplishments; that this was all due to God's grace, His gift to those outside His will. But it told me something entirely different: that regardless of what I do, pray or not pray, good deeds or not, treating folk right or not, the way had already been laid for achievement. Since the origin of my quest was God-inspired, my steps, my decisions, the doors I had to go through were already ordered. Success was pre-ordained.

I could do no wrong.

CB   BO

It's not that I wasn't religious, far from it. I was raised in a church-going family that went to services *every* Sunday. Unless you were dead or in a coma, you went to church. It's just that the rituals involved and the dogma that was preached didn't seem to make too much difference in people's everyday lives.

Also, I knew that as a person with a scientific aptitude, I would have to find a way to align my religious and spiritual precepts with the hard facts of science.

I had been instructed to always "put on your best for God!" So, on church mornings, we would put on our best clothes, our best shoes and our best hats. We made sure that this shirt was pressed just right or that blouse was just the right color, that there was not a speck of dirt anywhere. We were buffed to a glow. This was a Saturday evening custom practiced by church folk everywhere. As it turned out, this Sunday morning ritual of people "putting on their best for God" became more like a fashion show. Those weekly meetings had become society struts, fashion fairs and gossip parties where "putting on your best for God!" had become a metaphor for showing off and talking about each other.

This ritualized vanity could easily have caused me to become disillusioned, but that didn't happen. What did happen is that I took it upon myself to redefine "putting on your best for God!" I came to define it as putting on my best spirit, letting the best part of my mind and heart and personality be available.

It occurred to me that belief in an Almighty Creator, in a Divine Being, ought not be restricted to a weekly get-together of like-minded folk. It seemed to me that folk ought to express this belief daily and constantly, as well as at that weekly get-together. I had become convinced that people did not praise and worship daily because they felt that their religious duty was done at the conclusion of the weekly gathering; a couple hours spent just before the ball game and the spiritual gas tank was full for the week. How, uninteresting, uninspiring and drab.

I decided to offer daily those parts of me that are uplifting and moving, spiritual and inspirational.

The services did require organized moments of prayer, a reading of the Scriptures, a few songs and an inspired message from the pastor. Though this was good, it seemed that the church ought to have been actively trying to instill in us the lifestyle of Christ. That prayer, the constant seeking of His presence, ought to be a minute-by-minute effort, not just organized, weekly moments. That the process of trying to discern His will for us is through seeking His Holy Counsel.

Without ceasing.

CB   BD

As I moved toward completing the Biochem course, I'd decided to go to graduate school while waiting to re-apply to med school. I was accepted into NC State's graduate program of Physiology and in the fall of 1980, I began to work as a teaching assistant in the undergraduate Biology section while taking coursework toward a Master's degree in Physiology. Because the stipend didn't pay too much I also took a job at Dorothea Dix Hospital as a Psychiatric Technician.

Getting into the graduate school, getting the TA position, getting the Psych Tech job was effortless; all I had to do was put in the paperwork. If there were others trying to get in, if there was competition for those spots, I didn't notice it. These were just pieces of the puzzle that fell into their correct places. Nothing interfered with my progress.

Johnny Boy, an unwitting participant in an act of confirmation, was starting to live in Raleigh. By some confluence of events, he was taking a job there at about the same time I was starting school, so it only made sense that we would be roommates. He was my coolest pal.

"What time is your test tomorrow?" he asked

"About 9:00, why?"

"I mean, it's already after 11:00 and it don't help matters by smoking the rest of this joint; we're already buzzed up…"

"No shit."

"…so you oughta go on to bed. We can save this 'til tomorrow."

"Okay, John Lee!"—an off-hand reference to his namesake, our father. We laughed at that because I was obliquely saying he's trying to be my daddy, which wasn't likely. The only thing those two had in common was their name. "Okay, let's do that. It's some pretty good weed and ain't no need a just smokin' it just because it's there."

"No doubt. Besides, I got to go to work in the morning. By the way, you got company this weekend?"

"I do? Shit, I don't know, I didn't think so. Why? You sure are on my ass this p.m., You wanna holla at my people when they get here or what?"

"Well, she is kind a tight but, no, I was just being curious. I was thinking about going home this weekend and thought you might want to come along."

"Nah, I'm a hang around here this weekend and get some work done. I got some serious studying to do as well as some serious fucking, so I reckon I'll just stay here!"

CB ED

Our home life had changed about five years before this, in the fall of 1975. On Thanksgiving weekend, during my freshman year, Mom left Dad. Although it wasn't a divorce, it was a permanent separation. She vowed, "I'm never going back." And she didn't.

When I arrived home for Thanksgiving that weekend, there was all of this moving of boxes and people hustling and bustling, carrying this and wrapping that. I was really caught off guard. Her leaving had been long contemplated, primarily as a result of our constant urgings.

Dad's drinking had made our home life miserable. We didn't want our friends to come over, Mom could hardly have a civil conversation with him without him absolutely exploding and it would hurt us tremendously because it wasn't in her nature to raise her voice or aggressively defend herself. All he needed was a good ass-kicking, we knew it and she knew it, but she held us back, on more than one occasion, from tapping that ass. A little peace offering it would have been, from us to him. We love you, Daddy. *Pow!!*

When she left, he never knew what hit him. Because he took her kindness for weakness, he had no clue that she had already purchased a house long before she ever packed her first bag. In fact, he was sure that he had her cowed. He thought she would never do it, that she was just spouting empty threats. She had given him fair warning more than once.

"John, if you don't stop this drinking and cussing, I'm gonna leave you."

"Go ahead! Leave!! You'll just come crawling back like you ain't got no sense in the first place. You can't take care of yourself without me so, go ahead, leave!"

"I'm telling you John. You think this is some kind of joke. Well, it's not. I can and I will make it on my own. The only reason I've stayed here this long is for these children, so that they could have an opportunity to grow up in a home with both parents, but now that they're grown, if you don't change, I'm gone!"

He never changed…and she went.

ひ&んひ&

Dad was left with the house we grew up in, most of the furniture and a few dishes, a few pots and pans and all of the appliances. After two carloads, her move was complete. And I was really impressed by the new place, even though its location had been kept a secret until the decision to move had been made. Johnetta was her First Lieutenant and Comrade-at-Arms. Many of the logistics required for the move were under her tutelage. The two of them made a formidable alliance, one that Dad could not contend with.

The new place was in a part of town that was sort of upscale for middle class Black folk and Momma's choice of places to live made it clear that she wasn't nothing to trifle with. Since then, "going home" came to mean going to Momma's house up in Northwood Estates.

We would look forward to those times because home life had become much more pleasant. We missed the house we grew up in and looked on it with nostalgia when we would pass by occasionally, but without Mom there, it just wasn't the same. It didn't have that "home" feeling anymore. I had become accustomed to them being apart and no longer felt that great urge to "go home."

So, while going home regularly was welcome, it was far from necessary. She had become comfortable in her new surroundings and with her new neighbors and could look forward to her later years being filled with joy as opposed to them being filled with dread.

A big portion of that forward-looking happiness would be due to my eventual acceptance to and success with med school.

og so

Going to grad school, being a Teaching Assistant, and working at Dorothea Dix was a heavy load, but one that I welcomed. I figured med school would be more demanding than that so, for two semesters, from the fall of '80 to the spring of '81, that's what I did.

This time, when I re-applied, I only applied to *two* schools: UNC and Wake Forest.

When I did get my letter of acceptance, I was quite pleased, but not ecstatic. This was the way things were supposed to go. It was a part of a predetermined, maybe even supernatural, plan and that was that.

After completing my first year in grad school, my advisors there suggested that I finish my Master's requirements, putting med school on hold for a year; a good suggestion, but one that I disagreed with.

I began to make all the arrangements to close out my part of the apartment with Johnny Boy.

"So, you're outta here, huh?" he said to me. "I always knew you were the smart one out of all of us and you've really impressed me. You've kept your focus, you never lost your drive, you remained determined and stayed the course and now, here's the result. There's a lesson in here for everybody."

"I don't know what it is you want, giving me all of these compliments, but whatever it is, I ain't got it! I might have it in four

30

years or so, when I get outta school but, right now, I ain't got it!!" I said, and we both busted out laughing.

He and I had a great time living together, money had not been an issue and we had similar habits. He liked weed, I liked weed. He didn't drink much, I didn't drink much. He was a jock, I was a jock-wannabe and both of us would spend time at the clubhouse where there was a sauna, weight room, basketball and racquetball courts. He liked the girls and I liked the girls, though we never did get around to sharing them like the would-be-studs we thought we were.

Plus, he was game, he would try stuff. If it seemed reasonable and not too harmful, he'd try it and that rubbed off on me. On one occasion, we had met a guy out at the complex who needed a ride to Dunn, which was about 45 minutes from Raleigh. He said that as soon as we got there he'd turn us on to some stuff and, sure enough, once we got inside the door to his place he went into another room and returned with a white, crystalline powder that looked like cocaine, but wasn't. He said it was crystal meth or crank (I'd never heard of it) and you could snort it but the best way to do it was to inject it. Well, I'd never shot up, but Johnny Boy seemed to know something about it so I agreed to do it.

"Is it gonna hurt?" A reasonable question, I thought.

"Boy, what is you talkin' about. It might sting a little, but it ain't gonna, like, sho'nuf hurt." Johnny Boy saying this while Charlie is tying my arm. I looked around helplessly. There's no way I could back out now and be a pussy in big brother's eyes. No fuckin' way.

"Clinch your fist." Charlie instructed me. He'd already prepared the fix. He had taken a portion of the powder and put it in a spoon, then he put in a few drops of water to dissolve it all. A bit of cotton was dropped into the liquid and the needle tip was put in it; I couldn't figure out what that was for.

"What's the cotton for?"

"That's to keep the tip from getting dulled at the bottom of the spoon and to filter out any particulates that may be in the dope."

"Oh."

He pulled the head of the plunger in the syringe and the liquid squirted into the barrel where it took on a slightly beige hue; rather pretty looking, as he held it up against the light. He flicked the barrel with his finger, dislodging any bubbles that may have been lurking. I'd heard what a bubble could do. From television.

"Alright, you ready?" Charlie asked. And nearly in chorus, Johnny Boy asked, "You ready?"

I looked at them stupidly, having no clue to what was about to befall me. Charlie slid the needle into my arm expertly, though there was a noticeable pinch.

"Ow!"

"Aw hush you little baby, that shit didn't hurt," my brother declared.

"Yes, it did!" I said petulantly. "You just wait 'til it's your turn."

Charlie had emptied the contents of the syringe during this little exchange and then, blast-off occurred. This was the most intense, most powerful high I'd ever known and it came upon me like a 50-foot tidal wave. I mean, it just dropped me over and over, bathing me with a supreme sense of serenity and tranquility, which seemed to be based in a cavern of rushing sound. It was so ecstatic, exhilarating and downright blissful, I thought I was going to cry. It might as well have been a religious experience.

The euphoria was so strong, I knew I'd want to try it again.

I didn't know what that meant at the time, but I did know that money was short and you had to pay for the stuff. Still, after we got back to Raleigh, I thought about how to get some more and do that thing all over again. But that whole process was so convoluted I just couldn't deal with it, especially with what I had going on. There was no way I could spend my time looking for this stuff and all that went with it and do my school work at the same time. Just no way.

But, my God, what a blast that was!

THREE

My plans for the summer revolved around driving to California to visit my older brother, Winston, and having a good time on the West Coast. Not unexpectedly, Johnny Boy was a little curious about this.

"You mean, you're going to drive from momma's house to Winston's house by yourself."

"Absolutely. I remember when you and Perry drove to California and how that seemed adventurous and a little risky, so I'm a take it to the next level. I'm a do it solo! And furthermore, I ain't gonna even call Winston when I get to San Jose. I'm just gonna show up on his doorstep. I bet that'll get him!"

"Well, that's a helluva idea. Just be on your P's and Q's. Anything can happen. Trust your instincts and use your best judgment is all I can say."

I had no misgivings or second thoughts about going; I knew I'd be safe. I was on a God-given mission that couldn't be stopped, though Mom was not quite as convinced.

"Well, Ricky, that's quite a distance, isn't it? How long do you think it will take?"

"The AAA maps say 48 hours straight driving time with no stops. I figure to drive, maybe, 12 hours a day which should work out to four or five days. I'm in no hurry. This is likely to be my last vacation for a while."

"Well son, I can't begin to tell you how excited I am about your getting in school. You said this would happen. Though I may have had my doubts at times, you saw this thing through and I am so pleased. You deserve a vacation of your own choosing."

"I've said more than once Ma, this thing's got a mind of its own. I'm just an actor playing a part. Watch what happens. We both know I don't have money for tuition right now, but I'm a get a job out there doing something. I'm gonna make however much I can while I'm there. But, just watch and see. Something else, I don't know what, is going to happen to make my tuition secure."

"I certainly hope so. Your Daddy and I could only come up with part of what you need for the year so…"

I cut right in. "Ma, don't even worry about it. Something will happen."

Actually, I had no clue as to how tuition was going to be paid. My words were an attempt to assuage her anxieties about money for school. She had already put the four of us through school (with some help from Dad) and now here's this little booger who wants to be a doctor, who's really smart and is doing everything he can to make this thing work out. She was so proud and it was troubling for her not to have an immediate answer for this tuition question. My hope was to allay some of those uncertainties.

"Now you know I'm not comfortable with this 'something's gonna happen' stuff. That's just too imprecise. I need something a little more concrete before I can relax."

"I don't know what to tell you, Ma. Surely, if things have gone well this far, they will continue to do so. That's my opinion."

Forever the optimist, that's me. I believed my optimism to be infectious and I was not hesitant in being the primary vector in the spread of this oftentimes contagious disorder. It was completely irrational to think that just because things had gone well in the past, that they would continue to do so. Yet, this small piece of illogic had a home with me.

ॐ ॐ

I started driving on a Friday afternoon with $500, a fifth of Bacardi and an ounce of weed. Clearly, I had my priorities in order.

Once you get a good buzz going against the purr of the engine and the whine of the road beneath, you entered a semi-hypnotized state. Those miles just melted away.

I had not a clue how big *and* beautiful this country was. Until you see it up close, you miss out on all its glory. I will never forget the panoramic view that unfolded before me as I came out of the Appalachian Mountains down into the Tennessee Valley, how the land just opened up and spread out as I made the descent out of the mountains to the flatlands below.

So, this is what was on the other side of Grandfather Mountain, huh? It was as if the land rose up to meet me, as though I were making a slow, prolonged landing out of the sky. Absolutely stunning.

For the next three days, all I could see were open flatlands and widely spaced fields. As I moved through Oklahoma, New Mexico and Nevada, the horizon that seemed to be "just over there" was actually hundreds of miles away. Honestly, you really can't grasp the dimensions of this land from the air (I had made the trip on American Airlines when I was 16, my first flight), you needed to be up close and personal to fully appreciate it.

It is this kind of freedom, this ability to get up and go anywhere in the country you choose, on a whim, that is part of what makes America great. It was this sense of freedom that I felt all the way there. Not a care in the world. The car performed flawlessly and I rested whenever and wherever I wanted. Never in a motel, usually in the car. I ate when and where I wanted and if I ever needed any companionship, it showed up.

 ‘’

The Scenic Overlook was where I was treated to an up close of one of the true wonders of nature. I mean, awesome or exhilarating or magnificent don't begin to express what I really felt.

The fact is, I was witnessing one of God's marvels as I looked down into the bottom of the canyon. Couple that with a sweeping side-to-side gaze at the colorful striations of rock making up the walls of the canyon and I had forever an experience extraordinaire. This undulating, oversized trench snaked to the left and to the right as far as the eye could see, going on and on. Truly a world's wonder.

As I reached Las Vegas, the sun had already settled and darkness was fast approaching. I was putting on the headlights when, as I crested a rise in the highway, I could see twinklings of light on the horizon. And, in an instant of *deja vu* reminiscent of my descent out of the Appalachians, a dazzling spectacle came into view. A sparkling, bejeweled show of light arose slowly from the desert floor, an act of metropolitan levitation—the city itself rising up to meet me on the now-leveling highway.

"Man, check this shit out!" I exclaimed to myself.

As I drove the Strip, I marveled at the milling throngs of people, taxi horns blaring and music coming from everywhere. Bright lights flashing, water fountains burbling and spouting. I bet their electric bill in a month was more than I'd make in a year.

Wonder what's it like inside, I mused. Nah, I'd better go 'head, I got some place to be. I didn't go in, but at least I could say, "I been there!"

Ψ ∞

"You mean, you didn't even go inside?" Winston asked when I showed up on his doorstep later that day, somewhat incredulously.

"Nah, I'd already decided to bring it on in and I didn't want to delay my arrival any longer."

"So, Doc, you ready for school? I sure am proud of your efforts, but really, it's no more than what I expected anyway. I knew you'd do good."

"Yeah, but if I don't get no money then all I'll have is just a good effort and nothing to show for it, so I gotta get a job. Right away."

"Well, a friend of mine told me about a psych hospital down the road a piece. I'd been telling him about your school and work experiences. This place might be a good place to start."

Good looking out, I thought. So, that's what I did.

The hospital was located in Morgan Hill, a small town about 20 miles south of San Jose. I never became acquainted with the town, but I did get the job at the hospital. It was organized the same as those I'd worked in Hampton and Raleigh: observe patient behavior, make chart notes, take vital signs. This kind of across-the-country organization, with similar policies and procedures, made it possible for me to go right in and start, knowing already what was required of me.

Winston was appropriately nonplussed at my hiring. It simply fit in with his concept—and mine—of my charmed, can-do-no-wrong, can-not-fail life.

As he and I socialized throughout the summer, he would introduce me to various friends of his, one of whom was a speed freak. This young lady's thing was crystal meth, that same blast I got in Raleigh.

She was quite generous in sharing her fondness for this stuff and I, being The Supplicant, willingly accepted her gifts. It was a natural consequence that I would bring this contraband into the house; the privacy afforded by living with Winston and his kids being gone was without parallel. Yet, when he happened to see me in the process of preparing a hit, all he could say with some chagrin was, "I hope you know what you're doing."

☙ ☟

As the summer came to an end and the August deadline for registration was fast approaching, I checked my cash stash and found I had a little over $500.00 to go back with and to start school with. Pretty much like I figured.

I'd had a good time and did not deny myself opportunities for pleasure. Carmella had come out from her summer sabbatical in Michigan and we really did enjoy ourselves, so just having enough to get back on was a blessing. I was supremely confident. In fact, there was a peace of mind that said to me, not so much in words, but in feelings and impressions, everything's going to work out. So, I got in the car and said my goodbyes.

☙ ☟

Upon my arrival at the campus, I made visits to the various administrative posts: the medical school itself, for orientation, the dormitory for housing and the dreaded financial aid office for, in my case, permission to run me out of town since I didn't have any money. All of these stops proved to be routine, though the financial aid office did say that it would have to get back to me. That didn't sound too good.

After I settled in, I went for a walk to familiarize myself with my immediate surroundings and to do some local sightseeing. Without a doubt, the only sights I was really trying to see were the girls, where they might be and how might I get to them. Not to my surprise, this place was jam-packed, stacked floor-to-ceiling, with girls.

I mean, just because I was in professional school didn't mean that I was gonna stop doing my natural thing, that I wasn't supposed to get my groove on anymore. The kind of guy I had become dictated that I pursue the girls. Although my prime directive was to get an M.D., the directive right next to it was to screw all the girls I could.

My party scene had not changed at all. It still consisted of a little weed and maybe a beer. None of the hard stuff, that just wasn't me.

I figured I'd do here like I did at Hampton: get some study done between the fun. Come to find out, I was not alone. There were many hearty souls here who believed you could have a life and get an advanced degree at the same time. Looked like I was in good company.

Classes began the following week and it was helpful that I had taken the courses at the medical school the previous summer (UNC had an introductory program that gave prospective M.D. candidates an idea of what medical education was all about). Those experiences helped me to stay afloat with the first years' subject matter. At the very least, I wasn't being thrown into ice water, I had a little heads-up on what to expect. Still, the amount of work involved was startling. The tremendous volume of reading material, study guides and syllabi to be consumed was not to be taken carelessly. Because I studied, stayed current and contributed to lecture discussions, I felt like I was an effective student. Yet, like everybody else, I fell immediately behind. You couldn't stay current in this game, you had to stay ahead. An irreconcilable dichotomy, impossible to sustain, yet one to be pursued with relentless passion.

※ ※

Upon my return from classes one afternoon, there was a letter waiting for me from the financial aid office. I knew what this was and I did not look forward to reading what it had to say. Boy, Mom and Dad were sure gonna be disappointed that I had to come home until I could get money to attend. I'd talked about it to a couple of second- and third-year students who said that it was common practice for them to allow you to pick up some funds and, then, return to school. I bet they were just kidding.

Well, they did say that they had to get back to me. I was just hoping it'd be after I passed my first year courses. At least I'd have something to show for myself.

I opened the letter and it read:

> *Congratulations Mr. Moore, you are one of the two recipients of our annual McDowell financial aid scholarships. All books, tuition and fees are paid for the first year upon your acceptance of this award. Please contact us at our office for further information.*

What? This had to be some kind a joke, but the letterhead sure looked legit. Finally, it dawned on me...

HALLELUJAH!! I toldja! I toldja! I knew something would happen, I just *knew* it. I'd been saying it all along, this was a Divine Plan and there's nothing that could stop it. I did absolutely nothing to get this award, I didn't apply, I didn't inquire, which meant it had to be from Heaven.

Well, wouldn't Mom and Dad be relieved, especially Mom. This would be one phone call that I would be happy to make.

"Ma, I told you, once they accept you, they do all they can to keep you and make sure you graduate. The only way you don't graduate is if you can't keep up with the work. Money is not an issue." Like I really knew this to be true.

"Well, I sure am glad to hear that. I've been on my knees ever since you went out to see Winston. All of that 'something's gonna turn up' thinking wasn't getting it for me. No, sir, I had to go to my Lord and have a little talk with Jesus. I knew he'd make it right. Still, I'm going to send what little I can, so everything will work out."

"Aw, momma, don't sweat it. Don't do nothing out of the ordinary. Like I've said, this thing has a mind of its own. All we have to do is sit back and ride!"

"It sure seems that way."

She had really been supportive throughout all of my traveling and schooling and girls everywhere. I recalled a comment she had made, "Ricky, why do you have so many girls calling you?" and I said, "Ma, I guess you'd rather have a bunch a guys calling me, huh?" with a gleam in my eyes. That ended all of that line of inquiry. But her support, both financial and more importantly as a counselor and guide, was without compromise. She was right there by my side.

Even Dad surprised everybody. He did his part by supplying gas and oil for the car or some food to take back whenever I'd come home. He wasn't much on the mail, but I knew if I ever really needed anything, he'd do his best to get it.

I could hear him say to his buddies, "That boy a mine talkin' 'bout he wanna be a doctor. I declare! I don't know where he got such a idea. Ain't nobody I knowed of in mine or Florence's family ever did anything like that. I'm jus' gone have to do the bes' I can."

They'd all made it clear to me that if they were going to do their part, I sure would have to do mine. And this part was a real challenge. Sure, I was told to learn to enjoy and look forward to late nights of study, study all through the weekend, study during the holidays, study at home, study in the car. Whenever and wherever I might find myself, make sure to have a book and study, study, study! But, be sure to know that this level of commitment would be insignificant compared to the 80, 90, even, 100 hour work week as a resident. That would be the real joy I could look forward to.

I was able to do the study part quite well, though the reading required was intense. Sometimes with comprehension, sometimes without. Many times just staring at the page, reading the same thing over and over, the information barely registering. I could not reconcile this as being any easier than that residency part. I mean, how could anything be harder than all of this reading and studying. Geez, did it get tedious. Anatomy, Biochemistry, Microbiology, Physiology, on a professional school level, are big bites to chew, but chew them I did. And swallowed and digested. I was able to demonstrate my new ability to masticate by the test scores I received. The grading system was based on the pass/fail system which means that when all the tests are graded, the scores are added and an average is determined. The infamous *class average*. If your individual test score was above the calculated average, you passed. If it wasn't, you didn't.

Now, I understood the concept of academic competition. *Everybody*, every one of the hundred and twenty-some people, was striving to beat that class average. It was clear and unambiguous that there would be those who would be above the class average and, unfortunately, there would be those below it. Woe and shame unto those that fell below. It wasn't gonna be me, that's for sure. I couldn't see it, I couldn't even grasp the thought. However, the lifestyle that I was living gave all the indications that I didn't give school too much attention, let alone the class average.

I had it going on, just like at Hampton. The McDowell grant allowed me to get an apartment and some furniture. It also provided a monthly stipend, which allowed me some freedom of movement because of the extra cash. I'd met a few girls and things were ticking along rather nicely. I still had the Capri and it ran just as good as it did when I went to and from California. Sure I studied, but it did not interfere with my social life, not one bit.

ଓ ଔ

I began to realize and acknowledge that I had real value in the world, that people would really have to deal with me, i.e., I had become, in my eyes, a "Big Dog".

A Black man, young, healthy, smart, easy to get along with, who didn't have a snooty or I'm-better-than-the-next-guy attitude and in professional school, be it law, dentistry, or medicine, was an attractive package. This seemed irresistible to the ladies in Chapel Hill, where it seemed these qualities were valued even more than other places. Either I was meeting the wrong girls in Winston-Salem or I wasn't there long enough to meet the right ones because whenever I did come home, my social life came to screeching halt.

I mean, I had learned how to get girls, I had lost much of my freshman-year insecurities and had become accustomed to a certain quality and variety of woman, which seemed to be weirdly unavailable to me at home. The logical conclusion was a no-brainer: I'd spend most of my time in Chapel Hill where the grass was greener, like a good little boy.

Simple.

ଓ ଔ

"Hey, Rick!"

"Hey, girl. Whatcha been doing? Did you miss me?

"You know I did."

Dionne was a special girl. I'd met her during orientation after I'd gotten back from my cross-country tours. She was a Chapel Hill native and worked as a secretary in the UNC hospitals. The Student union had a dance the weekend before classes were to start and she, on a lark, decided to come. Ordinarily, she would never have come, these events having been a part of her growing up, but she made a fateful decision that evening. She met me.

She lived at home with her mother and sister. Her part of the residence had a separate entrance to it and gave her the kind of privacy that a twenty-something ought to have. We also shared time at my place, but her place had more of a homey atmosphere to it, so that's where we spent much of our togetherness.

"Did work go good for you?" I asked. She really appreciated a man she could talk to. One who seemed to be genuinely interested in her goings and comings. Somebody, she often said, "with some sense!"

"Yeah, about the same. Those nurses on 4-South still try to make like they're better than everybody else and I do my best to let it go, but it's so irritating to be around people with their head stuck up their butt, makes me want to scream."

"Shoot, you know I know what you're talkin' about. I know what time it is. Look where I am. Ain't nothing but asshole over there, Black and White!"

"I know that's right." She said with a knowing smile. And that smile of hers was electrifying, a real work of art. Just like the rest of her.

She was a little shorter than me with a nice, tight butt and a narrow waist. She was a little small at the top, but it was a firm, juicy smallness. She had just enough for a mouthful. Really neat. She had a head full of flowing, curly hair that was so well maintained you'd have thought it was a wig. She was a natural beauty, though I could never convince her of it. Never much make-up at all, it wasn't needed. Maybe a little lip gloss now and then, some clear nail polish, but that was about it. Very nice.

"So what are we gonna do tonight?" I asked. "Is there anything in particular you had in mind?"

"No, not really. We can stay around here if you want, I know you've got work to do."

"As always. That, my dear, will never change. But for you, I'll make some time. Come here."

As she walked toward me, I stepped to her. I put both arms around her waist and she draped hers over my shoulders. We just stood there, holding each other for a long moment. We did that a lot because, for me, it wasn't always about sex, but it was *always* about intimacy and closeness. Being able to separate the two added a special quality to our relationship that affirmed we could be intimate and sensual without it having to go all the way.

"I like this part." she said. "I've always wanted to be like this in a relationship. I mean, I get horny too, but that don't mean just because I want to do something, we can't be close until we do. Most guys think that because you want to hold or touch or be close that you want to screw, too. Which may be true, just not right then, y'see, and I appreciate you being able to understand that."

"Well, if I do, it's because I have you to share it with."

"And you always come up with the right things to say at just the right time." We both laugh at this because when we first met, my little rap towards her was so corny. But, she went for it and we made it. She overlooked my words and saw me for what I was, just a nice guy trying to meet a girl.

"Well," I said, "you're so easily impressed, whatever anybody says that sounds halfway decent, you just fall right for it."

"I do not!"

"Well then, I am sadly mistaken. I can only believe that my dazzling smile and extraordinarily shocking good looks turned you on."

"Boy, you know that wasn't it!"

We both howled with laughter. And so it went on a typical evening during the course of that first year. Although I did some wandering, Dionne was my constant.

At the end of the first year came the push for final exams. I'd had similar experiences at Hampton, so I didn't see this as being that much different. I studied a little more diligently and researched a little more thoroughly than I had in previous years but, for the most part, it was a repeat of what I had already been through. I really didn't see how I, or anybody else for that matter, could miss the cut off.

And I didn't.

When the scores came out the following week, I searched for my ID number. There it was: 6630—73, class average—72.

Well, alright. Get down, Rick! I knew there could be no other outcome. It simply was preordained for me to become a doctor and there I was living this Divinely Inspired dream and being successful at it.

Out of the 14 Black students in the class, I was one of the three that passed the exams outright. This meant that I did not have to take the summer make-up courses required of those that did not make the cut off. Oh, there were seven or eight White students that didn't make the average, but that's out of 120-some students. The numbers, however, spoke for themselves. Black students, generally, did not have a history of doing well in professional school. Some did, but the majority needed help. Kudos to American medical schools because they took the time and made the effort to coach and support those students as needed.

But, I wasn't one of the ones that needed the extra boost. I could just hear the rumblings of those that gave me those fake-ass smiles. "I wonder how he made it with his non-studying, going-to-the-party self." And I did get my groove on. But I also did my work.

Going into the summer, I looked forward to a summer internship with a local physician in Winston-Salem. The school encouraged its young doctors to get as much practical, hands-on experience as possible and they would pay for it as a stipend. So, I stayed with Momma and went to work in the doctor's office during the day. She was thrilled.

"Well, Ricky, this is so nice, seeing you go out to Dr. Cromwell's office."

"Ma, I am just so full of myself, I don't know what to do. Things couldn't be going any better for me." Although I didn't have my white lab coat or my clipboard, I was well on the way, as far as I could tell.

So, the summer went by rather cheerfully. With me making the commute to Chapel Hill on weekends to see Dionne, I was living the life. My apartment mate had gone for the summer and when I was there, I had the crib to myself. This meant that I had considerable time on my hands and because I was one ever open to something different, something curious, the idea came that I ought to try cocaine intravenously, just for kicks, sort of as a treat to myself for having done so well thus far. Since I wasn't new to the IV thing, it couldn't be all that tough.

I'd heard that if you shot up some coke, it would be a wild ride and a top-notch high that didn't have the hours-long edge of crystal methedrine. So I made a purchase, got a syringe from the hospital and tried to remember how I'd seen it done before. This was truly uncharted waters for me, but I wasn't worried, I only had curiosity about this thing. Like all the other things I'd tried, in no way could this become a problem.

I put some of what I'd purchased in a spoon with a bit of water and a dab of cotton from a Q-tip. I figured I'd heat it just a little to get rid of the particulates I could see, then pull the rest up into the syringe.

My first problem was in finding a vein. After I'd filled the syringe and checked out its hue, I tapped the barrel to dislodge any suspect bubbles lurking. I tied my arm with a belt (like I saw them do on TV) and laid the tip of the needle on top of the big vein running down my forearm then, gently, pushed it into the skin and ouch! that really stung, but the pain was momentary. I pulled on the plunger and nothing happened, no blood squirting into the barrel, no air, no nothing. I guessed that meant I had to dig deeper and *ooouch!!* that hurt even worse.

Shit, I didn't know what the hell I was doing. What I learned, after many tries, is that the angle at which the needle is pushed into the vein is very important.

When I finally did get a jet of blood, I readied myself. Surely, once I pushed the plunger, this would be a lot of fun. So, I pushed. All of it. The entire contents of the syringe, about half a barrel. All at once.

And nothing happened.

What the fuck? I thought this was supposed to *be* something. A few more seconds and still nothing. I began to think, maybe the guy sold me some bullshit 'cause I ain't feelin' a goddamned thing.

Right about then, I began to feel a tingling sensation, sort of under my brain, rising slowly toward the top of my head. And, on the heels of that, I began to have a medicine-like taste in the back of my mouth. At that point, there came a sound with steadily increasing intensity, a piercing sound of escalating pitch that went higher and higher and higher until there was a single-pitched sound screaming throughout my head. My eyes blurred, my heart lost its steady rhythm and my whole world rocked.

It was bliss. damn! damn!! damn!!! That shit was good!

The sound carried with it feelings of a mounting and increasing euphoria, an ecstasy that slammed me and caressed me and caught me completely off-guard. I was totally unprepared for such a grand experience. Then, momentarily, it all began to fade, to wash away, and to withdraw from me. I nearly wept.

Whew!! That shit was *baaadd*, I got to do that again. And check it out, I've found a new way to recreate, something I hadn't counted on and something that really worked. Besides, I ain't got nothing to worry about. Somebody had said this stuff was habit-forming, but that's hardly the truth.

Can't nothing bad happen anyway: I'm covered by Divine Authority.

FOUR

Summer came to an end and second year started.

The coursework was even more daunting than before: Pharmacology, Immunology, Pathology, Oncology, Neurology were all presented in the same dispassionate, non-emotional manner as the first year. I felt that I was pursuing the coursework with all the same vigor and enthusiasm as the previous year; that as the professors droned in their monotones, I continued to shine superlative.

But I was carrying a friend along this time, an extra burden to go along with my already full load.

After that first hit, which really turned my world upside down, I let it go for a while. For a couple of weeks, I didn't do anything, which gave the illusion that this stuff really wasn't habit-forming. There was no anxiety or fear related to my new-found pattern of getting a hit, then chilling for a while; getting a hit, then chilling for a while. That worked really well for a time.

Because I'd convinced myself that I was untouchable, I thought it was just a normal course of action when my pattern of use increased from once in a while to every other day to daily.

I was just making room for my new friend, that's all.

Going to school and supporting a serious drug habit are not compatible venues of pursuit, even though I thought I was handling things. When I didn't make the cut-off on a test for the first time since I'd been there, I blamed it on not having fully applied myself, not because I had a problem. I figured I could make up for the lost time by the end of the year.

Money was becoming more and more scarce. It turned out that recreation of this nature was expensive! And since I didn't have extra cash just lying around, I began to make up little stories about why I would need money and impose these half-truths on my unsuspecting mom and dad. Either I'd need a new book and, boy, you know those things cost a lot, or my electric bill was higher than I expected because, geez, you know, with all of this late-night studying and everything, I guess the electric company is taking advantage of us in school. Half-truths I say, because I might give a good and correct reason for needing money, but would use it instead toward the support of my new friend.

I found myself on many occasions pacing and prowling about the apartment after I had used and had run out of money, left with the hype, but not the high. This would go on all night, as I would think and scheme and try to figure out how to get more. The dawn would come and it would be time for class, yet I'd had no sleep or anything to eat. I'd go to school broke and would ask my classmates for small change, totally ignoring this cardinal rule of personal respect: never ask classmates for money. This makes for great gossip and an unpleasant reputation.

Dionne learned of my recreation, but because I was still in school, still studying, still giving the illusion of the good, solid student, I was able to downplay the significance of my situation, even to myself. I could tell, though, that she was concerned.

"Rick, I really don't understand how you think you can do drugs and go to school at the same time."

"Do drugs? What do you mean 'do drugs'? I don't do drugs. I might use from time to time because it's fun, but I ain't no addict or nothing like that, if that's what you're talking about. I mean, it don't interfere with school or anything, so what's the deal?"

"What's the deal? How can you be so blind? Ain't nobody gonna want a doctor that's on dope or has a name for drugs and that's where you're headed. Either you're gonna hurt yourself or hurt somebody else, that's what's happening. I mean, it's already clear to me your judgment is off, even right now."

"Off?"

"That's right, off. You're so distorted, you can't see it. C'mon man, can't you let it go? For me? All I want is for us to be together and live a good, clean life. I mean, do I crowd you?"

"No."

"Or make demands of you?"

"No."

"That's right, I don't, because I love you. We've been together almost 18 months now and I'm a tell you, this is the best time I've ever had in a relationship and I don't want to lose it behind no drugs. This thing you got going, this recreation is not cool. Not at all. I don't know where you get it or how you get it, but you need to take a chill pill, for real."

"Look, Dionne, I know you're concerned and I love you for that, but you saw how I breezed through last year. This science stuff comes naturally to me and as far as cocaine goes, I can take it or leave it."

"Oh, yeah."

"Yeah."

"Then, why don't you leave it. Just show me you can put it down."

"I *can* put it down!"

"Then prove it. Show me. Show me you can leave that stuff alone for a week, no, two weeks. Just two little measly weeks, 14 teeny-weenie days, and make a liar out of me, and you know I ain't no liar. I don't believe you can do it."

"Alright then, I'll show you. But, how're you gonna keep a check to know if I've cheated or not?"

"Keep a check? Shoot boy, it's not on me, it's on you. If you say you've let it go, I'll take your word for it, you've let it go. But remember, it's a thing *you* have to deal with, not me."

Now, that was a slick move on her part. I never suspected her to be so shrewd, having me be accountable to myself. She must have known intuitively that if I couldn't be honest with me, there was no way I could be honest with her. Psych 101.

It went on this way, these occasional confrontations. After a date would pass, she'd give me one of those "see-I-told-you-so" looks and I'd glance at her with such nonchalance that she wouldn't know what to make of it. Or so I thought. When she would ask me outright if I'd been able to keep my word, I'd be so deceptive that not only she, but Ray Charles and Stevie Wonder could have seen right through my castle in the sky. She had to believe that her love and support could do more for me than I could do for myself. That had to be the only thing that kept her from leaving me all together.

ж ʃ

As second year finals approached, I recognized that I was sorely unprepared. I'd been seriously considering a way out of this mess I had created. I knew I couldn't pass those tests in the shape I was in, so what was I to do? So, the week before finals were to be given, I made an appointment with Ms. Johnson in the Administrative Office.

"Mr. Moore," she said when I stood in front of her.

Hmmm, I wonder what's with that tone of voice. And check out that look in her eye; I wonder if she's heard or if she knows.

"Look, what do I have to do to withdraw from this year and come back in the fall and repeat my second year?" My plan was to get out before the finals were given so that, at least, I would not have failed them. My other tests during the year had gone on miserably, very sub-par, and there was no real reason for me to think that by taking the year over I, somehow, would come back in fighting form. As long as I carried "my new friend" around with me, I would always be out of order. But, hey, being reasonable or in order was not a part of my repertoire right then. Survival was.

"Why do you wish to withdraw?"

"Well, I have a personal issue going on that has distracted me and I feel that I can resolve it between now and next August plus I don't believe I'm prepared to pass next week's finals. So, it would be in my best interest, I think, to start fresh in the fall."

"Mr. Moore, you state your case well. However, I would like to know the nature of this 'personal issue' you say you have."

I *say* I have! Who is she to question me, I'd like to know? She sure is being nosy, wanting to know the real deal. Maybe, she already knows. I can't tell, but I'm not gonna confirm it, no sir-ee. I guess, maybe, folks have been talking around here because even I can tell the changes in me; all the little stupid shit I've been doing and the little dumb-ass comments I've made to some classmates. White folk at that. I bet something's been said. It shows, my dysfunction.

"All I can say is that it's personal and that I hope you can respect my privacy about this especially since it affects me and not the school."

"You must understand our concern whenever a student goes off-course. We do realize that life does not stop because of being in school and that this level of education is a challenge. This is not for everyone. There is some adjustment required, more for some than others." She paused for a few moments, organizing her thoughts, letting that sink in while looking at me like I might want to consider myself some kind of dumb-ass. Then she gives me this real hard stare. "Mr. Moore, I appreciate your feelings and your need for privacy in this matter, so I'm going to recommend your request to withdraw. I truly hope that things will work out for you. You will get formal notice in the mail in a couple of days."

Whew!

Well, that was done. Now, if I could just get it together by next August, I'd be alright. I'd already secured a lab technician job in one of the research labs until school started. I just had to wait until the formal withdrawal notification had been sent before I could start working. Always some kind of technicality in the way.

During this time, beginning in April when I saw Ms. Johnson, until August when classes started again, I made no real effort to deal with what was steadily becoming a big problem. Dionne was right. I couldn't let it go because whatever extra cash I had went toward that and whatever spare time I had went toward that too.

It got so that I would shoot up anywhere, this just being part of my recreation and the way I carried my friend around with me, is how I rationalized it. It was a secret thrill to take my paraphernalia onto the school grounds and find some stairwell or some empty room to get off in. I was out of control and didn't know it. I felt intrinsically that what I was doing was wrong, but I could do nothing to stop myself. I craved that shit so hard.

I couldn't tell my family the real reason I had to withdraw; they would've stopped everything right then and there. I had to cling to the hope that I would survive this episode as I had survived so many others. I held on to the fiction that I was bigger than this thing and that it wasn't going to handle me, I was going to handle it. Hah, now that was some real bullshit right there.

I didn't see how I could go to treatment, mainly because I was still in school. I saw no options other than to stay the course and hope and pray that things would turn out as they always had.

This was the bedrock of my hardheadedness: my belief that somehow, everything would turn out good.

Even though I had never gotten down on my knees in prayer, things had turned out pretty good so far. The way that I perceived God's Plan was, apparently, the right way. It didn't require a whole lot of bowing and gesticulating and begging, just a quiet reverence for Him and His creation; the acknowledgement that there is a Power greater than oneself. I felt like I was in His good graces to be able to withstand the turmoil I had subjected myself to thus far. Certainly, He would not turn His back on me when I needed Him most. For sure, because this had to be part of His Divine Plan for me as well and I was convinced He would not fail me.

ߙ ߚ

August came entirely too soon.

The job that I had taken had been quite an education. It was the kind of job I could see for myself. Creating experimental designs specifically for the testing of an idea, employing complex and delicate instruments to quantify and calculate these designs and, finally, the interpretation of the collected data.

All of this I observed during that interim. It was science in action, where you could see the day-by-day, hands-on labor required to demonstrate one, just one, indisputable, verifiable fact. It was a commentary on how tedious and exacting the Sciences can be.

And I was thinking that, maybe, if all else went wrong, this was something I could do.

My second second year was about to begin and I found myself undeniably adrift. I was loose at the moorings. Sure, I'd had a break from school and was gainfully employed the entire time, but I was on that shit the whole time, too. What else should I have expected?

My original classmates had moved on to their third year clinical rotations and I became a part of the sea of unrecognizable faces that had been the class behind me. It didn't matter, though, I was just going through the motions. I believed that just by hanging in there that the drive to win would return. Pure folly.

As classes began and textbooks were opened, I found that my interest in the subject matter just was not there. I was in school in body only. I was there because being a student was all I knew how to do.

My real interest had become cocaine, more cocaine, an unlimited supply, if you would, with an order of fresh syringes to the side, if you please.

ᚳ ᚹ

Because finances were such an obstacle and because I had no other real skills to make money, I began to make small time sales. I would sell a fifty here, a twenty-five there, hand-to-hand transactions to help support my now undeniably strong habit. These dealings caused me to come into contact with a whole other type of person, one who was smart and street savvy, way more than me.

Now, a fellow of meager resources and little sophistication handling felonious amounts of narcotic among folk he hardly knew was a recipe for disaster. Other than what happened at Hampton, I had no idea what I was doing. Selling narcotics out in the general public was completely different than selling to one's comrades and pals in school.

This was a clear indication of my dope-dealing IQ: zero. I didn't know shit.

Since it appeared that my progress in school, this time around, would be no better than it was when I took my withdrawal, I began to have, for the first time in my life, doubt. I began to question my invincibility, the divine rightness of my quest. A kind of intellectual lethargy set in, a mental constipation that usurped all of my efforts at academic reconstruction. A new feeling, a different mood began to unfold. The sense that I was living outside of His Will seeped in. And it frightened me.

What remained of my personality craved relief. I craved relief from the rat-race of school, relief from the necessity of doing right all the time, relief that could only be found in the poison that caused all of this turmoil in the first place. But, I had to go on.

Although I was living a false prosperity and a perpetual lie, I finally found the connection that would make it all work out.

A middle-aged white guy who happened to be riding through the parking lot of the apartments pulled up to where I was, as I was about to go inside my place. He drove a ratty looking Chevy pickup and seemed to be "looking."

I never questioned his authenticity. Must be like my lucky day.

"Hey yo, what's up?" I asked, as he pulled into a parking space.

"Nothing really. What you up to?" Kind of a Dixie drawl, country folk, for sure.

"I'm just on my way inside. You don't look familiar, I haven't seen you around. What's on your mind?" Hoping and praying that he'd say the magic words, I didn't give a shit who he was.

"Naw. I ain't from around here, but I was thinking I could run into somebody that would know where something is around here."

"Well, depending on what kind a something you talkin' about, we might could talk." My feeble attempt at being cautious.

"You know where some powder is? That's what I'm talking about." There, he said it.

"Maybe so. Why don't you come on inside so we can talk some more."

He got out and came on in and as we talked, it became clear that he wasn't interested in no one or two fifty-dollar pieces, no sir, he wanted to make multiple purchases of an ounce or more and I just so happened to know the guy to deal with. He pulled out 10 hundred dollar bills right then and there and I was only happy to oblige. I went off, out the door and across the parking lot. The dude I dealt with just happened to live in the complex.

Hot damn! I got me a real spender, no more of that nickel-and-dime bullshit for me. I'm going straight to the top!

I knocked and he came to the door.

"Yo, what up, Rick." He stood aside and I came on in.

"What up, Terry. You straight?"

"What you talkin' about?"

"How 'bout a O-Z?"

"You got a grand?" I pulled out that wad of bills and he exclaimed, "Oh shit, Rick done went out and robbed somebody! Boy, you done hit the jackpot, ain't you?"

"Sort of, yeah."

"Alright, then."

When I got back to my place, I gave that farmer the package and I was nearly prancing with anticipation to get my little cut for making the run. "Well, whatcha think?" I asked expectantly, silently begging for him to put some on the table for me.

"This looks pretty good." He dabbed a bit onto his tongue. "Tastes good, too. Got a nice freeze to it. I'm satisfied. I'll call you later to let you know when I want another one."

"But what about me?" I whine. "You gonna just take it and not leave me none? That shit ain't right."

"I know, but you're gonna have to bear with me here, I've got some other people to deal with and if it don't weigh out right when I get back then I've got a problem. I'll get you right next time, I just got to do it this way right now."

"I don't know, man. Your people would understand if you had to pay your connection with a little bit. You're s'posed to leave me something, especially on a sale like that. This ain't right." I could tell, I could hear it in my voice how pitiful I was coming off, but I didn't care, I wanted a hit.

"I'll make up for it next time, I promise. It'll all work out, you'll see, but I gotta go. I got people waiting."

Damn! I ain't get shit! I don't like this type a shit, not one bit. He s'posed to give me some and he knows it. I did my part and everything and for what?

"Alright dude. I'll see ya later."

ଓ ଽ

My performance at school continued its dismal decline. I was scrabbling at thin air, hoping some miracle would save this sinking ship.

So when word came through the grapevine that I was wanted by local Law Enforcement, I didn't panic. I calmly walked off school grounds and never looked back. No way was I going to let them arrest me in class; that would be the ultimate in embarrassment, worse that panhandling classmates for petty change.

I went to Dionne's.

"You know the police been looking for you."

"Yeah, I heard."

"Well, whatcha gonna do?"

"I don't know. Looks like school's a done deal, huh?"

"Nah, really? Nah, I bet they gone wait for you 'til you get out of this trouble you're in, don'tcha think?" She gave me a look that said we might be a done deal, too. "Of course school's a done deal."

"And I really don't want to go to jail right now…"

"But, you know, eventually, you're gonna have to."

"…so I'm gonna try to get into some kind of treatment center somewhere 'til all of this blows over. At least, it'll look like I'm trying to do something about this thing."

"In other words, go hide."

"Yep, that's about it, unless you have another idea."

"Yeah, how about turning yourself in and getting this over with. You can't run forever. You know you're all messed up. I've seen the changes come over you in the last year or so, and it's not been fun to watch."

"Nah, I ain't ready to go to jail just yet, see…"

"Why not? You know your career is over, you've just pissed on that and now you've got to answer for it. They got warrants out for you and they're not gonna stop until they get you locked up."

She says this purposefully and with strength, able to intuit the direction this thing must go. A kind of no-nonsense determination seemed to kick in.

"...if I can make it to a treatment center, they gotta wait 'til I get out. They won't serve warrants on me while I'm in a treatment center or hospital or something. Plus, it'll look good when I do go to court, that I've made some attempt to help myself."

The magnitude of my failing had not hit me, but I knew things weren't pretty. I didn't hate myself, but I was humiliated to have to go out like this.

"If you just want to buy yourself some time sure, go ahead. But you're silly if you think they won't come to wherever you are to serve those warrants on you. If you was on the moon, they'd catch the next shuttle up there to get you. They're gonna track you down, they already been here and I ain't said nothing to them, so how they know you're over here a lot? See what I'm saying. Them folks be knowing things we don't think they know."

"Well, maybe they do, but this is one time when they're gonna have to prove to me how well-connected they are. In the meantime, let's find a place that will accept an impaired medical professional."

"'Impaired medical professional?'"

"I figure if it's explained like this to whoever is in charge, they might be more willing to listen. We know I ain't got no money and I know there are programs for people just like me."

Boy, what a departure from the norm. My lifestyle, the way I went about my daily business, was about to be drastically altered. I knew I was just buying time, but I also knew that I had to get my ducks in a row so that when I went to court the judge would be encouraged towards leniency. Maybe even probation and a stiff fine. I could deal with that. I mean, really, what could they do? I was on my way to becoming a doctor and, due to the stresses of my profession, I fell prey to substance abuse, a common affliction among those in my calling. Plus I didn't have a record in North Carolina. So, to me, all of this was ample reason for me to thwart their detection for as long as I could.

That I might have been an addict was not the issue. I mean, how could I be an addict? I was enrolled at a prestigious university, I had a good place to live, came from a good family, had my own car, so how could I possibly be an addict? I'll admit that I had developed a fondness for the stuff, but that didn't make me no addict.

After a few pages turned and a few phone calls made, Pinehurst Treatment Center in Pinehurst, NC, agreed to accept me on an emergency basis. I could come right then, without delay.

Dionne and I made our way down east, to Pinehurst. Got there and she dropped me off with a loving hug and a sensuous kiss. "Bye, Rick. You know I'll always be there for you. I'll come down to visit after a week or so, okay. And remember, I love you and I'm very proud of you making this stand right here. Even though you were forced into it, I think it'll be for the best."

"Ok, Dionne, see you later. You know I love you, too, and I will always appreciate how you've been right by my side through this little rough patch in my life."

"Well, I guess that's what love'll do for you, huh? Make you do stuff you never in a million years thought you would!"

જી ૪૦

I had been at Pinehurst for about three weeks, learning about powerlessness and coming to believe and making a decision to turn my life and my will over to God and how all of that related to addiction, when the hospital administrator came to me and said, "Mr. Moore, we've been contacted by the police in Chapel Hill about your whereabouts. Because of confidentiality reasons, I could not disclose whether or not you were here. I felt it best to inform you personally, so that if there are any arrangements you need to make, you might want to get started. There is nothing the hospital can do to protect you should they show up here with a warrant."

Well, so much for my theory. The cavalry was on the way. It was time for me to go.

I called Dionne and she came down that evening. Talk about a period of pins and needles, geez, I looked at every car that came into the drive, trying not to seem nervous, but was scared as hell. She couldn't get there soon enough.

After a little discussion, we agreed to call the police as soon as we got back. I was booked in at the Orange County Jail under a $12,000 bond, facing two counts of Trafficking and six counts of Sale and Delivery. I figured I'd better call home, let them know why they hadn't heard from me in such a while.

"Well, Ma, I'm in jail."

"Jail! What for?"

"I got busted for selling drugs. I sold some to an undercover officer a couple of months ago and I just found out about it a few weeks ago."

"Selling drugs? Boy, what's the matter with you! Didn't you learn nothing after what happened at Hampton?"

"Ma, this is a little different. At Hampton, I didn't really go off the deep end."

"What do you mean?"

"This time, I experimented a little. I tried some because I didn't believe it would really affect me. Then, it seemed like, all of a sudden, one time wasn't enough, it was like I couldn't get enough. I did it over and over and over 'til I ran out of money and then I still couldn't stop. So, I ran into this guy that wanted to buy some and, thinking this would provide for my need, he turned out to be the police. In other words, I went off the deep end."

"My Lord!"

"As far as school is concerned, that's over with, at least until I can get this legal stuff behind me."

"Son, I am so sorry to hear this. I felt it in my bones, something wasn't right with you. I just couldn't put my finger on what it was."

"Yeah Ma, something just wasn't right."

"At least you're alive and in your right mind, not like your Aunt Clotelle. You know how she comes and goes." Momma's sister had had bouts of manic depression and schizophrenia off and on for years, so it wasn't such a long jump to think it was something in the bloodline. "At least you've got a chance for a second try."

There goes mom, always the optimist.

"How much is your bond?"

"$12,000."

"Alright then, we'll be up there tomorrow and get you out. You can just come home for a while."

Ah, the love of a mother for her child.

CR ☙

I did go home that summer and waited for my court date in September because Mom was as good as her word. She came right up and got me out on bond and that turned out to be a flavorful period in my life, the summer of '84. I just kicked back around the house and made attempts to have a normal life. I'd cut the grass and do the dishes and vacuum around the house, basically just piddle around.

My sister Johnetta, God bless her, invited me to a party for one of her friends and while I was there I met Roberta. My sister had gotten tired of seeing me just doing nothing, so she had a little mercy on me because I needed to get out; having left Dionne in Chapel Hill slowed my social life greatly.

Now this Roberta girl was somebody I could get used to being with. Very pretty, very stylish and *very* sexy. She was a school teacher, elementary school, so we had lots to talk about. Her sense of humor enticed me and I hoped that this thing could move along. Come to find out we'd been neighbors all along, but had never crossed paths. How quaint. A romance began to bud, but I had real concern about that. See, I had a secret.

"You know, it never fails," she said after I had told her, "that when I meet somebody I like, there's always another circumstance in the way, always something to disappoint me."

"Well, it won't be forever and I might even get off with probation. But regardless of what happens in court, the result won't last a lifetime. Maybe a couple of years at the most."

"How can you be so sure?"

"I can't be, but I come from a long line of optimists and we have a tendency to see the brighter side of things, a tendency to see the silver lining in dark clouds. No, I can't be so sure, but I believe in the eventual rightness of things."

"I sure hope you're right. I never expected this thing between us to turn out so well. I'm mildly surprised."

"Oh, surprised that you might like somebody so close to home or somebody that's not six feet tall and drop-dead gorgeous."

"No, none of that."

"Yeah, well, I'm pretty sure things are gonna work out."

We stood there in her backyard, just talking and enjoying the out-of-doors. She lived with her mom and dad and they had a Shepherd-mixed mutt that they kept leashed and we kind of played with it, but really our thoughts were on each other and the dark cloud looming on the horizon of our future.

FIVE

Southern Correctional Center is a medium custody facility located in Troy, NC. I found myself on a bus headed to this place after my September 14 court date.

Apparently I was lucky to have received only eight years, this having come as a result of "substantially cooperating" with the authorities in the "identification and/or conviction of other individuals in the narcotics trade."

In other words, I snitched.

This was nothing to be proud of but, hey, I didn't know any better, plus the police had my ass in a sling: either do this and qualify for First Offender Status (that incident in Hampton being conveniently forgotten), giving the judge more latitude in sentencing, or keep up the facade of a righteous, straight-up, I-ain't-no-snitch type fella and watch what would happen. I didn't like the tone of that, so I had to go along.

I was facing over 100 years without this part of the plea agreement and I needed to have a hedge against the judge going crazy and declaring some astronomical number as my time to serve. It was a crap shoot anyway, but being a First Offender did mean less time. I just hoped I wouldn't bump into any of the people involved in my case at this place.

It was a large facility with seven fifty-foot gun towers, double rows of chain linked, razor-topped fencing and five separate housing units or wings that radiated outward from the central processing and administrative areas. We were brought into the intake area where everything in our possession, including underwear and socks, was placed in a cardboard box to be mailed home. At our expense. If you didn't have a home, that property would be discarded or placed in the clothes house for anyone who might get out of prison. If you didn't have any money, they would charge the shipping to your account until, if and when some money came.

Once you were undressed, you submitted to a total body search. Mouth, armpits, hair on the head and then the dreaded "bend over and cough" procedure. And those guys actually looked!

Each man was given a delousing solution to lather into all hairy areas and then a cold shower to rinse this off. Now, I think the cold shower part was just to get a laugh on their part. The facility was nearly new and we knew they had warm water, they were just being assholes.

We were supplied with sheets, a towel, a change of clothing and toiletries (soap, toilet tissue, shampoo, toothpaste, etc.) after which we were herded to our pre-assigned housing units.

During all of this, there were about twenty of us who had gotten off the transfer bus together. No one was saying anything to anyone else and I hoped that no one would say anything to me. Overall, I had to admit, this whole process was looking rather well-organized, my first visit to a state penal institution.

As we moved toward our housing units, I couldn't help but notice how spotless, almost neurotically clean the place was. Obsessive was the thought that rang loud in my head. The hallways gleamed and shined with fresh wax, there was not a speck of dust anywhere.

And where was the noise? It was absolutely quiet. This shit was getting downright spooky. The place reminded me of the buildings at Hampton that would whisper quietly, exuding confidence and strength, good planning and good organization. If these were the qualities that the State wanted you to recognize that it had, it did a magnificent job in doing so. Unmistakably, you were in the bowels of an impregnable, supremely efficient, totally indifferent colossus.

When we got to the housing area, it got a little noisier, though by not much, and I could see why. Each wing was actually a self-contained block of thirty-two rooms that you entered only when the officer in the central control tower for that wing allowed you. He had an array of buttons and lights that indicated and directed what door to open or what door remained open too long.

Each man had his own cell in a two-tiered dormitory which was equipped with cable TV and central air. Although the showers and toilets were in an enclosed area at one end of the dorm and the TV area was at the other end, all sleeping, writing and personal activity could be done privately.

This can't be prison, I said to myself. Those fences must be there to keep folk out, not to keep folk in. I bet there are those who would not mind spending the rest of their lives in a place like this.

It had its own medical and dental facility and a pharmacy where you picked up your prescriptions the doctor ordered for you. A modern weight room and a full-length indoor basketball court, a pool room, Ping-Pong tables and a shuffleboard area. I started to ask where the heated pool and the tennis courts were, but I figured they'd let me know.

Because of my education, I was given a job as a clerk in their law library. This gave me an opportunity to meet many of the guys under quasi-professional circumstances. They would tell me their stories in the feeble hope that I could help them get out of what was really a luxury resort community. Being the new guy meant I might be able to shed some light on old, musty cases, cases that had been tossed and turned countless times. These guys were just looking for some hope, any kind of hope. This arrangement gave me status that I otherwise would not have had. As a result of this and the benefits of the facility, my stay turned into an educational rather than a punitive experience.

ഇ ഇ

During the 10 months I spent at Southern, I continued to perform juggling acts with the girls, as though I was on the street. Dionne came on the weekends when my family did not come, not knowing another girl came with my family many of those weekends. Likewise Roberta did not know that I was having a visitor on her off weekend. Quite often, she would make the drive alone, just to spend a few moments with me, without the distractions of family.

This went on for most of my stay at Southern and it gave me no small amount of sorrow. What with the sudden loss of female intimacy and the pressing memories of the fantastic sex I had with those two, I found myself dealing with personal sexual issues I had never dealt with before. I mean, how does one deal with sex in an environment that, by its nature, is hostile to healthy sexual conduct? This was a place that was socially unnatural (that being hundreds of men confined to a limited space with their movements tightly controlled) and was against any and all sexual conduct and contact. What, exactly, does one do for relief?

There were people who engaged in same-sex behavior and they had most people's attention. A great many of the population had been inside for eight, ten, twelve years or more and dealing with a man on a sexual level was, by their standard, considered normal. I just couldn't see it.

Still, what does one do? Those weekend visits were pure torture. They served, it seemed to me, only to whet my desires into an almost intolerable frenzy. Though intimate touching was not allowed, our conversations would be X-rated plus some touching, but only of the brush-the-surface-of-your-clothes type. I could sneak a feel between her legs on the sly and we'd both giggle and laugh, but what did that do? Boy, was I a horny motherfucker those days. I guess that rule, keep your hands on top of the table, served a purpose, but I had cooty-cat to play with and titties to rub, so I couldn't be bothered by no crazy-ass prison rules. Fuck that. By the same token, this sneaking around up under the table wasn't gonna get it either. So, the question remained…what to do?

That thing called self-gratification was nearly as foreign to me as homosexuality. I mean, I hadn't had any dealings with myself since, as kids, a few of us would gather around and we'd pull our little things out to see what each other had. I guess I was twelve or thirteen, everybody had a itty-bitty hard-on and we were all goo-goo eyed standing there looking at each other. Real innocent. Nothing malicious, nothing negative. Just young boys trying to figure it out. Nobody touched anybody, we just held on to ourselves trying to see who had the most hair or who was bigger than the other, giggling the whole time. I don't know how, but somehow, this thing about jacking off was weird. It was strange and was something I couldn't seem to get comfortable with.

Maybe it would eventually become something that I could be familiar with because, I tell you the truth, when your testosterone gets up and there is no adequate way to satisfy that urge, it seems like there is a tornado in your crotch. Any little thought or any little contact, however inadvertent that contact may be, would make your dick hard. And who wants to walk around all day long with their dick all hard? The sexual urge has physical as well as mental components that can become a cocktail of colliding emotions and feelings searching for expression.

Boy, was I glad to make it to minimum custody and get transferred to the facility in Winston-Salem. Relief was just around the corner!!

Going to minimum happened at just the right time. I was beginning to rationalize how a guy might become involved with another guy. I mean the pressures were there and they were real. Although I had not crossed that line, it began to seem like not such a crazy thought after all. I could see how it *could* happen. Maybe that's what it takes for some guys to make it and, if so, who am I to judge? I'm just glad I was leaving.

Now that I was going to Cherry Street, I could look forward to some up close and personal contact visits where some *real* hanky-panky, some *real* touch-me-right-there, could happen.

છ ৪৩

Up to the point of my custody change, my visitors consisted of mom, Johnetta and Roberta, with Dionne and me having come to an end a couple of months ago. It happened so indelicately. She came to visit on a weekend that I had not planned for; Roberta had been there a few minutes and there I was, caught in the middle.

"So, Rick, this is how you treat me after all that we've been through? And you know we've been through a lot."

Uh-oh.

"I met you in '81 and here it is three years later an' I'm coming to see you, in prison of all places. I took care of you when you were sick, gave you a hideout when you were running from the law and loved you unconditionally. You had total access to my car, my home, an' my love an' now you've got another girl?"

All this going on kinda loudly right there in the visitation room, in front of everybody.

"Nigga, YOU AIN'T SHIT!!"

I saw her contorted expression, I saw the pain on her face and it rattled me. Because of where we were, I couldn't let that scenario become a full-blown scene. I hated to, but I had to give her the upper hand. Roberta didn't say a word, just sat there quietly assessing the situation, wondering what the outcome would be.

I said, "I didn't have the courage to tell you..."

"Yeah, I know. You've shown me how good you are at running and hiding."

"...so, when I came to prison and Roberta wanted to be a part of this, I had to try to work out how these visits could be arranged. I didn't tell her about you, nor you about her."

Roberta still sitting there silently, taking it all in. I didn't bother to introduce them.

"I just thought things would work themselves out."

"Well, they certainly have. So, what's up? What're you gonna do? Is it gonna be me or her 'cause it ain't gonna be both me *and* her, that's for damn sure."

"What? You gonna make me choose right here, right now?" I looked at Roberta, trying to read her expression. I looked at Dionne, knowing how she felt. But, she was right. I had to make a choice. I knew who was better suited for me, who I had more in common with and who, in the long run, would make me happiest. I paused for another moment. "Well, right now, I'm gonna spend some time with Roberta. Maybe next week, if you decide to come, we can talk some more, see if we can get on the same page."

"Talk some more, huh? Get on the same page, huh?" She looked at Roberta and said, "I don't know what you're gonna do about this guy here, but I'm outta here." Then, she turned back to me. "Rick, you're dumber than I thought. I ain't fixin' to stay around and wait on you like I have to be second. No, that I don't have to be."

She left and I never saw her again.

ଔ ଓ

"Hey, baby girl, guess where I am!"

"No."

"Yep!"

"For real?"

"Yep."

"Well, when can I come?" Roberta asked anxiously.

Already I could feel the charge, the excitement of what we had planned coming together. There was the distinctly pleasant sensation of a bulge occurring and I had to disengage my thinking so that I could remain decent on the telephone, standing at the telephone bank among all those guys.

"I guess you can come this weekend if you want to. You know Momma is gonna want to come, too."

"That's only right. She should come if she wants to."

"Yeah, but what about us?" Whining. My selfishness out front and unappealing.

"Well, I think we'll be alright. We've waited this long, we can wait some more."

"You say that shit, but be for real."

"I am. You know your momma knows how to be cool about things. I bet she'll just come and stay for a little while and then leave, watch and see." She waited a minute to see if I could process this insurrection. "So, you made it up there already, huh?"

"Yeah," I said rather unhappily. "I told you it wasn't gonna be so bad, didn't I?"

"Yeah, you did and I didn't think it was gonna go by fast enough, but it did, didn't it!" she said with real enthusiasm.

"Yes, it did." Surely, she couldn't misplace my growing discontent.

"So...?"

"So what?" I asked, truly unable to comprehend.

"Are you ready?"

"Ready? Ready for what?"

"Boy, you are so silly. What do you think?"

"I mean, you already said Momma probably will come, so I let all that go."

"You are so-o-o dumb, you ain't got no faith at all. I already talked to your momma. She said she'll wait 'til next weekend."

I gasped kind of loud, but I didn't care. "Ah-h, girl, you ain't shit. You played me! Here I am about to bust and you playin' games. You gonna come up this weekend for real?"

"Yeah, boy."

"So, it's on then..." I said, somewhat under my breath. I could feel it all over my body. My balls were tingling, my skin was flushed and the weekend couldn't come soon enough. Horniness is an animal with a character and personality all its own.

"Yep. So, you say Saturday afternoon, huh, around 2:00, right? Think you can make it?" she said, giggling like a teen-ager.

"You know I'm gonna be there. I been waitin' on this for a while."

"Me, too."

"Okay, see ya then."

I was set. I was home, my family was well and my girl was coming to see me and we both had great expectations. This visit's gonna be *so* live!

ଔ ଓ

Surprisingly, the urge to use, the cravings that were at one time so strong, had abated and I began to feel my old self returning. This period of enforced abstinence, courtesy of the State of North Carolina, played an important role in the return of the old me. That guy, who at one time was on a divine mission to become a doctor, was back! That out-of-sight, out-of-mind psychology proved to be quite effective in helping me over the rough spots.

I had no clue as to how I was going return to medicine, I just knew that one day I would. My hand had always been in His hand. The presence of His spirit in my life had been a balm for my sin-sick soul and a bridge over deeply troubled waters. He would, without a shadow of doubt, make a way out of no way.

Maybe drugs were available in prison, maybe they weren't. I didn't know and I didn't go through any changes to find out. I just wasn't interested. I'd come full circle, from school to jail to prison and had returned to Winston reasonably intact. The program for proceeding through the system and out to freedom had been explained to me and drugs were the last thing on my mind.

Oddly enough, the regret or remorse that I should have felt since I had destroyed (or, at least, seriously delayed) my professional career was strangely silent. There I was, Inmate #0288782, kind of excited about where I was at that time, having made a journey through the State's penal system and found out that it wasn't all *that* bad. A confident optimism began to pervade my outlook and I was struck by the knowledge that this bag of lemons I had given to myself would turn into a jar of lemonade.

Upon my arrival, my interests immediately turned to the Community Volunteer and Work-Release Programs, which offered tangible, concrete consequences for good behavior and strong incentives for getting out.

My arrival heralded a new beginning in my life. It was attended by my family, which was well on its way to wellness, and the addition of another one, who seemed to fit right in. Our first visit in Winston-Salem was about to start and I was really excited.

"Hey, Momma!"

"Hi Ricky, how you doing?"

"Hey, Johnetta!"

"Hey, boy."

"What's up, Roberta?" I looked at her strangely. I didn't expect all these people and from the look on her face, neither did she.

"Hey, Rick."

"Well, I sure am glad y'all finally decided to get up here. I been waiting since yesterday. Y'all bring somethin' to eat?"

Momma had a box of KFC and Roberta had *our* picnic basket. Though it didn't look like food would be a problem, it seemed that other interests might be.

Johnetta said, "If we had known Roberta was gonna bring a whole basket, we would've saved that bit of money."

Momma added, "Or I could just take this home since it looks like you and Roberta have enough. I can eat this later on."

"Why don't you do that Mrs. Moore?" Roberta said.

Momma nodded. "Well, anyway, this is going to work out just as good. And, you know what? I'm really glad I don't have to make that drive down to Troy anymore, Ricky. This is much better, having you here."

"Absolutely, Ma. I'm glad I'm here, too. But, who woulda ever thought that I'd be up here on Cherry St.? Not in my wildest dreams did I ever see this scenario in on the horizon."

"No, I would never have thought this would happen either." she said. "Maybe, through all of this, God has a work planned for you that none of us can see. Because, son, you sure look good."

"And I feel good too, Ma."

Johnetta joined in. "He does look good, Momma, but one thing's for sure: we all had our hopes built up about having a doctor in the family and I for one am not pleased about this outcome." She looked around the table, trying to get nods of agreement. "I mean, there is no way you can convince anybody that God would approve of you using drugs. I think Ricky did what he did by being arrogant, self-centered and totally out of the will of God. Just plain ol' disobedience and these are the fruits of that disobedience."

That's just like Johnetta, she'd be the one for a reality check. Shit, all I wanted to do was to say hello to everybody, get something to eat and try to feel up my girl's panties, not get into a philosophical debate about my drug habit.

"This," she went on, as she gestured with her hand all about the visiting yard, a look of mild discomfort on her face, "is something that never should have been."

"Yeah, Johnetta, I can't argue with that. But I refuse to believe this is what God has for me. There's gotta be more to it. There's gotta be a silver lining to this dark cloud."

"What kind of silver lining?" Johnetta said, her skepticism still shining through. "What's that supposed to mean?"

"Well, let's be straight up. Momma, Roberta, what y'all say? Let's be straight up."

They both nodded.

I began, "I have been reasonably successful in my academic pursuits, even though I smoked a little pot and drank a little alcohol. Those things never interfered with what I was trying to do; they merely served as a form recreation. Well, when I passed my first year, I knew I could do this medical school thing. Even though I went to parties with my classmates where all kinds of stuff went on, none of that would deter me. So, I had heard about this cocaine thing, that if you'd put it in a needle and shoot it up, it'd really be a fun experience. So, that's what I did, just to see if that's what would happen. I knew I couldn't get hooked on it because I had been so successful otherwise, you see? Pure curiosity."

"And what did you learn?" my sister asked.

"That I really liked what it did to me and that, by its nature, it makes you do it again and again. I also learned it's something I can't mess with in the future. God has been merciful enough to restore me to my right self and I'll never cross that bridge again. I just want a second chance."

Roberta said, "Well, Rick, I can see that you're one of the smartest people I've met and that being a doctor is so *you*. It must be that there is another side to this story that has yet to unfold."

I continued, "And look, what about Roberta?"

"What do you mean?" Johnetta asked, still not one hundred percent willing to grant me any grace.

"Oh come on, Johnetta. What I'm saying is that there seems to be sort of a spiritual conspiracy of events that caused you to ask me to that party then, to place Roberta there to be introduced to me out of all the other guys there and, to top it off, for her to actually dig me. There's got to be something more planned, more of a Divine Plan, than what we see because God has surely blessed me with her."

"And speaking about that," Momma said, "they make the cutest couple don't they, Johnetta?"

"They really do, Momma."

"It's good to see you stand by my son like this. Not everyone would have been so willing to overlook his incarceration, but you looked beyond his fault."

"Well, I appreciate that Mrs. Moore. He's the kind of guy I don't mind standing by."

"Yeah, long as we don't stand by too long 'cause y'all really need to quit pretending like everybody on the same page." I gave Roberta a conspiratorial look. Apparently, this didn't escape Mom and Johnetta.

"Well, son, I guess we better be going now so you two can talk alone for a while."

"Aw, Ma, y'all ain't gotta rush." Me, trying to play it off, knowing I was lying, wishing they would *hurry up* and go. I was just trying to be polite. "I ain't seen y'all in a couple a weeks, so it ain't no hurry." Boy, I was really piling that shit high.

"Well, now that you're home, we don't have to be in a rush to see you. Come on, Johnetta, let's stop by the mall on the way home."

As they walked away from the visitation yard, Roberta and I looked at each other with that very special gleam in our eyes. I think, at that moment, the whole world stopped and instantaneously we knew each other's thoughts.

"So, what's up?" I said.

"I don't know, you tell me."

"I know I can't wait to get my hands on you."

"What you wanna do that for?" she said, with a reserved, demure smile.

"The better to know you, my dear," I say, feeling rather eager and very much in season. We both chuckle to ourselves as we began to fix our places. She brought out a cloth that flowed over both sides of the table. We put the food out and thought we would eat, but neither of us was really interested in food. It was just a decoy.

SIX

After satisfying some of my more urgent physical needs, my second goal was to find some kind of employment, which was a major step in getting back into the real world.

I had already created nightmare scenarios about employers being too reluctant to hire anybody with a felony background, but I found out that that was the furthest thing from the truth. In fact, the first place I inquired, a local Kentucky Fried Chicken, picked me right up. It was entry-level fast food and experience was not required. It did not come close to what my true abilities were worth and that was okay. Hey, you had to crawl before you walked, so this was as good a start as I could expect.

It was about this time that I met Tim at a weekly meeting of Yokefellows, an organization of Christian men and women who volunteer in prisons. It is present in most, if not all, prisons in North Carolina and has been a part of prison outreach for many years. At weekly meetings, guys are encouraged to fellowship in this Christian atmosphere where the concern is the spiritual quality of life for incarcerated individuals.

Tim had been a regular volunteer, was always there and always had a word of encouragement. He was a white guy, maybe seven or eight years older than me, who had an engaging smile and an infectious laugh. It was a warm summer evening and we were standing outside as he was going to the parking lot for home, having one of our regular conversations, when I happened to notice some paperwork in his hand. It had a Wake Forest letterhead and I inquired—just out of curiosity—about his work.

"I'm an associate professor over at Bowman Gray. I operate a lab there."

What? No, he didn't just say that, did he? Thinking I could not have heard him correctly, I asked him a couple of off-hand questions.

"Really. That ought to be interesting work, you being in a lab and all. What kinda stuff do you do? Research?" I was atremble with excitement.

"Well, it's pretty interesting. We do a biochemical test on reproductive tissue tumors in women. Those samples are biopsied material that we receive from all of the area hospitals. From them we try to see how one form of treatment works as opposed to another."

"So, what are you, M.D. or Ph.D.?"

"I'm Ph.D. Why do you ask?"

Hallelujah! I knew it, I just knew it!

"Just wait right here, Tim."

I flew down the steps to the dorm, jogged to my locker and got my resume. In like fashion, I returned and handed him my paperwork. He looked it over briefly, then looked up with a perplexed—even stunned—expression and asked, "Is this you?"

"Yeah, that's what I've done up to right now, excluding, for obvious reasons I think, my current imprisonment. I hope the document speaks for itself."

"I'll say it does. Look, you're just the person I've been looking for. For the life of me, I couldn't figure out how I was going to replace Rena. She's my current assistant and she's eight months pregnant. I didn't want to, but I'd eventually have to go down to personnel and get a file to replace her."

"Well, what's wrong with that?"

"Because you're dealing with unknowns. They'll send you somebody that's qualified, for sure, but you don't have any idea who they are or where they come from or what their values are. I knew Rena before I hired her and that's how I prefer to do it. But going through personnel, geez, that's like walking through a minefield."

"And, lo and behold, I show up!"

"And lo and behold, you show up." He shook his head and I could see from his smile that, like me, he was seeing a Divine hand in all this. "So, what I want you to do is to go on over to personnel in the Hanes Building on Hawthorne. Fill out your application and don't forget to put 'yes' on your felony history question. I'll come to personnel myself and get your paperwork. Won't be a problem."

"Are you serious. Just like that?"

"Just like that, but you need to get right on it. I'm looking for her to go any time now and we've got to get you trained before she goes, so don't wait around."

And with that, he not only left the facility, he left me stupefied as well. I mean, I knew this was going to happen and I thought it might take a little more time but, boy, when God makes a power move, He makes one! I declare, this is the handiwork of God Almighty, clear as pure water. For such a confluence of events to occur, for so many wide-ranging variables to intersect at this time and place, it can only be Divine Intervention. Suppose I hadn't paid any attention to his letterhead? Suppose Rena had already gone to the hospital? Suppose I hadn't made minimum when I did? I mean, I could go on and on with the "what ifs" and still not be able to highlight this event, because that's what this was, an Event. The possibilities were endless. I gotta tell somebody. I gotta call my Momma.

悆 悃

"Momma!"

"What, boy?"

"Guess what."

"I can't guess. What?"

"Guess anyway."

"What, boy!"

"I got a job at Bowman Gray."

There was a long pause, a charged, expectant silence, a silence so majestic it seemed as though it was about to release something spectacular. I couldn't tell if she was still on the phone, but I hadn't heard it click. Then, I heard her.

"No."

"Yes."

"No!"

"Yes!"   /

"Well, I swanee, it never fails. I shouldn't be surprised, though. God can do anything! I've been telling you that haven't I, Ricky."

"Yeah, Momma, but..."

"This is one of the better deals that He's done and I've seen Him do some mighty interesting stuff, but this is pretty good right here. And so soon, too."

"But, Ma, I been telling you the same thing, ain't that right? This is just confirmation of what we both been saying all along."

"Yes, that is so right. Well, tell me. How did this happen? What did you do?"

I told her the story and concluded, "Ain't that somethin'?"

"It sure is. I can't wait to tell Johnetta. She'll be knocked off her feet."

"I know that's right."

"It's almost like a dream. I still can't believe it."

"It is dream-like ain't it, Ma. But, you know what? What this experience is teaching me is that living in this world, with all of its unexpected consequences, is based on spiritual principles that have very little to do with religion or church-going or any of the religious institutions man has created," I said. "Just like blessings fall down to the criminal and the evil-doer, accidents and catastrophe happen to the saint and the child of God. It just might be that little of what we go through and experience on a day-to-day basis have to do with a Supreme Being interfering in our lives."

"Well, Ricky, to say Divine Intervention is unrelated to going to church or believing in God, well, I just don't know. When you talk like this son, sometimes you bother me. I don't know where you get it from."

"Well, Ma, these aren't simple questions, so there aren't going to be simple answers. It's clear to me that there is Something beyond human institutions, human ways of doing things, at work here in this world. I tell you the truth, Ma, any doubt that I might have ever had..."

"I can only imagine your doubt because I surely have had mine." she put in.

"...has been completely obliterated. I don't now and have never, since I've been an adult, ever gotten down on my knees to pray. I just lift Him up in my thoughts daily, giving reverence and worship to all that He has done for me."

"What do you mean you don't get down on your knees when you pray?"

"I mean, I don't pray in the way you taught me to pray. It seems that God is far more interested in what we *do* than in what we *say* we're gonna do or in what we want Him to do for us. It seems to me these events today speak to *something* that I must be doing right, don'tcha think?"

I don't think Momma was convinced, but we left it at that.

☓ ☣

Bowman Gray School of Medicine/Baptist Hospital is the medical school/teaching hospital facility away from the main campus of Wake Forest University. It is across town from the unit on Hawthorne Road in a leafy, tree-lined suburban area with its own atmosphere of the educationally and socially elite. If it got out around the facility that I was in prison, I might be looked on with great trepidation. It turned out that Dr. Kotke was good for discretion. I mean, Bowman Gray was not known for its community activism on my side of the tracks, so it was a big deal to everybody when one of us got hired to do more than serve or clean up.

When I went in to personnel, I didn't have the insecurity of not knowing if I'd get a call back or if I had to make a follow-up phone call to check on my application. And sure enough, he called me over for the interview the next day after I let him know the application was in.

Tim was right. Rena was as big as a baby elephant. She could go at any minute. She was a petite woman, but being nine months pregnant, she waddled around the lab and introduced me to everybody and all of the equipment and told me to just hang tight, that we could get this worked out in a couple of days flat. I didn't think she had that long, it seemed to me.

Tim joined in and said that we would get started bright and early and that I should try to be in by eight or eight-thirty each day. He went on to say that, eventually, I would be traveling to the various hospitals (Lexington, High Point, the three in Winston-Salem) to pick up their surgical biopsy samples. It would be necessary for me to get my driver's license, as traveling is part of the job.

And so it came to pass that I was afforded a unique and almost unheard of opportunity for a guy in my situation. Being incarcerated, but working at a highly respected medical institution seemed incomprehensible, yet there I was. I left the KFC that very day and the next day joined the tremendous work force of the Bowman Gray School of Medicine/Baptist Hospital complex where there were over 5,000 regular employees. I stepped right into the organized mayhem that is characteristic of top-notch institutions of research and knowledge without missing a beat.

I was comfortable. I was home.

Ψ ∞

Leaving the prison gates every day, going to a job that was as nice or nicer than the prison job the guards had may have inspired some enmity, but either I was too simple or too indifferent to see it. Actually, I didn't give a shit about what they thought. The guys may also have had some feelings in this regard, but I was never privy to it. In fact, it seemed that I was held in a little brighter light than before because, apparently, the grapevine stories about that guy, Rick, who was almost a doctor had turned out to have some merit.

My social interactions on the camp certainly did not change and although my appetite for cocaine had gone on sabbatical, I still felt that a little weed wouldn't hurt a thing. I'd concluded categorically that cocaine was my particular problem, nothing else.

Weed was in a class all by itself. To me, it had none of the negative outcomes associated with it as did cocaine and so was considered relatively harmless. I'd smoked a little bit at Southern, but nothing extraordinary. When I got to Cherry Street, I began to associate with one or two of the guys who did smoke because I enjoyed catching a buzz now and then. It seemed to add an aspect to prison life where you would be there in body, but not in mind. A little puff tilted the world just a bit. This was escapism at its best.

Doing time and smoking weed were inseparable buddies.

Since I never thought one could be dependent on weed, false dependency was never considered. In retrospect, I was unable or unwilling to accept life on life's terms and took the coward's way out by escaping. This would have consequences beyond anything I could see at the time.

Since weed had become, unbeknownst to me at the time, the substitute for what I really wanted, I'd persuaded myself that I was through with cocaine.

Though I didn't smoke at work or on the way to work, occasionally, one or two of us would go with the Chaplain to his home church on Sundays. His church was located in Walkertown, a small, rural community outside Winston-Salem. I'd known Doug Smith from Mt. Zion where we were members. It was a personal pleasure to be in his company. Donald Johnson, on the other hand, I'd met on the unit. He was a likeable guy and was the unit barber. We got along mainly because we shared a goofy, off-color sense of humor. And a fondness for weed.

"You got that thang, boy!"

"Nah, nigga, I'm just out here doin' nothin'," I said, as I pulled out a joint. "Where's the flame at, Don? We ain't got no flame, we ain't got no smoke."

"Oh, my nigga, I got the flame. Shit, I just wanted to be sure you had the weed."

"Oh, really."

"Yeah, really. Look, gimme that thang so I can get my blaze on."

"You know God's watchin' you, standin' out in front of His house, getting' tuned up."

"He better be. I'm gonna need somebody to watch me 'cause I sho' can't watch myself!"

We laughed like hyenas, standing out there in the country in front of a small, whitewashed, country church, it being just like one on a post card. Seemingly doing no harm, but each of us harboring a seed of guilt for committing such a trespass on church grounds. I knew where that kind of thinking came from and I fought the discussion of it because we had a more immediate concern.

The aroma of marijuana is a unique perfume. It has a signature that indicates without a doubt that it's there. Church would be getting out shortly and it would be a scandal if, when the congregants did come out, they were to notice that pungent bouquet that enveloped their holy ground. We'd never hear the end of it.

"Boy, this some good weed. This on the camp?"

"Yep, that's where I got it. It's kinda loud though, ain't it; maybe we ought to wrap things up before they come out, that way everything'll be straight."

"Boy, you ain't 'noid is you?" he said with a chuckle. "Ain't no need a worryin' about them inside; we ain't been out here but a couple a minutes anyway."

"Yeah, but suppose somebody does come out, then what?" My paranoia, becoming comically obvious, was written all over my face.

"Boy, you is a trip! Ain't nobody gonna come out. You hear all that shoutin' in there. Ain't nobody thinkin' about us. Here, hit this while me and God watch out for you since you so concerned. We got this, ain't we God!" He laughed as I look at him stupidly.

"Y'all better 'cause I need to chill."

"So look, how is that job over there at Baptist?"

"Man, I couldn't have written a better script. Ain't a doubt in my mind that God is real 'cause ain't no way this was supposed to happen so soon."

"I'm saying, though, what kind of work you do?"

"Man, this the shit I went to school for. I work in a lab with test tubes and computers and all kinds of sophisticated equipment. You gotta be taught how to use it, but you also gotta know what it's used for. I'm tellin' you, I'm in my natural element. Why, what you been hearing?"

"Nothin', man, other than that you was really qualified and was really smart and that if nobody could get a job over there, you could. That's about it. Motherfuckas is really impressed with that shit you're doing over there."

"Well, I'm just tryin' to maintain."

We finished the last bit of the joint and shortly after that the first few congregants began to leave the sanctuary to come into the church yard.

"Well, good afternoon, sisters. How'd y'all enjoy this morning's service?"

"Oh, just fine. Pastor Doug always gives us a good word. How are you two?"

Good and buzzed up. "We're fine, just waiting for the chaplain to leave. He's pastor to you, but he's chaplain to us. We're visiting from up on Cherry Street."

"Oh, yes. That's so nice. Reverend Smith works hard at staying close to those that are less fortunate or have come onto misfortune. He has a heart for that. He often quotes Hebrews 13:3 on visiting those that are in prison. You all are lucky to have him."

"Oh, don't we know it," said Don. "Chaplain is a genuinely concerned man and I have grown just by being in his company. We are proud to have him with us while we can as well. Looks like we all got share him, huh?"

Everybody laughed.

"Well, that's just fine. You young men take care and we'll be on our way."

"Okay, you all. God bless!"

I just hoped we passed the test and they didn't notice anything; they sure stayed long enough.

When we got to the unit, Chaplain Doug signed us in at the Sergeant's Office and headed to his next destination. We thanked him profusely for his kindness and vowed to be ever vigilant, that our spirits remain true to the idea of doing for others as he so willingly does. We went through the usual, cursory pat down. However, this time, they decide to check a little more thoroughly. This is to be expected. Occasionally, they do random, more intense searches just to keep the guys on their toes. The officer went through Don's pockets, no problem. He went through my pockets and...

...Uh-oh.

"Well, Mr. Moore, what do we have here?"

I was dumbfounded, I had no idea. Maybe he planted something on me that quickly. I'd heard they did that from time to time. Still, I had not a clue and looked at him as though he were speaking a foreign language. I couldn't seem to understand what he was saying.

"What. What did you say?" I answered, my legs feeling tremulous and rubbery, my mouth running dry. I'm scared, for real.

"I know you're not coming in here with reefer on you, I just know better than that, don't I? Just came from church, too. With the chaplain, at that. Tell me this is not reefer I've got out of your pocket."

Shit! I had completely forgotten about the couple of joints I had left in my pocket, the ones we didn't smoke. Just fuckin' slipped my mind. Boy, this is gonna look bad.

"Well, sir, I can tell you it's not my stuff. I'd never bring anything contraband in here. I mean, I'm on work release and everything, I wouldn't risk messing that up for no reefer."

"So, what's it doing in your pocket, huh?" He seemed to be having a good time with this, my guilt seeming so obvious. "Nah, I gotta believe this yourn. You just hang on to that idea right there, now hold your hands out."

I look at Don and he looked at me and we both want to laugh because this whole scene was so stupid, but what could we do? It was my own dumbness, my own inattentiveness that was at fault and now I'm really gonna have to dance to the music.

They put handcuffs on me and we marched across the yard to segregation. Me. Rick, who had it going on so swell, look at his dumb-ass now, I could just hear the guys saying. The yard was wide open, it was afternoon and everybody was out on that nice day, watching me go to the hole. It is a most ridiculously humiliating feeling to be in prison and be such a dullard as to not be able to keep handcuffs off you, even in there.

Damn! Damn! Damn! I ain't been on the job a month and here I am, going to the hole for some really silly shit. How am I going to be able to explain this to anybody? I know Momma and Johnetta ain't trying to hear nothing. Opportunity done gone straight to hell behind my senselessness. Damn!

As they closed the door to seg, I put my hands out through the tray slot so that they can remove my handcuffs and I mumbled to myself, nigga you ain't shit.

Now, who's gonna do the lab work? Rena had already taken her leave and it was just me and Tim in the lab. I had to get somebody to call him to let him know what was going on, then I could begin my prayer vigil that he wouldn't fire me. The segregation area was inside the largest dorm and was an iron rebar-enclosed area. Everybody could walk by and see who was in and stop and talk if they chose.

Here comes Don. "Damn, Rick, why didn't you let me know you had some more, we could a stashed that somewhere."

"Man, I just fuckin' forgot. That's all there is to it. I mean, I was gonna smoke some more, but then church got out and we had to go. Things just went by and I didn't pay attention."

"Well, is there anything you need for me to do?" he asked, as a small crowd had gathered around behind him. Everybody wanted to know what the hell happened, why was Rick in the hole.

"After a while, I might get you to call my job, okay."

"A'ight, man, Just let me know what you need."

"A'ight, bet."

Later that evening, I got the write-up. Sarge told me they would dispose of it the next day. I'd be looking at some hole time, extra duty, loss of levels, passes, work release, everything gone. Just be thankful they didn't take out a warrant for Possession of Marijuana in a State Facility. Now, that would've been a helluva thing.

I decided to ride it out without calling anybody. I hadn't had any write-ups my entire time, so that might be helpful.

Next day, I met with the camp superintendent and he made me a deal: if I'd plead guilty to it, say it was mine, he'd give me all of the punishments recommended, but suspend them for ninety days. Shoot, I wasn't about to turn down a deal like that, so that's what I did and that's what he did.

Little did I know that my pleading guilty would put a smear on the face of the chaplain. Since I was with him when this happened, the camp officials could really sit back and gloat and have a good laugh. He being a Black chaplain in a good ol' boy system made him look bad when this kind of thing happened, even if he had nothing to do with it. I'm sure I would have made the same choice, even if I'd known this is what would be the result. Maybe I was desperate, maybe I didn't have a strong sense of character, who knows, but when your ass gets in a dangle, all that "values" shit goes out the window.

To really put an interesting twist on these events, the local parole officer, Jim Goff, paid me a visit while I was in the hole. After I had pled guilty and gotten a suspended sentence, I had to wait to be released from seg. Mr. Goff had no idea what my status was, he was just following instructions from his superiors at the Parole Commission in Raleigh. He called me to the bars at the tray slot where we discussed the rule and regulations of parole. Little did I know he had already checked on my home plan with my Mom.

A couple of hours later, I walked not only out of the hole, but out of prison! Just like that.

I was amazed at how, through no actions or words of my own, my fortunes had gone from sugar to shit and back to sugar in a matter of forty-eight hours. What is it that causes life to be so arbitrary, so fickle in its bestowal of favors and equally so unpredictable in its bestowal of misfortune? Surely, there is a pattern of living that can be divined that would lead people to a constant reality of one or the other, favor or misfortune. But, who would want a reality of constant misfortune? And, obviously, no one can have a reality of constant favor, so what's the operating principle?

There's got to be an answer.

SEVEN

It was surreal, coming into the neighborhood after so long an absence. Everything seemed so fresh and clean, as though I'd never been on these streets. Mr. Goff made the turn onto my street and there it was, my long-lost-hadn't-been-seen-in-many-moons home.

As we pulled into the drive, he gave my last instructions on how to contact him, how to get started on my community service and basically how not to get violated. Don't want that to happen. That would require a lot of other scenarios to take place, none of them pleasant. He said absconding was the most common violation, so be sure to stay in touch and inform him of all moves I might make or even think of making. I thanked him for his time and as I was getting out, Momma came to the door.

"I thought I heard somebody out here."

"Hey, Momma!"

"Boy, what are you doing here?"

"Ma, that's my parole officer, Mr. Goff. He's just dropping me off."

"Dropping you off? Why? What do you mean?"

"Ma, please! I just made parole today so here I am."

"Well, do wonders never cease? Welcome home son. God is good! I knew my God was an awesome God and that it was just a matter of time before this thing got worked out. Come on in and let's talk."

I hadn't been in the house in so-o-o long, I was caught off-guard by how good it felt just to be at home again. No way I'd do anything to spoil this, it was too good. At first, out under the carport with Momma and the cool breeze running through the maples and hickories in the yard and then, with Momma going inside, I was reminded of how truly lucky I was and the importance of maintaining good family ties. When we got inside, she gave me a warm, motherly embrace and I kinda snuggled up close in her arms. Real tender, a mother and her Prodigal Son, having come home from his riotous living.

She said, "I was about to call Roberta and ask if she'd heard from you since you hadn't called her for a couple of days. But, from the looks of things, you've been too busy to call."

If she only knew. Ain't no way I'd tell her just how chaotic the last couple of days had been.

"Actually, Ma, I have been rather busy what with the job and going on passes on the weekend. We went over to Doug's church in Walkertown Sunday."

"Oh, you did! That's nice. How was his service?"

"Real nice, Ma. And then, having to make preparations when they told me about this parole, I've been kinda caught up. I hadn't talked to Rob, either. I guess I'll call her after a while. I just want to get reacquainted with the house and all."

When she bought the house in '79, it was a no-frills, nothing-fancy cottage of red brick with white shutters. But Momma couldn't leave it at that, oh no. We all accused her of giving in to a moment of conceit and self-importance when she had the inside done in a style that reminded us of homes in *Better Homes and Gardens*. She had redone the living room and kitchen. In fact, she had one whole wall removed and installed deep-pile carpeting in what had become a great room where the den, living room and kitchen were all open into a common area. Very nice, very spacious. As we walked through the great room, we came to the hallway.

"Geez Ma, you really did it up this time, didn't you. I mean, these changes are what's happening."

"You like it?"

"For real. This is really good."

Going down the hallway, the first bedroom was mine and there was a sign on the door that said "Ricky's Room." As we stood in the doorway, she said, "You know what I noticed the most about your room while you were gone?"

"No, tell me."

"I've never closed the door and occasionally, I would look in as I would pass by and, you know what? Your shoes would never move."

I looked on the floor and there they were, right at the foot of the bed where I last saw them two years earlier. She could've just as easily picked my clothes to focus on, but clothes don't possess the aura of movement and action that shoes have. Clothes hang, but shoes move and I hadn't been home in years for my shoes to move.

"From time to time, I'd glance in here and see these shoes still in the same place and it would remind me of you and how long it had been since you'd been here. I'd never adjusted to it and, until now, never realized how used I am to seeing your shoes move around. Sounds strange, but it's true."

"Actually, Ma, it's kinda touching, really, because it is such an uncommon observation to make."

"Yes it is."

"If it's okay with you, I'd like to stay here for a while 'til I get straightened out. Hope you don't mind."

"No, I don't mind. I think I'd rather enjoy having the company and all. What with you going out to work daily, it'll be like a regular home around here once again!"

"But, Ma..."

"What?"

"We gotta get a dog."

"A dog? Well, we can deal with that later. Don't you think you ought to call Roberta here shortly?"

"Yeah, I was gonna do that in a little bit after I got settled in."

"And you might as well get it in your mind you're going to church and I do wish you'd join the choir, Ricky, we really could use your talents. So, don't think you're going to sit around here on Sundays, nosiree. This is not going to be another vacation, uh-uh."

"And Ma, that's really what I have in mind. It's because of my spiritual life, I believe, that I've been resurrected in such a fashion."

"Well, I'm glad to hear it. Sounds like you've given this some thought."

"Of course I have. All that time away from home, I'd better have given something some thought. Anyway, I gotta do what I can to get settled in. I've gotta be at work in the morning plus I need to call Roberta."

"What are you going to do for transportation?"

"Well, Ma, if things ain't changed too much, the bus that goes down Carver Road goes all the way to Baptist Hospital..."

"Yes, it sure does."

"...so it only makes sense to ride the bus 'til I can do better, that way I won't bother nobody."

"There you go son, you've got the right idea!"

We hug again and I say, "Well, Ma, I'm a call Roberta here shortly so whatcha got to eat?"

"About the same thing, son. I'll go in here and see what I can come up with."

There was a phone extension in the kitchen and in her bedroom. Since she was going to fix something in the kitchen, I decided to use the one in her room.

"What up, Rob!"

"Rick! Hey there, what's up with you?"

"Oh, I ain't been doing nothing unusual, just thinking about you and wanted to see you."

"Oh, that's so nice. You know I'm coming up there Saturday, so don't worry. I would've come to Yokefellows tonight but we've got parent-teacher conferences so I'll be at school, but Saturday for sure, I'll be up there."

"Well, that's not good enough. I want to see you now. Right now."

"Uh-oh, I've heard that tone of voice before. Whatcha wanna see me 'right now' for?" she said, with a shade of thinly veiled eagerness.

"I tell you what, why don't you come by Momma's house, that way I can show you *exactly* what I want."

There was a huge quietness on the other end and then, an explosion of elation. "Ahhh, Ricky! You're home!!"

"Now, how did you figure that out so easily?"

"This is so nice! I'm gonna stop by there on the way to school and I should be by there in just a few minutes, okay."

"Damn right, okay."

"Boy, you know we can't do nothing."

"Why not?"

"'Cause I've got to be at school and we won't have time."

"No excuse."

"Well, that's just how it is. When I get finished with my last conference, I'll stop back by here on the way home and we can talk about what we can or cannot do."

"So, because you have the upper hand, you're gonna make me wait?"

"Absolutely! Good things come to those who wait. You know, that kind a thing."

Well, this is all good. Momma's in a good space, Roberta's in a good space and I'm in a good space. Looks like the only thing to do is to make this work.

Cß ß?

"Hey Rick, I'd begun to wonder what had happened to you," Tim said Tuesday when I showed up. "I got a phone call from somebody up at the camp who said you were in a bit of trouble. But here it is Tuesday and you show up. What happened?"

"Well, Tim, I'm gonna tell you the truth. I got put into the hole for something I really didn't have anything to do with. I went to church with the chaplain on Sunday and wore somebody else's jacket. Little did I know that the owner had a couple of joints in his pocket that *he'd* forgotten about. So, when we came back to get checked in, they do a routine search and found those couple of joints and charged me with it."

"My, my. So, what did they do about it?"

I told him the remainder of the story as we walked down the hallway from his office to the lab.

"Well, I'm glad to have you back. Let's get you to work. I've already stopped the reactions yesterday and spun them down. You've got to get them counted in the machine and crunch the numbers. We've got another set of tumors to grind and assay, so it might be wise to start those before you count the last ones. That's just an idea. You do it however you choose."

"Okay then, I'll get started right now. Are the new tumors in the same freezer?"

"Yep, nothing's changed."

"Good, you'll be down the hall in case I need you."

"Right."

The Hanes Building is the big research facility on the School of Medicine's main campus. Its hallways are as long as a football field and as wide as a mobile home. It is a six-story behemoth, squared off at all four corners and is all labs and offices. It faced Hawthorne Road, but linked to all other areas of the hospital via a maze of interconnecting hallways.

This environment was identical to what I'd left in Chapel Hill. Though it was of a smaller size, the intensity, the drive, the competitive atmosphere, nevertheless, spoke as loudly there as at any other nationally ranked school. Every person, every experiment, each lab struggling for recognition, for accomplishment, for pre-eminence in their respective field of inquiry. Our lab, The Steroid Receptor Lab, was no different.

Tim's entire career had been devoted to the development of a bioassay for steroid receptors on cancer tissues. His test became the gold standard in the industry for receptor site quantitative analysis. It became the best way to define a tumor's susceptibility to a hormonal analog because the more receptor sites a cell has the more vulnerable it is to hormonal therapy. This means that cell growth can be inhibited, i.e., tumor shrinkage can be promoted, by the blocking of the hormonal receptor site. In effect, the analog "gets in the way" of the normal molecule and tissue growth is blocked.

Tamoxifen was the most popularly effective blocker and, in many cases, tumor size reductions were dramatic. They occurred in a variety of patients and on a variety of susceptible tumors (not only breast, but also uterine, cervical and ovarian), so the usefulness of this relatively non-toxic, low side effect treatment was quite high. The alternative was chemotherapy, radiation and/or surgery.

I found myself being involved in the advancement of a novel and innovative therapeutic technique where the research about it was sparse and the labs that were performing it were just coming on line. I was getting in, if not on the ground floor, very close to it. Steroid receptor blockade, as a therapeutic approach, was fast becoming a reliable and dependable method to be used in conjunction with traditional treatments for female reproductive cancer. And the test that I was doing determined those that would benefit from it as opposed to those that wouldn't.

For me, it couldn't get no better than this. Hallelujah!

 CB EO

Though the bus stop was only a five-minute walk from my front door and took me directly to the Hanes Building, I knew I needed— or, more honestly, wanted—a car. The bus was convenient and economical, but it couldn't touch independence. I was still getting rides from Roberta whenever we went out, plus it wasn't a thing I could do on my own without having to ask somebody.

After talking it over with Mom, I did my homework and found a good used car I could afford. Well, okay, it was better than a good used car. It was a Dodge Daytona Turbo-Z that was no joke, for real. I mean, this car was the truth! Black lacquer exterior, tan leather interior, fully loaded. A dream car. At least for a guy like me, just getting out of prison, this being the first car he is buying and paying for. I could just see me in it, too. Boy, I could really get my shine on in this thing! Just gettin' out the joint and drop on the set with a phat-ass ride like this, man, that shit would be the bomb! Showin' off, that's what I'm talkin' about. This car would be that real ego statement.

While I was feeding my ego and building my independence, I was taking care of my parole requirements in a fun, yet helpful, way by volunteering at a local recreation center. I was participating in church and its choir, the drama club, and other meetings. Roberta and I would take turns in attending each other's services. Over time, she became as familiar a figure in Mt. Zion as I became in Grace Presbyterian, her home church. All of us would go out to restaurants and just have a good time. Me, Momma, Roberta, Johnetta and her husband Paul would visit one another at our places and would also visit mutual friends. I was simply enjoying life on life's terms. And loving it.

Cocaine no longer had a place at the table.

Added to this was the real sense of purpose in living that occurs when a man gets into the daily to and fro of work and home. I had a job that I enjoyed and looked forward to going to every day. Even when I felt a little bit under the weather, I went to work anyway. I never used a sick day or a vacation day while I was there.

This idyllic existence, of having meaningful work, a love of God and family, of having a sense of responsibility and purpose, this oh, so American lifestyle continued until after I got off parole after one year.

Using drugs was not anywhere close to being a part of my life. It never occurred to me that I would or could return to active use and everything that I was doing indicated this. I didn't buy no coke, didn't use no coke, didn't want no coke. Smoked a little weed now and then, drank a little beer once in a while, that was it. Same thing I did in college and grad school. In my mind, weed and beer weren't *real* drugs, that was cocaine and heroin. Weed and beer were just forms of entertainment. There was no upheaval, no calamitous or notorious behavior going on in my life, just smooth sailing.

Until one day, a couple of weeks after I got off parole.

☙ ❧

Keith and I had been hanging out at his place in Lakeside apartments for a while. He was my buddy from church and high school and we shared similar tastes and attitudes in many areas. Neither of us was prone to loud outbursts nor were we looking to be seen or thought highly of. Just two regular guys who liked a variety of girls, some good weed and a couple of beers. Because he lived alone and had more personal privacy than I, his place became the meeting spot for all manner of entertainment that would come to pass. We would cookout or have a couple of girls over or catch a buzz. His recreation was exclusively pot and beer and, because we had been pals so long, he could not understand how cocaine had thrown me so far off track nor how I could have tried the stuff in the first place.

Those were cool days. On many occasions, he and I would just sit back and talk, and that's really what life was all about. Good conversation, good friends, good family, good job, everything in place and under control just like it used to be. No loose ends.

My life had begun to rebuild professionally and that was really something to see. The lab was being featured at some of the conferences I attended at Research Triangle Park. This was at Tim's insistence. Being ever mindful of my scientific aptitude and interests, he made sure that I'd go. My inquiries to the school of medicine were being met with moderate interest and it was starting to look like I was in possession of a real comeback story.

So, it occurred to me since my life was once more in good and decent order that maybe, what I went through, as far as being out of control, was just a fluke. I mean, c'mon, that shit couldn't be *that* awesome. Three years had gone by since I'd last had some. Surely, enough time had passed for me to be straight.

So, I tried it again.

EIGHT

"Rick, look, we've got to stop those reactions now and I mean right now. We've got an emergency pick-up over at Forsyth and they want the results by Friday. This barely gives the sample time to incubate, so after you do the charcoal step, come get me."

I was somewhat hesitant about coming to work after my little escapade, but things weren't so bad. It was all in my mind, thinking that somehow, he'd know about it.

After I got my dope and did my thing, the feeling it gave me was just as awesome as ever, just as good as it was the first time. But this time was even better because now, I got some control. See, that was the problem the first time. I had lost control, but now I still had my job, my girl, my home life and my right mind. The world did not end and my life did not come crashing down around me just because I did some dope.

Hell, this shit just might work out after all! I thought to myself.

Going out to Forsyth was no big thing, even the early reaction stops was no problem. I'd become so adept at the running of the lab that little wrinkles like this were handled rather adroitly, it was simply a matter of course. So, after I put the charcoal in to stop the reactions, I called Tim.

"Okay," I said, "the reactions have been stopped and I'm ready to start the new sample. When do you want me to go over to Forsyth?"

"Right now, if you're at a point you can get away."

"I am."

"Okay then, go on down to the van, here's the keys. Run on over to Forsyth and get the sample and come on back. I've got some other things to do around here. It may be a late night, but it's what's got to be done."

"No problem, Tim, I've got it covered. We should have the results by or before Friday."

Although this particular errand at this time of the week was unusual, it was one of my responsibilities to retrieve biopsy samples from local hospitals. This was done on a regularly scheduled rotating basis and it afforded me time away from the lab and, on many occasions, opportunities to get into mischief. I might stop by Roberta's or I might see somebody on the street and stop to talk or I might buy some dope and do my thing. It just depended on what I felt like doing. I was on a loose time schedule, so my absences were not noticed.

Since I had always been prompt and straightforward in my travels for the lab, there was never any suspicion directed toward me if I were a little late. Having my own key to the lab allowed me to come and go as I pleased. Needless to say, I had free reign in what I did, with little oversight by anyone. And why should I have oversight? It was a professional environment where everyone had to have, by necessity, an ability to work independently. Trustworthiness never enters into the equation when you work in a high-powered place like a medical research laboratory.

Up to this point, all of this was true, but now I was courting my one true archenemy with whom all hell had broken loose in the past. Bowman Gray School of Medicine, that staid, austere institution of higher learning, had no clue that one of its members was fast becoming a dope fiend and an outlaw. Again.

Ψ Ѫ

Over time, it occurred to me that I could do my thing right there in the lab. I didn't have to go to try to find a local shooting gallery in the 'hood or sneak around in Mom's house after she went to bed, trying to get off. I could get down right there! I could be in the lab late night or at any time after normal working hours, doing my thing, and not raise any suspicions. My presence wouldn't raise a second glance.

I was new to having to find a discrete place to shoot up. I had been used to the immediate access and privacy of my own place in Chapel Hill. But being out on the dope scene in Winston-Salem created an entirely different experience with an entirely different character of people. The whole dynamic of getting dope, from where you get it and who you get it from to where you go to use and how you get there, was new and different for me, even scary.

As it turned out, I didn't have to worry. I had the lab. All I had to do was get my shit and my problems getting high were over.

┊ ┊

Addiction, being the cruel paymaster that he is, demands, little by little, slowly but surely, his kickback of chaos and heartbreak, of broken lives and shattered dreams.

Inevitably, a time came to pass that my normal and regular comings and goings had, inexorably, become my abnormal and irregular comings and goings. This gradual decline became so obvious that Mom had begun to take notice, in a suspicion-free kind of way, without my noticing that she was even paying attention.

"Hey, Ma. Whatcha up to?" I inquired, rather innocently, after coming in late from one of my evening debaucheries. Ordinarily, she did not wait up for me.

"I called Roberta." There was a long pause.

"And..."

"And you weren't there and hadn't been there. See, this has been happening for a while now and I want to know what's really going on."

"What do you mean 'what's really going on'."

You can't fool your momma. I knew what she was talking about, but I was gonna play it off as long as I could. I wasn't ready to give up my bright and shining facade, not without a few lies. Roberta had also been asking the same type questions about where I'd been and why I couldn't be where I said I would be, stuff like that. They must have been talking to each other from time to time in order for them to have such similar inquiries.

"You know, what used to be the dependable comings and goings for you have, here lately, become erratic and unusual. It looks like it could be drugs and I want to know if it is."

Like I'm really going to tell the truth.

"If what is, Ma?" I asked, trying to maintain an attitude of disbelief.

"Are you using drugs?"

"No, Ma! Why would you say that?"

"You've just been behaving strangely around here lately, that's all. And I tell you, if it is, me and you got some things we're gonna have to work out!"

"I mean, really Ma, how could I be on drugs? I got a nice car that I'm paying for, a nice girl who loves me dearly, a nice home, a great family, a good job. I mean, people on drugs don't have all of this. They be on the streets walkin' around beggin' and stealin' all the time. Is that what I'm doing?"

"No, you're not, but I'm not convinced either. I'm telling you right now, young man, I'm not at all comfortable about what I'm seeing or what you're telling me. You better make doggone sure you're doing right, you hear, or it's going to be real trouble!"

☙ ❧

The thing of it is, I was paid on a bi-weekly basis. Though I had no rent or no real bills other than that car payment, I began to find myself short of money. At first, when this dope thing jumped off, after I'd paid whatever I might owe, I'd buy some and have a little bit of money left over. But, after a short while, the frequency increased so much that I began to let my bills go just to buy dope to satisfy that urge.

I felt myself going over the edge into that chasm of incessant craving. The euphoria that cocaine gives also creates a compulsion to repeat the experience over and over, the endless cycle of perpetual use being stitched into your bones. I was being driven to do what I didn't want to do, knowing full well that what I was doing was harmful. Yet, I did it anyway. This is the hidden, evil spirit of drug use and addiction that drags everyone under its spell to their doom. It was just a matter of time before my glass house would shatter.

Though I was holding my job duties down and maintaining my social and work relationships I, on many occasions, would come up questionable regarding issues of personal decorum.

From time to time, we would attend conferences at Research Triangle Park and I would be asked to drive. No one knew (how could they have known?) that I'd had no sleep the night before. So, while at the wheel, I'd nod off. The car would drift and Tim and the other passengers (all Ph.D.'s) would give a startled cry and my eyes would fly open. I'd over-correct causing an even greater sense of dread as the car shimmied and swerved back onto the pavement. I'd be relieved of those duties, climb my strung-out ass in the back seat and wouldn't wake up until somebody told me we had arrived.

Not looking too good, at all. In fact, looking rather shabby, to be honest.

Many times, my all-nighters would be at home after Mom had gone to bed. Trying my best to keep decent hours, I'd come in late, sometimes from the lab, sometimes from Keith's apartment, all highed up with a little bit left just to keep it going as long as I could. When she would go to her room, I'd lay in my bed until I felt like she was asleep and then get up to fix me a hit. I'd do this under cover of dim light in the kitchen away from her room. I'd get that blast and end up creeping around the house, wacked out of my head, trying not to awaken her, listening very intently to the high-pitched scream in my head that this drug-induced cerebral climax brings. It is so intense that it is simultaneously hypnotic and ecstatic. I'd have two or three syringes, each half full of dope, lined up for duty, ready to be discharged as soon as the trumpet sounded and the high began to wear down.

But, sooner or later, you run out.

ಅ ಖ

My drug connection was a family man. Four, five and six in the morning was way too early to go to his house, even if I had money. Most times I didn't, so what could I do? Nothing but go to bed. And that's what I would do, not having any way to go to sleep at all. I'd just wait, eyes wide open. Waiting for dawn.

Cocaine, being the stimulant that it is, keeps you hyped. But the amount I was using had me tossing and turning and being supremely uncomfortable, the edginess of it having taken over. This is where the real drama in your life begins to occur because dope is the only thing that can soothe this raw, open wound in your psyche. Since getting more dope required money, something had to give. Somehow, you've got to come to a reckoning with that demon inside. Usually, a good stiff drink would make it manageable, but I didn't find out about that for years because, really, I didn't like alcohol. Right then, at that moment and all the others like it, I was just miserable.

It should have been enough to discourage anybody from putting themselves through that kind of torture. Not me though.

I'd do it again. Every time.

03 80

By then, Mom had become really suspicious. I was hardly getting up on time for work. As the cocaine would wear off, drowsiness would set in, but it was time to go to work and I hadn't yet slept. A battle was shaping up about this and I was no longer able to keep lying about it. I came in one evening and Mom called me to her.

"Ricky, come here!" She was sitting in her favorite lounger with a resolute and implacable look about her. "Roll up your sleeves."

"Do what?"

"Boy, you do what I tell you! Now, roll up your sleeves!!"

Man, oh man. She was dead on it and I didn't have the first bit of wiggle room. So, reluctantly, hesitantly, even nervously, I rolled up my shirt sleeve. And there was the evidence.

"Lord, have mercy! Boy, what is this?"

"Ma, what?" Even in the face of imminent disaster, I tried to be evasive. The ship was taking on water and sinking fast, but I still thought I could bail fast enough.

"This!" She pointed. "And this!" She traced the outline of those tell-tale signs. "According to this scarring on your arms, where your veins *used* to be, I'd say you've been doing this a while, huh? You might as well tell me."

She really believed in the redemptive value of truth-telling, that confessing your sins would make it all better.

"Well, Ma, sounds like you already know what the deal is." Real contrite like.

"I don't want to 'sound like' I know what the deal is, I want to *know* what the deal is and I want *you* to tell me."

It really is not easy to admit your wrong-doings, even in the face of overwhelming evidence, when all of your lies have been exposed. It is a humiliating experience when the flaw, the warp, in your character is made plain for all to see.

Maybe that was her intent, to humiliate me in the hope that my conscience would prevent me from further calamity. By insisting that I confess, this may have unwittingly set us up for what was to become an endless series of admissions and confessions. Maybe all of it played into her rock-solid belief that any child of hers could and would correct their errors when they were shown the futility of such untruthfulness. That such foolishness could be erased simply by being shown what it is, foolishness.

It was all predicated on my actually having a conscience. But, addiction can really deter good, conscientious behavior. One essentially becomes a sociopath, the conscience having been relegated to that strange nether-world of addiction.

Then, I began to see a way out.

"Go ahead, tell me."

I looked at her. It was so quiet in the room, the hush was loud. I knew there was an option here, I just had to figure it out.

"I mean, Ma, what can I say? I been using."

"Using what?"

"Cocaine."

"With a needle?"

"Yeah."

"Lord, have mercy." She looked at me with an expression of sadness and compassion, a lost and forlorn look that would belie the resolve that she would ultimately display. I saw this and tried to bear a countenance of pity and distress, as though I was at the end of my rope and could go no further, doing my best to arouse as much empathy as I could. My creative light bulb began to flash.

"Well, we've got to find you a treatment center. What does Dr. Kotke think about all of this?"

"He doesn't know."

"Doesn't know? Hah, you'd be surprised. If the way you've been handling yourself around here is any indication, I'm sure he suspects something."

"Why would you say that?"

"Going to work late most of the time. You used to get on out of here before 8:00, now it's more toward 8:30. Not having any extra money for lunch, knowing full well you don't have any bills. You think he can't see all of that? And I bet you get sleepy, too. Oh sure, he doesn't know. That's just what you think."

೪ ೫

She was right, of course, but I would never admit, not ever, what had happened the day I had misjudged Tim's departure for the day. It was after 5:00, his normal time of leaving. I'd had a delivery from my supplier and had planned to do just a bit before hitting the road. I had all of my tools (syringes, cotton balls, test tubes) out on my desk and had put a 50cc sample into my first needle.

I was just about to put it in my arm when I heard a key in the door.

GODDAMN! It could only be Tim. What to do, what to do!

Panicking, I tried to hide under a work bench just as he was coming in the door, but it was too late. He could see the preparations out in full view and, as he turned to look around, saw me. Under a table, looking stupid. Well, I said to myself, as I got to my feet, it was a pretty good job, I sure am gonna miss working here.

"Aw, Rick." he said with no small amount of concern. "It doesn't have to be this way."

He extended his hand and, as I took it, he pulled me to him in a comforting embrace. I stood there totally embarrassed, not sure of what to say or do. I was a wreck on the inside. Not so much over the possibility of losing my job or getting busted by my boss, but for having to let that hit go because it was gonna be a damn good one!

The whole experience of getting high at that moment, after having begun to mentally retreat to that cocoon of my inner comfort

102

zone, was totally destroyed. It became the user's nightmare, all of the reasons for ever being paranoid in the first place, coming true.

"C'mon, man, throw that thing away." Tim said gently, but firmly.

I did this dutifully, solemnly, carefully making sure that I paid attention to where it landed in the trash can. Pretending, really trying to show remorse, but actually just wanting him to hurry up and go. So far, I had not said a word. Instead, I relied on my rather persuasive skills of the actor. I was completely devoid of emotion, just waiting for my opportunity.

"You don't ever have to go out like this man. All your talent and skill just going to waste? Nah, that's not for you. Promise me that this is over, that this won't ever happen again."

I looked him dead in the eye and said, "That's my word, Tim, as of right this minute. There's no way I could continue to do this knowing what's at stake. I'm just glad you came when you did."

"Me, too. Now look, you go on and lock up and I'll see you tomorrow. We've been doing real well since you've been here and I wouldn't want to lose you because of these drugs. Just let it alone, okay?"

"Okay, Tim, I'll lock up and put everything back right. Thanks a lot. You've been a real pal."

"Okay, Rick. I'm counting on you."

" 'Preciate it, Tim." I watch as he walked down the hallway a bit and then around the corner. Perfect.

I hurried up to close and lock the door. I couldn't wait to get back to that trash can. Though I was pleased that he gave me a reprieve and left so nicely, I didn't even care to see if it was a trick, that he might double-back to check. I didn't give a damn anyway, that syringe was half full of dope and I'd be damned if I wasn't going to put it in its proper place—my arm.

I mean, what else should I have done? Should I actually have closed the lab, locked up and gone home? Ought I have made, at that moment, the supreme effort at abstinence? Maybe so, but I was too far gone. There was no way I could possibly do anything so reasonable or so rational as that.

Besides, the lab offered comforts that I could not find anywhere else. Not only privacy, but also my own supply of syringes, a comfortable captain's chair at my desk, ample surface area on which to do my do and plenty of room to indulge. All of which helped to create a pleasant ambience and a more blissful narcotic experience. For months, the lab was where you could find me, late nights, with a needle stuck in my arm.

These elements, my own personal shooting gallery, a good supplier, adequate finances and my newly-acquired theatrical abilities, became the psychological foundation for my addiction. My circumstances were arranged in such a way that justified in my mind why I could self-medicate, even self-destruct, and get away with it: God provided it all, God would protect me from it all.

Apparently, doing 26 months in prison and having the world returned to me in a marvelous fashion meant absolutely nothing.

ՀՑ ՀՖ

"Well, if he does know," I said to my mom, "he hasn't said anything to me. I think I got that covered."

"Ricky, you can think anything you want to think, but we're gonna have to get you into a treatment center. This time, I'm gonna take you myself."

"Well, Ma, if we do that then he'll know for sure, won't he?"

"Boy, you're so far gone you can't even see what's happening to you. Your very life is at stake here, not to mention the salvation of your soul. If we don't get you some help, you're in danger of losing it all, not just some glorified job at Bowman Gray. This is serious. I wish I had known this when you were at Chapel Hill like I know now. I'd have pulled you out of school so fast, your head would have been spinning."

I had gone out onto the precipice and stood, once again, on the edge of a fearsome and terrifying abyss.

Somehow, I had to avoid this treatment center thing.

NINE

"Where you been, Rick?" I had stopped off at Roberta's place after one of my binges and she wasn't too happy about my absences. My lack of presence lately had pressed her hard.

"At the lab. Why?"

"Because I'm not happy with the way things are going. I think you're on drugs and I think it's become more important to you than anything else. Plus, your mom tells me that you and she have talked about finding a treatment center, which I think is a move in the right direction, but it also tells me that things are quite serious. I just wonder if it's too late."

"Too late for what?"

"Too late for us, too late for you to get a grip, too late for your job..." she mused. "Look, I don't know. I just don't think a person can stop using drugs or stop doing anything if they don't want to do it themselves. Can't nobody stop doing something for somebody else, it has to be for themselves."

"You sayin' I'm on drugs, is that what you sayin'?"

"What I'm saying is just because me and your momma want you to quit don't mean that's what you want to do, that's all."

"First of all," I say, "what makes you think the jury is still out on this thing? I mean, what makes you the Knower of all Facts?"

She exploded. "Look boy, don't try to play me! You think because I don't say anything that nothing's wrong? That everything's just fine just because I haven't confronted you? Well, it ain't just fine and this is the confrontation. If you can't be straight with me, maybe it's time for this to be over."

Not words I wanted to hear. She was a good person and had been with me throughout my entire incarceration. That alone deserved some respect and honesty. Sure, things went well the first year or so after I got out. We had high hopes that the relationship would go all the way, so side-stepping big issues and playing bullshit-ass games should not have been any part of my offerings to her. She deserved more, she deserved better.

I came clean. "Yeah, me and Momma talkin' about a treatment center and, right now, I'm waiting to see what ARCA has to say."

"Well, that's good. It's a step in the right direction. But, there still remains the point of whether you're going because you really want to quit or you're going because all of us want you to quit. Nobody knows that but you. If you haven't made up your mind that it's over, then going to treatment will be absolutely meaningless."

"I ain't gone front, Rob. Trying to let that shit go is like trying to stop being horny, it's a helluva thing and hard to do. On one hand, I say I want to be clean then, on the other hand, I can't wait to get some dope. It's like I'm torn right down the middle between doing what I want to do and doing what I need to do. So far, doing what my addiction tells me to do has reigned supreme and that's not good. Right now, I don't have any answers and I'm really and truly hoping ARCA will have some."

"Listen," she said, "be straight up. What is it about getting high that you like so much. I mean, what is it?"

"How can I tell you? It's hard to describe. I mean, what can I say because all of this has taken me completely by surprise."

"How do you mean?"

"I had actually convinced myself that after doing that prison time and then getting on at Bowman Gray, that somehow what I went through in Chapel Hill was a fluke. I figured I could do it again and be alright, but it looks like that shit is too much to contain. I reckon I like it too much 'cause it's really getting in the way."

"But why cocaine? I mean, we've smoked plenty weed and had a few drinks to go with it and all that was cool…"

"Right."

"... and we've been doing this as a part of our growing up since high school. Maybe even a little acid here and there and nothing like this has happened. Now that we're all grown up, it seems this cocaine thing has become a real problem. For a lot a people."

"Look Rob, I have absolutely no explanation. Everything you said is true. I guess some of us are more susceptible to compulsive behavior than others and this particular drug brings it out." I opened up to Roberta, telling her as clearly as I could what it was like to use the way I did and the culture that came with it. I told her that IV drug use was a secretive endeavor that could only take place through evasion and elusion. And because only a certain type of person and environment were involved, it became its own culture, a subculture, so to speak, with a set of rules and a language all its own.

While those who smoked pot or snorted powder could socialize together, those who used a syringe were pariahs of the drug-use scene. They were total outcasts. The air-headed, slightly wacky atmosphere you find when potheads or snorters get high was largely absent with people who shot up. There wasn't much conversation. It was a silent, personal, introspective affair, the user's attention being fixed inwardly. No one who shot up was trying to talk. It was the intensity of the IV cocaine high would captivate you and take you over to the other side.

The downside is the experience is so complete and visceral, that you go to extremes to get it again and you end up chasing an endless dream, a dream that will never return you to where you think you ought to be. But you keep trying.

Roberta is watching me go through this explanation, my tendency toward theatrics amplified, and when I finish, she sits there for a moment.

"That has got to be the biggest piece of shit I've ever heard. You need your fuckin' head examined, for real! You are lost and you gotta find yourself somehow."

"Look, Rob, this drug scene is something else. Something new and completely different that I never even knew existed. Now, I'm still on the periphery. But, the whole thing intrigues me. I'm still able to keep my job and have a good family life, so..."

"So, what? Still able? Are you saying you're just waiting to blow it all? You're just going to have this little 'intrigue' until it loses its appeal to you? You actually think that you're gonna be able to just walk away? Just because you haven't lost your job don't mean that you won't and just because you haven't lost your family don't mean that you won't."

"Wait, Rob! You ain't even gave me a chance to finish."

A look of undisguised contempt clouded her face. "Go ahead and finish."

"What I'm saying is that, yeah, unless I straighten up that, yeah, I'm gonna blow it and probably move from the periphery of this thing to the mainstream. I'm just really hoping and praying that this treatment situation will somehow fix or get rid of this craving. See, it's the craving that drives everything and tortures me so terribly. I'm hoping to be okay when I get discharged."

"You ought to know there ain't no easy answers to anything complicated and it sounds like what you've gotten yourself into is complicated, so don't just expect to be all better when the treatment is over. At least you're able to admit that you have a real problem..."

"Yeah, I guess I do."

"...and that's the beginning of real healing, first admitting that there is a problem. But do *you* want to be clean? Because it has to come from inside you. Nobody else."

"I mean, hell yeah, I want to be clean. But, more than that, I want this craving, this never-ending, constantly grinding *urge* to go away! I want that to leave me alone more than anything else 'cause if I don't have the urge, then I won't use."

"But, I'm not so sure that can be fixed," she said. "It may be that you'll have to learn how to live with the craving. It's like my cigarettes. Shit, I've tried on numerous occasions to quit."

"Yeah."

"Yet I go right back, knowing that shit is aging me faster than I would ordinarily. *Because* of that craving. So, I can identify."

"So, why don't you try a patch or something. Maybe chew some a that nicotine gum sometimes. It ain't nothing but the nicotine calling you, that's all."

"And I agree" she said. "But, I bet you ain't gonna be able to get you no cocaine patch!"

We laugh out loud at this.

My efforts at recovery were not lost on her. She knew that this addiction thing really masked my true self. But, I was in the throes of a compulsion so overwhelmingly powerful, so cunning and treacherous that this time, just like in Chapel Hill, I had no more clue about what I was up against than Samson had with Delilah.

The problem then became how to go to treatment and keep my job. Since Tim had given me a Class A reprieve when he caught me in the lab, I felt uncomfortable, just a few weeks later, in telling him that I needed to go to treatment. In other words, I just couldn't quit. I felt he would consider me a liability—which I was—dismiss me outright and not take any further risks. Which is what I would have done if it had been me. A real quandary, this was.

As it turned out, I had been developing a mild fever. I knew something was amiss, but I played it off like it wasn't nothing, that it was just some passing something that would go away. Even as it gradually worsened, I depended on my history of having always been healthy to see me through because visits to the doctor were strange to me. So in my denial, I began to justify this bit of ill-health as symptomatic of "withdrawal".

In my mind, I could say with complete equanimity, "See, I told y'all I was stopping. Look at this temperature I have!"

From my addled point of view, the fever was confirmation that I was really making the effort to get off drugs, on my own, without a treatment center. But that's not how cocaine withdrawal presents itself. It's all psychological and is alleviated only by the passage of time. And still I continued to decline, the fever getting worse and worse 'til everybody around me began to complain, "Boy, you look sick. What's wrong with you? You need to go see a doctor, for real."

Momma, either tiring of my withdrawal charade or fearful of seeing me in the midst of a general health failure, finally said, "Ricky, I'm taking you to see Dr. Alford."

Which was cool with me because I felt terrible.

☙ ❧

"Mrs. Moore, we're going to put your son in the hospital right this minute. He has full blown pneumonia and requires immediate medical attention."

Shit. I didn't give a damn. I'd been walking around half-dead looking, couldn't hardly hold my head up, didn't have no appetite, just miserable. This type of pneumonia didn't present with a cough, like most types of lung infections. The reason why no one thought my questionable health was that bad was because there was nothing conspicuous to indicate it. The doctor said it was due to septicemia. An organism had gotten into my blood stream whose population began to explode in my lungs rendering me listless, lifeless and generally useless.

"Well, Dr. Alford," Momma asked, sensing the gravity in his voice, "how long will his stay be? Will he recover? Because he sure looks bad."

Dr. Alford had been our family physician since before I was born. He was not one to pull punches.

"Maybe if he had come in sooner I could give you a clearer picture of what may or may not happen. But as it is, he's waited so long and the pneumonia is so wide spread, I really hope we've caught it in time."

"What do you mean?" she said with some unease.

"Let's just get him to the hospital and go from there. He's very sick and needs to begin therapy just as soon as he gets a room assignment."

Upon my arrival at Forsyth Memorial Hospital, the details for my stay had already been arranged. I was admitted to Room 622, put straightaway into hospital garb and started on bilateral IV lines for the antibiotics, IVs in both arms.

At first, this presented a tricky issue because I didn't have any superficial veins, at least not any obvious ones. They'd been so constantly assaulted and terrorized, they just upped and quit, just collapsed. Fortunately, one of the staff had experience in dealing with this type of situation and so was able to get the infusions started without too much fuss. Were it not for her, I would've had to find a vein myself, which wouldn't have been a big deal, given my familiarity with the landscape of my arms.

When the lab results came back, there were real questions as to how this raging inferno in my chest got started in the first place. Since it was most likely me, what did I do to expose myself in this manner? My penchant for mischief was legion, so the possibilities were endless. For sure, I was in a lifestyle where personal behavior, more often than not, resulted in unforeseen and, many times, unpleasant circumstances. More than likely, the culprit was something that I deliberately, but most likely accidentally, introduced into my system as opposed to a chance or coincidental event. Still, what was it?

I did recall an occasion when I had copped some dope, a portion of which was already sold because I had another guys' money with mine. But, in order to maximize my take, I had to find some cut to stretch the quantity that I had. Usually mannitol, inositol, or vitamin B6 powder were used (never quinine, that was for heroin), so I looked around the lab and found some inositol.

Being the supreme, top-of-the-line, alpha addict, I was unable *not* to use a portion of that which I had prepared for the other guy. I said to myself, "Shit, I done went out and got all this shit done, I want me a fuckin' hit."

So, I put a measure into the spoon not knowing or caring that the contents of the inositol container were unsterile. Those microorganisms found their way into the most nutritious and tasty of environments: blood. From this good fortune, they were able to multiply unchecked and after a few days, I began to show signs of my first fever.

I was hooked up to IVs for six weeks, during which time there were real questions as to whether or not I would survive. There were episodes of profuse sweating followed by episodes of intense shivering known as "waxing and waning," the signature of truly virulent infections. And the coughing. The never-ending, always present, shake-you-to-your-bones cough filled with phlegm, two or three cups in a day I'd spit out. With the waxing and waning and all of this coughing, my bed clothing was being changed three to four times a day. I was in dire straits and I knew it. If there was any light at the end of the tunnel, it sure was dim.

That I was in a potentially fatal situation was out of my awareness. I mean, I didn't feel like I was dying. Yet, I would see Dr.

Alford and his colleague consult daily, hovering in a corner, speaking in hushed tones, seeming to calculate the odds of my continued existence. I had no idea how unsure they actually were about my survival; they put on the best face possible. They really didn't think I was going to make it.

But, I did.

CB BO

Although my recovery was nothing short of miraculous, I was quickly returned to the reality of the here-and-now when I found out I had no job. What I did not know, but should have known, was that upon my admission to the hospital, I should have taken a leave-of-absence from Bowman Gray. When I recovered, they would have been obligated to find me another job within the hospital complex. Since I didn't do my part, they were under no requirement to reinstate this guy who, most assuredly, was a disaster area. I'm sure there was much murmuring and opinion-making about me and my whereabouts in those hallowed hallways. Most likely, their thinking was good riddance.

Because of my sudden departure, Tim had to replace me so that the work of the lab could continue. There was no possible way he could have waited for me. He couldn't be blamed for not wanting to be bothered. My misbehavior had really soured relations there and rather than suffer any further humiliations, he decided to cut his losses. I mean, really. How could you expect a guy, because of his Christian ethic and desire to do what's right, who gave an ex-offender a chance, to do anything else? He had done his part, time to let Rick go. When I did get discharged, the person he had hired was up, running and working out well. There was no way, in good conscience, he could let that person go to re-hire someone with such a dubious personal pedigree. I wasn't mad, I did it to myself.

This meant that I could make no more excuses about going to treatment. I couldn't use the job, it was gone. I couldn't use my bills, I didn't have any. And I most certainly couldn't say I'd do it later. No, I had to go because I needed to go, even though I didn't want to go.

What's more telling, was that while I was in the hospital, on the most life-threatening journey I had ever known, I did my best, with

112

no luck, to get my brother Calvin to bring me some dope! In fact, after my discharge, from the moment I left the hospital, I was on a dope hunt.

Calvin had received an insurance settlement. His house had been destroyed by a malfunctioning furnace while he was out of town. We had always been fond of each other, I suppose, because of our mutual friendliness with substance abuse and the errant, unruly lifestyle that attended it and also because of our blood relationship.

Neither Johnetta, Johnny Boy nor Winston had ever hung out with him as I had, and they had no need to do so. Now that he had come into money and was spending it freely on my drug of choice, I found myself being pulled into the orbit of his planet, which was pock-marked by the meteors of my desire: women, dope, free access and an open door, come-as-you-please policy. My kind a guy.

He was in an apartment off Peters Creek Parkway where, by chance, a young lady friend of mine also lived. Since I was newly unemployed and had lots of spare time, I made regular "coke runs" to Fayetteville to get top quality at a decent price. Calvin supplied the money and I did the transporting, a neat little arrangement.

It was at this apartment where I had my first overdose.

We were getting high-quality product from a childhood friend of mine who had gone big time in the dope game. He and I grew up together, attended the same church and even, after college, had a reunion up on Cherry Street, where he was the baker in the kitchen. Shocked me. I hadn't seen him since college and it was strange to meet him in the penitentiary.

Who would a thought?

So, I would meet him in Fayetteville because this is where he moved after getting out. He'd have the powder, I'd have the cash. A quick swap and we'd go our separate ways.

Upon my return, Calvin and I would gather around the coffee table in the living room. I would, ceremoniously and with a flourish, bring out the package and put it on the table. He would give me a portion to sample and I, being unable or unwilling to gauge its purity, would put a goodly amount in the spoon. I'd end up with my normal 50cc shot, but sometimes it would be greatly concentrated and therefore highly potent.

He had learned how to turn powder into "rock" and that was his preferred method of use.   So, he would be doing his thing while I would be doing mine.

CҘ ҍ

An overdose is an odd experience. It comes totally unexpected and takes you completely by surprise. No one who is getting high purposefully tries to O.D. That would be a suicide and dope-heads desire greatly to live because they *want* to get high. So, when you go through the process of putting your hit into the syringe, finding a vein, putting the needle in and drawing back a flag (blood in the syringe), nothing is unusual. The anticipation is the same, the sense of relaxation is the same and all is well, so that when you push your normal dose, because things are so ordinary and so laid back, you find yourself just waiting for the "bells to ring" so you can get that blast. Slowly, you begin to get that slight tingly feeling in the brain and you begin to have that sweet, mediciny taste in the back of your mouth. This is when you really smile because you know you've got a good hit on the way. You give a barely audible sigh.

And, with everything going as it should, the needle hanging out of your arm, you take it in your hand and push the remaining dose, pull the syringe out and rinse it while you wait for that bliss to come.

Only this time, it comes so overwhelmingly powerful, so hard and intense, that it takes your breath away. It is stunning in its force.

You gasp. You look around wildly, your eyes bulging out of their sockets as you try your best to control this raging monster. But, there is no control. Once it's in, it can't come out. And you realize this. Instantaneously, the fear strikes because you now face the very great possibility of death.

You have unknowingly and unwittingly stepped off of the precipice out into the abyss and are hanging in mid-air. And it's scary.

Your heartbeat doubles and becomes completely erratic and out of rhythm. Involuntarily, your body rocks back and forth because your heart is slamming and banging around crazily in your chest.

You begin to ask yourself, Am I going to die? Oh God, please don't let me die! PLEASE DON'T LET ME DIE!!! Please, Please, please...

While the dope is rocketing through your body, your heart, the center of life, is doing the shimmy-shammy, totally out of control. This is quite unfamiliar and very disorienting, your heart's normal rhythm having been viciously chased away by the monster occupying your system. The jarring shock, the immediacy and intensity of the rush puts you "out there." You become engulfed in a web of silence. Your vision is blurred and the silence is accentuated by the sound of those "bells," that high, piercing scream which is the focus in all of getting high. This mosaic is weaved by the euphoria, the deliciously robust ecstasy that comes along, hand-in-hand, with those bells. And you are gone.

This is when you really begin to perceive the limits of your own mortality. What's really frightening about the whole ordeal is that once it starts, it can't be stopped. Either you live or you die. There are no alternatives.

And it was wonderful.

CB   BD

When I came back from that nothingness that is suspended in time and space, all the faces that were in Calvin's apartment were looking at me with a mixture of fear, concern and relief.

Calvin said to me, "Boy, I sure am glad you made it. You was shakin' and tremblin' and swingin' your arms around all wild, we didn't know what to do. Kim called herself doing something by putting her hands in your pants and stroking your balls—" (I remembered that part!) "—but I was about to put your ass outside and call the paramedics 'cause it wasn't shit I could do for you. That's for real."

I was still dazed, not really sure of what had happened. There were two or three somewhat familiar faces that were there earlier when me and Calvin divided up our portions. They happened to be witnesses to this, apparently, rare spectacle. One of them said, "Man, you was a shakin' and a jumpin', I knew it was a O.D. but I ain't never seen one before. That shit was a trip, dude. Word up!"

Another one said, "Man, I ain't never seen one a them before. I thought for sure you was gone die, the way that shit had you goin'. That must be some fuckin' good ass shit. I'm gonna smoke mine, I'm too scared to shoot it like you did."

Like I was some kind a hero.

As I collected myself and steadied my thinking, the buzz from the high still had me zooming. My body was warm all over from all of that shaking (which I later learned were seizures) but, before the high could wear down, I began to look for that syringe, ready to do battle again, ready to face those demons and monsters and go to that scary place just one more time. Surely, I was a man in deep trouble, carrying some kind of inevitable death wish.

A part of me wanted to stop, but a bigger part of me said no, you can't stop, this has to go on.

ɔ ɛ

After I made it home later that night, Momma announced, "Ricky, we've got your appointment at rehab tomorrow, so get whatever you're going to need in a suitcase and be ready to go in the morning."

My mother, God bless her, had been doing the necessary legwork to get me into treatment and, after that episode at Calvin's, I could honestly say that was the place I needed to be. I had a life to live, I truly didn't want to die. I just wanted to be able to get high and still live a normal life, that's what I wanted. Could treatment make that possible?

I began to ask more questions about God. These questions, about my role in life, about the nature of people, about being created in the image of God, began to arise and they demanded answers. If God is in control of all events and knows beforehand those that are to occur, why doesn't He step in and prevent those events that, most assuredly, will result in disaster? Since He is the author and Creator of all things, are not these blights His doings? He allows them, does nothing to interfere with them, they are elements in His total creation, so He must be responsible. But, this line of reasoning was contrary to my religious upbringing, i.e., that God is all-powerful and loves His creation, that He wants the best for us and desires only good to befall us.

Quite puzzling, this juxtaposition.

TEN

We pulled onto a sparsely populated, cracked asphalt, parking lot and Mom said, "Well, Ricky, we're here. It doesn't look like that bad of a place."

I detected a tinge of disappointment in her voice. Addiction Recovery Care Association (ARCA) was a renovated Army surplus depot and it looked like it; drab and gray with lifeless looking trees and grass.

With cheerless bravado, I said, "Yeah, Ma, it looks okay."

I'd had little to say on the ride. Much of my thinking swirled around how to get myself out of this bullshit trap I was in. But as we got my few belongings to the registration desk and got me signed in, I got out of myself long enough to recognize that Mom was hurting something fierce.

"Aw, Ma, don't look so sad. I'm gonna be okay, you just wait and see. I'm gonna come back a changed person."

Words of encouragement are always helpful, however empty they may be.

08 80

I was familiar with the curious groupspeak surrounding the 12-step concept, an incessant chatter about admitting powerlessness and making a decision and making amends and on and on. To be sure, the 12 steps had a good and clear record of helping people stay off drugs and alcohol when all else failed. So, what I had to do to come out on top of this situation was to find the magic formula and, abracadabra! I'd be cured.

I had to admit though, that there was a certain subtle beauty about those steps. They seemed to encompass the ideal philosophy of life and since it had always been a goal of mine to establish a code of living, they had a natural appeal to me. How this would translate to me staying off cocaine, I couldn't figure.

The theme threaded throughout the steps is based on the requirement for one to declare one's relationship to God (or a higher spiritual authority, for those uncomfortable with the God concept), to take the focus off of self by offering wisdom and knowledge to others and being willing to accept the same in return, and to make amends, that is, to apologize to those you had harmed. In other words, there is a real spiritual motif surrounding the steps.

What I learned was that through a short stay at a treatment facility, one could put some time and distance between himself and his drug of choice. This separation would be enhanced through education, nutrition, and rest. It was done this way in the hope that those who gave themselves to this new way of living would establish a foundation on which to build their sobriety. Although the rates of relapse were (and still are) alarming, this scenario did represent a flare of hope.

Sobriety education began with an in-depth study of the 12 steps in a classroom setting, followed by regular meetings that covered the variety of topics that can come out of learning to stay clean— honesty, open-mindedness, honesty, powerlessness, courage, wisdom, resentment and others. Insights or suggestions on how to deal with them were offered by those present, those who were willing to "share". It was in this "sharing" where you really could get some decent advice.

During my first few days, I had to decide if any of those steps applied to me. Certainly my time at Pinehurst did not come close to addressing the nature of my drug use, since I had concluded that the times in Chapel Hill were just an aberration. Now that I was *back* in treatment, voluntarily at that, I had to reassess. Something fundamental had to be amiss.

The first step asked if I could admit that I was powerless over cocaine; that I did what it told me to do and couldn't help it. But it was a two-part step, the other part asking me to further admit that, because of this powerlessness, my life had become disorganized, confused and chaotic. In other words, it had become unmanageable. In order for me to do this, I had to take personal inventory:

Let's see. I shot dope at home, in my car, at work, during the day and during the night. I spent all of my money on dope and nothing on the essentials or the necessities of life such as food, rent, or utilities. When I ran out, I would be in despair and total misery because I couldn't get more.

I'd say this qualified as powerlessness.

I got hospitalized with a life-threatening illness as a direct result of my drug use. I'd had an O.D. and although I had a job at the time, I was dependent on my mother for support, then, I lost my job. I'd say this sounded a whole lot like unmanageability. Obviously, the first step applied very well.

The second step asked if I could believe that a power greater than myself could restore me to sanity. Sanity? Now wait a minute, I gotta define this sanity thing because I was sane. Wasn't I? I mean, I didn't see things that weren't there or hear things nobody else heard nor did I talk to myself about things I didn't see or things I didn't hear. But, if a person does something, anything, over and over, and gets shitty results each time he does it thinking that if he does it *just one more time* he'll get better results, that he'll get an outcome different from the one he got the last time he did it, then he too, is watching a cartoon that doesn't match the real world. His grasp on reality is askew. He must be insane.

Even after a period of abstinence (for example, when you've crashed for a couple of days after a binge or when you stay for a couple of weeks in a treatment center) and you seem to think you've seen the error of your ways, you've convinced yourself that it's all just a peculiarity and you're gonna "go get just one more" and the next thing you know your lunch money is gone, your car payment is gone, even your gas money is gone and in a moment of hilarious hysteria you say "Damn, I did that same ol' dumb shit again!"

Only there's a piece of you that's not laughing.

The next step said that I had to make a decision to turn my will and my life over to the care of God, as I understood Him. I had a real problem with accepting defeat and "turning my life over" meant that I was defeated, a concept I was loath to acknowledge, which really was why I tried it again in the first place.

As a matter of fact, these principles are well thought-out, well-constructed canons that people everywhere could and should live by. They speak to the nature of the human spirit in a manner free of ambiguity and religious authority. This is the universal attraction of the group process, enabling people to work through their personal and family issues of addiction and compulsion within the context of a concise philosophic ethic. They provide a demonstrable method of mending one's self-esteem and made a way to restore one's sense of value and purpose in life.

But I was too far gone for any of this to matter.

The allure, the excitement, that juicy feeling you got in the heat of a get-high moment had not diminished. In fact, the desire to get high was the clear winner in the race over the desire to stay clean. After whining and begging my Higher Power to fix me, after a few good meals and some well-deserved rest, even after shit seemed to be getting back to normal, I just couldn't let that dope go. I had to admit it. I just couldn't front and say I didn't think about getting high. Shit, I thought about it *all* the time. That "thang" was in my flesh, it was in my skin. It had become as much a part of me as my own consciousness. Indeed, there might as well have been a whole other person inside of me who was me, yet was still a stranger. But, I was thinking, if I could finish this program, the magic would work, relief would come my way and I could go on and live like a regular guy.

So, when the whites of my eyes began to take on a yellowish tone, I couldn't help but wonder what in the world was wrong. My previous medical experiences prepared me to observe these signs in other people, not in myself. When the on-site nurse diagnosed probable hepatitis, I was rather befuddled as to who or what she was actually talking about. Surely, there'd been some mistake. A quick blood test confirmed the diagnosis but, facility policy and county health codes dictated that, due to the highly contagious nature of this illness, I had to be immediately discharged.

It was just as well, I was ready to go anyway. My fractured existence didn't lend itself to this kind of quasi-training camp mentality in the first place.

CR ⁊

Having just been discharged from the treatment center should have encouraged me to step up and ask Roberta to marry me. She had stood by me through very difficult circumstances, I should make it right by her, I should do the right thing. At least that was my take on things, but I was back to my same old habits. I was not, however, fooling her.

"Well, Rick, you know I don't misplace my stuff," she said on one such occasion when she was onto my same old habits. "Once it comes in this house, it stays where it's put, it just don't up and grow legs and walk away. Now, you say you haven't seen my necklace and that's all well and good, but you best be clear about one damn thing: I'm wondering about you. For real."

And she had reason to wonder. There was gonna be hell to pay or some clever maneuvering on my part when her checks began to bounce.

At first, I thought I was going to have some trouble at the bank, but why should that be? Proper ID, a look of casual unconcern and the teller was in my hip pocket. It all got started one day after I had come in the previous night very late. Roberta had gone to work and I began to despair for some dope, so I began rummaging through her things, just looking for anything of value. I came across her checks, still in their boxes.

Banks, being ever polite and hardly suspecting guile when they see a valid ID and adequate funds, assumed it was a straightforward, legitimate transaction. My initial anxieties were baseless as they cashed the check with hardly a passing glance and so began my first experience in the nefarious world of forgery and uttering.

Then Roberta inquired about her check book.

"Well, Rob, I really haven't seen it. I could offer some guesses, but that's all they would be. For real though, I'd tell you if I knew."

"I just bet you would."

"I mean, why you gotta say it like that, huh? Like you really ain't got no faith in me at all."

"You right, man, I ain't got no faith in you. That's how I'm sayin' it. I have not been pleased at all by your recent inconsistencies. You have been fickle and unreliable and your momma ain't happy about it either. We do talk, you know. What's worse is that I cannot just walk away from you. I thought we had something really good..."

"We do, Rob." I bleated plaintively.

"...but those streets can be so rough and that's not an element for which you are prepared. I'd hate to come home to some bad news. I mean, these checks and this money is bad news enough, but that can be replaced. You can't. I ain't stupid, there's no doubt in my mind that you found my checks and forged my name and that's what I've told your mother."

I kind a figured that, but I tried to keep her from focusing on such accusations. "What kind a bad news you talkin' about?"

Like I didn't already know. Being in those drug areas certainly exposed a person to all manner of harm. Out there on the corner, not being from the area, waiting for my car or walking around looking for somebody to get a little small piece from, did put me in unpredictably dangerous zones. You couldn't stay inside the places where you had smoked if you didn't have more dope. They'd tell you right quick if you ain't got no more dope, you gotta go. Just like that. Regardless of the time of day or night nor how much money in drugs or cigarettes or burgers or anything you may have spent with them. In the end all that mattered was, you got some more dope?

"Like something happening to you. A call from the hospital or the police or the morgue would really spoil my day."

"Just think of what it would do to my day," I say, in a woeful attempt at humor.

"Boy, please."

☙ ❧

And she was right, but standing out there amongst those strangers in a no man's land was almost comfortable for me.

I mean, those people were fiercely territorial and if you were their friend they stuck by you, but if you were their enemy, look out. I'd seen them chase away folks who might have been on the block earlier. These were people with whom they were familiar but, because they didn't have drugs at the time, were scolded away. Yet others who had just copped, but were complete strangers, were cordially invited in. Everybody was your friend as long as they had dope, even strangers.

This was odd psychology indeed, foreign stuff and difficult to grasp, but there it was. My ability to avoid the scenario of being the scorned, unwelcomed visitor were improved by sharing a portion, just a hit, to a head that might be in the area, whether he or she was in a house or not. In this way, I became someone they would look out for since, most times, I would share what I had. Not the usual behavior of folks on the block. In fact, I became quite literate in the ways of smoking outside and the etiquette involved because real heads rarely came inside to smoke. A piece of crack was so hard to come by, few people were going to share what they had unless the weather was really bad and they *had* to come inside.

Though Rob's anxieties were well-founded, I had developed a facility and a fondness for hanging out with these folks. However, I found it advantageous to perpetuate the illusion that I was out of my element and regularly faced a clear and unmistakable menace. Because I had been employed and had a nice car, I could get dope on credit. This endeared me to a few of the folks in the hood because I could, if it was really pressing, go to a dopeboy and get some by letting him use my car.

I'd seen folk run out of money and want a blast so bad that they'd go to the dopeman and try to make any kind of ol' raggedy-ass deal 'til the next day, 'til payday or 'til any day really. They'd have very little (usually nothing) to use as collateral and it'd be so pitiful to watch folk sell themselves out like that, just begging and pleading for another hit. When you're not from the 'hood and you've smoked your last blast, being on alien turf did encourage recreational violence. Young bucks, just wilding for some action, would make some out of your dumbass—just for being there.

Rob was right. I knew I had to straighten up, do right, be more careful. But how real was that? I knew how much she cared for me, from the time we first met, and how long and faithfully she had stood by me. I had to find a way to give her the respect she so splendidly deserved, but I was being swallowed whole by this dope thing, my outlook on life flopping and floundering like a fish out of water.

ELEVEN

I either had to go home and deal with Momma or go back to Roberta's and deal with her. Neither one of those choices was I looking forward to, but I had to come up with something. I knew Rob was pissed as hell and I knew Momma was gonna have this, that and the other to say about this bank situation.

I might just have to 'fess up about those checks, but this calling home ahead of time is really something I should do. She always telling me how much it worries her, how she can't stay asleep, always popping awake, when she hasn't heard from me and it's 2 or 3 o'clock in the morning. I tell her if she hadn't heard from me, then I must be alright, but she says I don't have children, so I just don't understand. I guess I don't.

Still, I ought to be able to do just this one little thing, ain't nothing but a phone call. Why can't I do just this one little thing to make my Momma a little bit comfortable in the face of all this chaos I'm causing?

She'll probably be asking me if I've been using again—like I've ever stopped—and what am I going to do about my problem and on and on. Maybe I ought not go home or over to Rob's right now. Maybe, if I hang out long enough, somebody might come by or something might come up so I can get a blast. Least I won't have to face that music right now, I'll just do all of that later. I'm a pull over 'til I decide what to do, maybe somebody might see me and I could get lucky.

Uh-oh, I wondered who this was walking up. I guess I oughta roll my window down...

"What up, man?" dude said.

"Yo, what up."

"I seen you just sittin' here so I just came over to holla. You, uh, doin' anything or you, uh, waitin' on sombody?"

"Nah, man, I'm just chillin'." I say with the reserved langour of one experienced in the streets. "I ain't doin' too much, just tryin' to see if I can get my drink on."

"Man, it's 4 o'clock in the morning, where you gonna get a drink this time a night?"

"Oh, you must not be from here, where you from?" I ask with studied nonchalance.

"Nah, I ain't, I'm from Walkertown, why."

"'Cause if you was from here, you'd know that there's always drinks somewhere. But, anyway, what you doing out here so late, you gotta walk home or something?"

"I mean, I could ask you the same thing about why you out here late like this talkin' to yourself in the car..."

"Yo, man, I was just working through some things, that's all."

"Whatever. But, yeah, I could use a ride home. My name's Mike and if I had a ride home, that's where I'd be."

"You mean out to Walkertown?"

"Yeah."

"You got any money?"

"Nah, but I thought we could make a little hustle, then money wouldn't be a problem."

"What kind a 'little hustle'?"

"Well, I know this person who will give me some money, but I don't have a way there."

"I thought you was tryin' to go home?"

"Well, I was, but I was really tryin' to get over to where I could get some money at and when I saw you sittin' there mumbling to yourself..."

"I wasn't mumbling to myself."

"Oh, yes you was."

"No, I wasn't."

"Well, who was you mumblin' to?"

"I wasn't mumblin'."

"Well, talkin' then, Mr. Exact. You was talkin' to somebody and since I don't see nobody else in the car, so you had to be talkin' to yourself."

"You sure mighty comfortable just meetin' me."

"So."

"Well, anyway..."

"Yeah, anyway, when I saw you, how 'bout this, just sittin' in your car by yourself, you like that better? I figured I'd come over and see what's up."

"So, you tell me: you want a ride home or a ride over there?"

"Okay, look, check it out. You get high?"

"What you mean?" I asked, faking like I really don't know what he's talking about. Talking to a total stranger in a low-income, high crime neighborhood at 4 o'clock in the morning, boy please, quit playing.

"You know what I'm saying. You, uh, smoke?"

"Yeah, I smoke."

"Well, then," he said happily, "let's get busy!"

ଔ ଷ

No doubt, let's get busy. This is what I've been waiting on since I pulled over, taking the chance that somebody might want to do something just like this: make a hustle, relatively legit, to get some dope money.

Many times in the past I could recall sitting in my car or just riding around fiending for some dope, jonesing real bad, looking for something or somebody to get me high and nothing would come up. After the blast has gone, all you get left with is this antsy hype that keeps you up and moving and wanting to do something, *anything* to keep it going.

Those would be the times when I really should have taken my ass on home, when the misery and downright disgust of doing dope became so apparent, but I just couldn't because if I went home, just as sure as the sun would rise, I figured somebody would come by who I could get with and I might miss out on a get high, so I just couldn't go in because I might miss getting blessed.

It was a sorry state of affairs, for sure.

Shortly the world would begin to wake up, folks would be getting ready for work, cars would begin creeping along thoroughfares. And there I'd be. Out there, looking stupid. Eventually, drowsiness would be my savior and I would succumb to fatigue. But just as soon as I'd wake up, I'd want a hit.

Now this dude has just walked into my frazzled little world. I knew that solace would come if I could get some more dope, so he showed up right on time. My only hope was that he wasn't bullshitting, that he would be correct on this deal because I sure was gonna give him a try.

We rode over to a pay phone where he, apparently, made a collect call. Had to be collect, didn't nobody have no money and he talked to whoever it was for a few minutes. I couldn't discern the context of the conversation but after he got in the car, he directed me to First and MLK Boulevard, where we made a left turn onto First and proceeded to a quaint, well-kept bungalow. The New Yorker in the drive, the unattached garage, and fresh paint on the house told me that whoever was the occupant was doing quite well indeed, thank you very much. My spirits waxed anew.

I didn't park behind the New Yorker, I stayed on the street, directly in front of the walkway to the front door. Mike got out, went to the door and tapped lightly, the soft lighting suggesting that he was expected. Presently, an older woman, well-kept, slightly graying, came to bring him inside; he stayed for a short while, then came back to the car.

I'm looking at him for some sign, some expression, some indication of his success or failure. Nothing. He maintained a poker face.

This kind of seemingly emotionless take on things was impossible for me. After I'd pull one of my stunts on Momma (because I'm positive that's what's happened here), the thrill of faking her out was nearly as intoxicating as the journey of going to cop. I had long ago resorted to this most odious form of manipulation.

"Well?"

"Well, what?" he said in return, trying to appear unperturbed.

"Look man, you seem cool and all, but I ain't up for no games right about now. Did you get straight or what?"

"Yeah, man, I got straight. I got a few bucks."

"Alrighty, then! That's what I'm talking about." I say with a grin and a look of relief because I knew I would've amped out if he had come up empty-handed; ain't nothing worse than being on a wild goose chase and dealing with a bullshittin' nigga when you're dope-hungry. I'd had my share of people who swear they gonna go over here and get this or go over there and do that and end up not getting or doing a damn thing, but burn up gas.

That shit pisses me off, but I aint' got to deal with that now. It's a brand new day.

"Where we gonna cop at?" I ask, trying to mask, though not so convincingly, my excitement.

He said, "I don't care. Shoot, we can go back to Lakeside."

"Well, that's what we'll do but, first of all, I need some gas so we going by the BP right now, before we run out."

"Okay."

CB BO

Lakeside Apartments is a complex of low-income housing for marginally employed people. It was located on a primary roadway linking more upscale suburbs to downtown Winston-Salem. It had a reputation for open air, 24-7, stop-and-cop drug sales and was one of the first places I cut my teeth on the drug scene and began to be known in those circles.

Many of the dopeboys from Cleveland Projects or Piedmont Circle would come to Lakeside and vice-versa. Commonly, heads would be looking for crack to buy and, depending on who you knew, could come off with a pretty good deal, maybe a two-for-one, from one of the dopeboys who was not from the Lakeside 'hood. Folks were constantly on the move in this scene, there was always an ebb and flow in the tide of humanity that passed those streets; you became known by the company you kept, the people you knew and those that knew you.

We parked in one of the several parking areas and got out. Apartments line the short roads throughout the complex and we found ourselves under the dim street light out front; a few heads milled about and one of them walked right up. This one I knew from being around.

"What up, Rick."

"What up, Reid."

"You lookin'?"

"I don't know yet." Although I did know that's what we were doing, by rights, it wasn't my money so I would have been out of order to speak on it.

Besides, the first ones to come up trying to make a sale usually have "dummies," especially late night, so it was good that I knew this guy. They know where the dope is and want to get high too, but don't have money, so they sell fake dope to get those few dollars. This can be dangerous because folk get mighty testy about giving their money up for junk, but if you don't know any better and get caught up in not knowing who you're dealing with, it can and will happen. I've seen heads sell dummies to people they knew and who knew them, sometimes real rocks right off the ground! But it was usually a cooked concoction of Goody Headache Powders laced with Anbesol, the medication for toothaches. When it hardened, you couldn't tell it from a real crack rock—until you tried to smoke it. It would give off this tremendously offensive odor and you would know immediately what it was but, by then, it was too late.

At twenty bucks a pop, this can be quite a risky undertaking. But that urge to use, that desire to get high, coupled with a good dose of desperation, would drive folk to do some strange things and expose themselves to all sort of unpleasantness. People out hustling up their ends, doing their best to get cop fare get pissed off when they get gypped out of their money like that, somebody selling them some fake shit. A nigga would bust your ass behind shit like that but, oddly, folk got away with it more than they got fucked up for it.

A hectic and hazardous lifestyle, for sure.

"Well, what's up then?" Street code for "what you doin' out here if you ain't coppin'?" Then he notices Mike who was just standing to the side, not really in the line of fire of this conversation.

"Oh, hey, my man! What's up with you? I seen you around here earlier but they tol' me you was tryin' to get to the crib."

"I was, but my plans changed. Looks like I'm a hang out a little while longer, got a couple things to tend to."

Oh, he Mr. Big now 'cause he got a little change in his pockets? That's niggas for you. Once they get what they want, they go the other way. Well, he did get me some gas and got us some drinks so I figured he'd be cool and do me right when we came to cop. Still, it's too early to tell. He could turn out to be one of those really unpleasant dickheads who change their colors after they get up on some money. A little while ago they was broke, fiending and begging for a hit, you could a bought them for two dollars. But once they get some money, you can't tell them shit, knowing good and well they couldn't have gotten straightened out without your help, then they gonna try and get all fly. That shit pisses me off.

Reid speaks up. "Well, if you're lookin', I got a little somethin' right here. You really ain't got to go nowhere if you want somethin'."

"What you got?" I inquire, suspecting what's up.

"Nah, man, I got this." Mike steps in with the weighty authority of the one that's got the money. I figured this might happen.

"A'ight, man, but check that shit first."

"What you mean 'check that shit', Rick? Don't come out here wit' that bullshit!"

"What? 'Cause I tell the man to check your shit? Nigga, if your shit is correct you ought a *want* a motherfucker to check it. Only them dummy-sellin', late-night ass niggas don't want nobody to check they shit. You one a them? You got dummies?"

"Nah, man, not this time. This shit straight."

Mike said, "Hold on, Rick. I said I got this. Look, Reid, let me see what you got."

"Yeah, Rick, hold on, he said he got this. Since it ain't your loot, you ain't got no real say-so anyway."

"Fuck that." I said. "Wouldn't be no loot if it wan't for the ride I gave my man, so I got say-so, you'n run nothin' here no way."

"Why don't you chill, Rick?" Mike said.

"I tell you what," I went on without missing a beat, "just take us to where the dope is and we'll look out for you for doing that."

"What for?" Reid said. "I got dope right here. Besides, Ray-Ray an' them went to the club and L'il Man say better not nobody come past his crib 'cause he chillin' with his girl. So, what y'all gone do?"

Mike said, "Let me see a twenty."

Reid goes into his pocket and brings out six or seven real nice looking pieces. I mean, that shit looked like real quality dope. Maybe L'il Man put him on to keep things rolling while he chilled. I hated to admit it, but maybe Reid *didn't* have dummies.

"Damn, Reid." I said, "That shit look pretty good. You musta tricked somebody into trusting you, huh. Still, let my man test that."

"A'ight. Here, my man, try this." He looks me in the eye and I don't miss his sarcasm. I try to give him as threatening a look as I can, but he just grins.

There are a couple of ways to tell if a piece of dope is counterfeit; a field test, so to speak. One is to rub it on your tongue or gum; it will numb you if it's real or it will "freeze" you if it's fake. You got to have a little experience to be able to tell the difference. Another way is to briefly flash a lighter across the surface of the rock. That burst of heat melts the surface ever so slightly, which then emits a pungent, sweetish smell if it's real or an acrid, unpleasant aroma if it's not. This is the most reliable method to use, though the other might be the quickest. You had to be up on your testing because even the most experienced smoker could be fooled. Besides, it was S.O.P. for every day, street-level buying and selling. The reality of it was that since the big boys tested theirs, we ought to test ours, too.

Mike took the rock, looked at it, rubbed it on his tongue and, after a moment, pronounced it legit. I sure hoped so because I was wanting a hit real bad.

"Yeah, man, it's good. Let me get two of 'em."

"A'ight." Reid allowed him to choose another one from the pieces gathered in his hand. This was done right out in the open, under the clear, but shadowy castings of the street light. A casual observer would recognize this as probably an illicit exchange of some nature. Though these thoughts occurred to everybody, whether you're going to cop, in the act of copping, or had already just copped, you always were subconsciously hoping—consciously dismissing the real possibility of it—that the police weren't in the bushes or in some abandoned apartment or just happen to be riding by on routine patrol. Always cat-and-mouse, this game.

ભ ફ

"Where we gonna smoke this at?" Mike inquired.

"Well, we could pull around back and sit in the car or we could go up to Pookie's house, but you know you're gonna have to give her somethin' if we go in there. Or we could go around to my man Keith's house. He don't smoke and he lives right around the corner, but he does work and I'd hate to wake him up just so we can blaze."

"Yeah, I'm hearing all that."

"So, on the other hand, we really could just sit in the car," I said. "That way we ain't got to share nothin' with nobody. We might not have the comforts of being inside, but we'll have the independence of not being tied down and we can come and go as we please. So, you make the call, it's your shit."

"I mean," Mike began, "it's really up to you. You got the car and everything and none of this would be possible without your having taken a chance on me, so whatever you think is cool is cool with me. You wanna hang out in the ride, we do that or you wanna go inside, we can do that. Whichever, it's on you."

I must say, he caught me off-guard with that bit of honesty. "Well look, what I want to know is, are we through or what? Is this all for the night? 'Cause, I mean, if it is then we can't do too much riding 'cause gas gonna be a problem."

"I don't know if I can get any more money, it'll just depend. So, maybe, this is it."

"A'ight, then we'll just sit in the car."

"Okay, that's cool."

We pulled into a little hidden cul-de-sac, a place made like it was just for smokers in a car. Since late-night police patrols weren't regular, you could sit in a car for hours and have a complete smoke out, totally on the down low. The trouble occurred when your solitude was broken up by the creeping in of a spontaneous, deeply irrational sense of terror. This is a state of mind that tells you something extraordinarily terrible is just about to occur when, in fact, no such thing is even happening. Being inside a house tended to keep paranoia at a distance but when you're outside and, particularly, when the dope was good, it could be quite disturbing.

"Well, this as good a spot as any," I said.

"Yeah, at least we off that main drag through the 'hood," Mike responded.

"Yeah. So look, you got a stem?"

"Yeah, but ain't you got one?"

"Yeah, well, I had one but I had to let it go."

"What you mean 'let it go'?"

"Yo, man, I wanted a hit so I sold it. You ain't never sold your stem?"

"Nah, dude. How am I gonna smoke if I ain't got no stem? I can't believe you sold your stem."

"Well, I did."

"Well, I guess we'll have to use mine, huh. I just hope you don't get stupid when you smoke. You don't get stupid do you? 'Cause if you do, that's really gonna piss me off."

I guess since he had the dope and the money, he could get a little jazzy with me.

"Just as long as you pass it to me when it's my turn, we'll be alright," he said. "You know what I mean, then after I get my hit, I'll pass it back to you. Okay? See, if you had yours, we wouldn't have to go through all this."

"No doubt, I was buggin' when I let my shit go like that but yo, man, I was fiendin' and didn't nobody want to go nowhere or nothing, so I was kind a stuck. But, on the real, I don't get weird or freeze up like I seen some folk do. That shit there is crazy as hell."

"That it is. I seen some weird shit like that before and it just fucks me up to see folk trip out like that. So, a'ight man, let's get down. You go ahead and break us off and I'll give you the glass so you can go first."

Damn, this dude trying to be real classy about it, gonna offer the pipe to me first and then let me break off the rock, too. He ain't so bad after all. Letting the other guy go first is a magnanimous gesture that tells all who are paying attention that an effort is being made to be gentlemanly and courteous in circumstances where such attributes are not regularly seen.

I took one of the pieces and broke it in half. I gave his half to him and he handed me the stem. This was done quietly, ceremoniously, almost religiously; a sharing of the elements, as it were.

Undoubtedly, this little scenario was being repeated around crack tables and amongst crackheads everywhere. It was a form of communion, was it not? Not unlike what would be done in church—the dividing of the Host, the passing around and sharing of the Host among the celebrants, done with an air of solemnity and graveness that made any given smoke scene an echo of a communion service.. However, this would be the Church of the Crack Rock or the Church of the Get High, wouldn't it? Blasphemy, for sure, but when you're struggling for understanding in an area of your life that's out of control, such comparisons seem normal. To me, God had become sometimey and unpredictable anyway.

Because of his great good gesture of offering me the pipe first, I then offered it to him so that he could go first which he graciously accepted. He put his half on, took the lighter and melted the dope onto the screening, put the opposite end to his lips, fired the lighter and took his hit. The handling and lighting of a piece of crack on a stem is no different than that of a cigarette. Other than holding the flame to the business end for a continual, longer period of time and inhaling the entire time you burn it, it's the same.

I watched as volumes of thick, white smoke roiled through the glass pipe. It was an aspect of smoking that was nearly uncontrollable: watching those clouds of smoke. Something about it was just mesmerizing.

After 20 or 30 seconds of continuous inhalation, he passed the pipe to me. During that time, I watched as he measured and evaluated the intensity of the flame against the end of the pipe, moving it back and forth, back and forth, coaxing the maximum amount from the hit. As the effect of the narcotic began to take, I saw his eyes glaze over and a vacant, distant look came onto his face.

For the few moments that I watched him smoke, in the darkened quiet of the car, without distractions or people to distract, I could just relax. This pseudo-serenity was comforting and was part of what made crack smoking so appealing. In the early morning hours, before dawn, just before the world would begin to awaken, a surprising peacefulness prevailed.

Now that it was my turn, I could look forward to a good, good hit. Given the way Mike was staring out into space, I knew I was due for a major blast. I broke my half in half, put that onto the screening and melted it. Like a prayer being answered, it gave off that dazzlingly sweet aroma and a hot sizzling sound while it melted onto the just used pipe. Even as I lighted it, the remnants of that sizzling sound came through as the flame consumed the rock.

Momentarily, I began to feel the first tingling fingers of pleasure caress my brain...then the rush. That sudden, cascading rapture cocaine brings and, along with it, an intensity that just goes and goes and goes.

Damn! I said to myself, that Reid got some good shit. I wonder where he got it from. Shit. Oh, shit! Man, this blast is really fucking me up.

Then, suddenly, I became aware that *somebody* was out there. Somebody was watching us. "Yo man. You hear that?" I asked, my voice spiked with uneasiness.

"Hear what?"

"Shhhhhhh! Listen!" I whisper loudly.

"I don't hear nothin'." Mike retorted, a look of frustration beginning to cloud his face.

"Shhh." I gestured to him with my hand. I was looking around, back and forth, side to side, in the rear view mirror, in the side mirror. Looking intently, straining even, as though by my looking, something or somebody would be forced to appear.

"Man, you trippin'!" Mike exclaimed. "Damn, man, I was kind a havin' a good time 'til you started this shit. I ain't had no peace and quiet like this all day and now you wants to trip. Damn! You fuckin' my high up."

"Mike, goddammit, be quiet so I can listen!" I whispered emphatically, still concentrating, waiting for whatever is going to appear to appear or whatever is going to happen to happen.

"Listen to what?" he said, and that seemed to ring a bell.

Damn, I must be tripping. The very thing I hate to see others doing, I end up doing myself. That shit makes me look so fucking stupid, I can't believe it. But, then, that there was a might, mighty good fucking hit and it put me into that zone I so loved to be in. I guess I just couldn't help myself.

"Hey, look," I say, "we better go, you know, before somethin' happens." A strange urgency creeping through my words.

"Man, ain't nothing gonna happen. But, if you want to go, we can. It just seems like this is such a cool spot and I'd hate to go and run into some bullshit down the road somewhere. But if it'll make you feel better, go ahead."

"Yeah, it will. Just moving to another spot somewhere else would make me feel a lot better."

I took a brief pause then started the car. As I pulled out of the little area we were in, a police cruiser eased by slowly—maybe he saw us, maybe he didn't. Scared the shit out of me right then and there, especially when I saw him go up the street and put his brake lights on. Shit, this some action I don't need.

"See that shit, I told you some ol' bullshit was liable to jump off 'cause we was cool where we was at!" Mike exclaimed.

"Man, don't start panicking just 'cause you see a police car, everything still cool."

"I ain't panicking, but they's the only folk that could give us a bad day, so let's just be cool and see what's going on. You got license?"

"What the fuck kind a dumbass question is that. You see this car I'm drivin'? Of course I got license, all my shit legit. Our only problem is that little bit of crack you got. You got a rock left ain't you?"

"Yeah."

"Well, just keep it in your hand in case you have to throw it or swallow it or somethin'. So let's just ride on up outta here if we can. If we can't, I'll handle the police." My sense of purpose and determination having returned as I could be facing a devastating and unpredictable encounter.

We went up the street and around the corner, following the direction the cop car went. As we headed toward the exit of the complex, we could see straight ahead, a license check. Not to worry, I had mine.

"Damn, what they doin' havin' a license check at 5 o'clock in the morning?" Mike asked plaintively, to no one in particular. Looks like it's his turn to be unnerved.

"I guess they tryin' to get as many strays as they can before shift change and, if we don't be careful, we could end up being one a them strays."

As we pulled up to the officers in the street, resplendent in their brightly striped orange-white reflector jackets, we saw that one was on foot patrol, another was monitoring traffic from the opposite direction and a third was patiently awaiting my car to stop. This early in the morning, there wasn't a lot of traffic coming or going, so it made our traveling at such an early hour seem suspicious, at least in my eyes. I guess we should have stayed put.

Coming to a stop, I rolled down the window. The officer leaned down and says, "Good morning, sir. Can I see your license and registration, please?"

"Sure." I wasn't worried. I knew my credentials were in order, but I also knew that they thrived on giving folks a hard time, especially in a neighborhood like this. And here I am, out here in the wee hours with this real nice car. I got the paperwork out of the glove box and handed it to him.

"Are you Mr. Moore?"

"Yes."

"Just a minute."

He went to his cruiser where he could go through the routine of calling in and checking me out. On this I was, again, unconcerned as I had not been in trouble with the law since my days in Chapel Hill.

But, on his return to the window, I tried to divine some meaning from his expression.

"Okay, Mr. Moore, you check out."

"Okay, thanks."

"But, could you tell me why you're coming out of here so early in the morning?"

"Well, I met Mike here last night and it just got late, time got by us and we decided to head on in. No particular reason other than headed home, that's about it."

"I see. Well, you ought to know that this is a designated high-crime area as you can see by the signs posted on the telephone poles at each entrance." I had not seen them or ever noticed them, but there they were. "This designation and public warning allows us to search any vehicle and its occupants at our discretion. So, if you don't mind, or even if you do, we're gonna have to search you, your friend and your vehicle."

This ain't looking too good.

"Hey, Ted. Get over here so we can search this vehicle and these men." Damn, what are we going to do about that dope and this stem? Damn.

"Okay passenger, what's your name?" the other officer asked when he came up to Mike's window.

"Mike Walkers."

"Okay, Mr. Walkers, you understand that this search by no means is an attempt to involve you in any illegal activity nor is it an infringement on your presumed innocence of any such activity, yet this is an option we can explore. So, I'm going to say to you, if either of you have any guns, drugs, open containers of alcohol, weapons of mass destruction or anything that could cause us a problem, tell us right now."

"No, I don't." Mike says confidently.

"Me, neither." I knew I still had Mike's pipe, but that was just a ticket, simple paraphernalia, I was cool with that.

"Well, my officer says he saw something come out of the passenger window back there a bit as you all were approaching, so we're gonna go down there and see if anything turns up, okay." With his polite ass, like if it ain't okay, he ain't gonna look for whatever he says his boy saw. Fuck him and his manners.

"Hey, Eddie!"

"Yo!"

"Go on down to where you saw that object come out of the car and look around while Ted and I frisk these gentlemen and search their vehicle."

"Okay, Andy."

"Ted, you get the driver and I'll get the passenger."

"Alrighty," Ted chirped, happy and content that he had the legal right to give somebody a bad day.

Andy tells Mike to step out of the car and Ted does the same for me. Andy goes through Mike's pockets, waistband, his socks down to the ankles, his shirt pockets and comes up empty. I guess he did throw that piece. Ted searched me and found the stem.

"Hey Andy, I got a crack pipe."

"Anything else?"

"Naw, nothing else."

"Well, go ahead and write that up. This passenger's clean as far as I can tell. Hey Eddie!"

"Yo!"

"You found anything?"

"Not yet, Andy. Still looking."

"Good man, keep it up. Alright fellas, step over here and sit in the curb. Ted, if you would, watch these gentlemen while I conduct a search of their vehicle."

"Will do, Andy."

Such nice guys.

He started on my side, using his flashlight to look on the floorboard, then feel under the seats. He pulled down the sun visors, then looked in the ash tray; he slaps the seats with his palm apparently looking for crumbs, small bits of crack that may have fallen off when the rock was being broken, to pop up. Then he went to the passenger side and did the same thing.

"Okay, what have we here?" he suddenly announces. My stomach did a little butterfly shuffle as he stepped away from the car with something pinched between his thumb and index finger. Probably one of those crumbs. "Hey Ted, go get me one a those field tests. Let's see what this is."

"Gotcha, Andy."

At that very moment, the ultimate snoop dog yells from down the street, "Hey Andy! I found something that looks like rock down here."

"Good Eddie, bring it on up."

"I guess we should test it, huh, just to make sure." he said breathlessly as soon as he got back to the, now, crime scene.

"May as well. I found a fragment in the car, so let's see what's up. Could be nothing, might be something."

A field test for law enforcement is a clear glass ampule with a liquid inside that turns blue in the presence of cocaine. This is standard procedure, nationwide. They take a portion of whatever they're questioning, put it in the ampule and crush it. If it turns blue, it's positive and is good enough for a felony arrest, possession of controlled substance.

"Well, there she goes, Andy. Looks like somebody didn't throw it far enough, huh? What does your fragment do?"

"Well, looks like I'm a need another tester and if it comes back good, we're gonna escort these fine gentlemen down to our detention center. Or to, what the regular folk like us call the jail house!"

They howl boisterously as though it's just the funniest thing they'd ever heard. But, it puts my life on an all-too-familiar-yet-totally-unavoidable course—back in trouble again.

Oh, well, it's only right. The way I've been going here lately, I sort of figured it would eventually come to these ends. There would be a cell with my name on it before too long.

Mike says to me in a low tone of voice, "How they gone accuse me of somethin' they found in the street? Somethin' they just picked up and say it's mine, how they gone do that?"

"Maybe they can't, maybe they can, but they did say they saw something come out the window on your side and all it takes is their word. I wish I'd a been paying attention, I'd a told you to swallow it. That little bit wouldna done nothin' to you anyway.

"But still," I went on, "you're the one that has to prove the shit wasn't yours in the first place. And how you gonna do that when *they* said they saw it with their own eyes come out the passenger side window? It's your word against theirs and you in a designated drug area, too. That looks questionable right there. That thing called 'innocent until proven guilty' is bullshit. The real deal is you're assumed guilty and you have to prove yourself innocent. That's the deal. The courts and the judge automatically believe you did whatever the police say you did. It's up to you to get out of it. Now, many times they be right and a lotta times they do good shit, but sometimes folks do a crime, get caught and still get out of it and that really pisses them off. Hopefully, that'll be the case here, but it just ain't no tellin'."

"How you know?"

"I been locked up, that's how I know. Been there, done that. Besides, look at my situation: here they find a crumb, a speck of dope in my car and they're gonna charge me with possession of a controlled substance. Now, what kind a bullshit is that? They won't even have enough left to bring to court as evidence, but yet and still, I got to go through all the changes, all the rigamarole of the system. I gotta get fingerprinted, see the magistrate, make bond, then make plans to go to court. For a crumb. Maybe it'll stick, maybe it won't, but they sure do make you go through all the motions."

"Daaammmnnnn."

"Yeah, damn. Ain't no big thing though, it's just part of doing business on the dope scene. You keep fuckin' around out here in this crack world and they gonna make room for your ass, too. Trust me, I know."

TWELVE

The Forsyth County Jail was an old structure that had been in use since the '30s. Though efforts had been made to modernize and expand the facility, it remained severely overcrowded and was in dire need of replacement. The receiving area, where potential, yet unwilling, inmates were brought in, was a fence-enclosed driveway. This was adjacent to the main entrance and was remotely operated from inside the building.

This being my first acquaintance with the justice system in Winston-Salem, I was acutely aware of my surroundings. After going inside with hands still cuffed behind my back, I was fingerprinted, photographed and booked by the magistrate who set my bond. I was allowed to make that one phone call to see if Momma would come get me, but the line was busy. Since there was the possibility that I could make bond, I was put in a holding cell.

Because of the relatively minor nature of the charge (simple possession) and because it was his first offense, Mike was able to leave on an unsecured bond meaning that he didn't have to put up any property or money, only his signature that he would show up for court. I, on the other hand, drew a higher bond, which had to be secured by a bondsman or by property. My prior record had come back to pay a visit.

I'm sure Momma was worried. She didn't know where I was, what I was doing or what kind of shape I might be in. It was so simple what she asked of me, just give her a call if I wasn't coming in.

But no, my pussy ass couldn't find the guts to call while I was in the midst of my frolicking. And now that I found myself in a bind, look who I was trying to call—it never failed. I bet if I had access to unlimited dope and money, I'd probably never call anybody just to let them know I was alright. No, I'd just smoke and smoke and smoke.

I wasn't too worried about staying in jail a long time. I figured Momma would come right on down and get me. If it turned out to be an overnight stay, well, so be it. I could hang that long.

"Frederick Moore."

I hear my name called out.

"Yeah."

"Step over here." A detention officer motioned me toward him and into a recessed anteroom full of linens, blankets, towels, washcloths and hygiene items. "Are you getting out this morning?"

It was going on 9:00 by then.

"Well, I don't know. I need to call back."

"What we're gonna do is this: we need this space right now, so we're gonna let you call from upstairs with the other fellas. Go ahead and get your linens and everything and follow me."

I knew I was allowed a phone call, but I wasn't gonna stress it. Maybe they really did need this space, so that could turn into brownie points somewhere, or maybe Momma wasn't home right now or suppose she just didn't feel like coming. At least, right here, I could relax a minute. Besides, I'd never been inside "The Dungeon" as it was known in the 'hood, so it'd be cool to see what it was like.

I got my belongings and followed the officer to an elevator, which took us up a couple of floors. The doors opened and I followed him dutifully through the cellblocks. They were arranged in a maze-like fashion that, until you got to know where you were going, made it nearly impossible to figure out where you came from. The cellblocks were constructed from steel rebar running from floor to ceiling with each block of cells (about eight blocks with four cells in each block) separated by a two-foot thick concrete wall.

When we got to the one I was assigned to, I realized I had not a clue how to get back to the elevator we had just gotten out of. The entrance to each cellblock is through a cast iron door. The officer produced a skeleton key, opened the door and I entered. The two cells in the middle of the block had four bunks, the ones on either end had two bunks meaning that the block was meant to house 12 men, but there were 15 or 16 inside, not including me. I guessed there'd have to be floor space somewhere, but this motherfucker was really crowded.

As I made this assessment, I knew I had to say my hellos to this strange and suspicious looking bunch. I was on my own, for sure. I looked around for the phone and spotted it. Maybe I could get through to Momma right about now 'cause this whole deal here was looking rather unnerving. I glanced around furtively and didn't see one familiar face. Geez.

"What up, fellas," I said, hoping the jitteriness and the anxiety I was feeling could not be heard in the tone of my voice.

"What up," a couple of voices rang out. Guys were playing cards or talking animatedly to one another in the cells; a few appeared to be sleeping, others were lounging along the bars looking bored as hell. No TV, no radio, no books, just a newspaper. Shit. A dungeon, for real. Some creepy-ass shit here.

"Hey, yo," I said out loud to no one in particular. "Where can I put this shit?" Referring to the generous donations from the county I was carrying.

"Just wherever, man." I didn't sense any hostility or animosity or anything so my guard began to relax a little. But, it was no telling when or how long those guys had been cramped up in there together. Whatever it was that was simmering just beneath the façade of those sad, impassive faces I didn't want to be a part of when it boiled over. I found a spot near the shower and went to use the phone.

"Ain't no needa that. Phones don't come on 'til eleven noway."

"Damn. A'ight, man, 'preciate it."

"You from here, dude?"

"Yeah, man, born and raised."

"Well, I ain't never seen you before, where you be at?"

"Pretty much mostly around Lakeside and Cleveland, that area, you know."

"Oh yeah?"

"Yeah."

"You know Reid?"

"Shee-it, who don't know Reid. I seen his dumb ass last night."

"Yeah, what was y'all doin'?"

"Well, I ain't gone front, I was out there getting' my smoke on and ended up buyin' some from Reid. Can you believe that shit?"

"What! Reid had some shit to sell? Reid?"

"That's exactly what I said. Fucked me up. What the fuck is goin' on, Reid with some real dope to sell? And to top it off, the shit was damn good! His dummy-sellin' ass had some dope. I figured it came from one of the fellas in the 'hood. But still, he had some to sell and hadn't smoked it all."

"No doubt. That's Reid. So he had some good shit, huh? Who he get it from?"

"He didn't say but, he did say L'il Man didn't want no company last night, so I figured he was giving Reid a chance to get on his feet. That's what I figure. Shit, if he act right, he could turn this into something, couldn't he."

"He sho' could, for real."

I said, "He a good hustler and everything, so maybe this'll give him a chance to quit beggin' and sellin' them dummies. I mean, it would really upgrade the set if people knew they could come over there and get a square deal without no hassle. Sellin' them dummies fucks the block up and people be hesitating about coming back."

"Damn sho' do, but they always come back."

"Don't they. That shit's crazy, too."

"I know that's right. What's your name, bruh?"

"Rick."

"My name's DJ."

"A'ight."

❧ ❧

It was the lunch that really brought into focus my being in jail.

It wasn't the food itself as much as it was when they brought the trays en masse for the whole floor, stacked 20 high, and passed them through a slot made in the bars that separated the cellblock from the hallway, just like on TV. Guys' arms dangling out all along those avenues. Jailers, trustees, other homeys going in or coming out. Just whoever. A cacophony of voices that suggested the asylum-like quality of being locked up. It was surreal, each person holding onto every atom of sanity possible in a decidedly insane and unnatural existence, those three meals a day being an event themselves. Guys set their internal clocks by when the food trays were being served. It wasn't bad food as much as it was the surroundings in which it was served and the cheerless, quiet moment in which I received it.

Cঽ ৪০

After lunch, I tried to call Mom. I had to wait because all the other guys in the block had been waiting first. There was some sort of hierarchy going on that I didn't understand.

"Hi, Mom."

"Hi."

"I guess you know where I am."

"I guess I do."

Silence.

A moment or two passed. Still, silence. I waited for her to say something and when she didn't, I said, "So, you're not interested in what I have to say."

"Why? Should I be?"

"Yeah, I mean, I know I messed up but I thought you'd be interested in what I have to say. Besides, there's nobody else for me to turn to."

"How lovely of you to think of only me at a time like this."

"Ma, that's not fair!"

"Probably not and it's probably a cheap shot too, but it's true nonetheless. How many times have I asked you to just call me at night when you're not coming home? How many times? And now that you're in a bit of trouble, you decide to call. Not for my benefit, no siree, but for yours and yours alone. This is how selfish you've become."

"Selfish? Ma, I'm not selfish."

"Oh, yes you are. If there's another word to describe why you're just now calling home after two or three days of no communication, I'd like to know what it is. The reason you're in the streets in the first place is not because you care about me or your family or Roberta, that poor precious girl, she loves you so much, but because you care more about the streets and whatever they have to offer."

"Ma, that's not true!"

"Oh, yes it is, son. Now, what do you want?"

"Dog, Ma, you make it seem like I ain't got no heart at all, that all I'm concerned about is just me, me, me."

"No, Ricky, *you* make it seem like all you're concerned about is you, you, you. Not me or anybody else."

More silence. Then, a recorded message in a tinny, computerized voice came on the line, "You have one minute remaining."

"Ma, the phone is about to cut off and I guess I was hoping that you'd think about coming to get me."

"Well, I knew that was coming, that's the only reason you called in the first place…"

"Ma!"

"What I will do is see if there are any probation options available that would release you to a treatment center as a part of your sentencing, but that's about it. As far as me just coming and bailing you out, I don't think so."

"So, does that mean you're not gonna come and get me?"

"Boy, something must really be wrong with you. Don't you know I can get some rest now? I don't have to worry about where you are or if you're going to call or if something's happened to you. I think you need to be right where you are."

Just when I thought I could say something to change the way the tide was turning, that same dispassionate voice came on the line. "Thank you for using Pay-Tel."

The phone went dead. And I still hadn't talked to Roberta.

Cß ꙮ

"I'm saying though, Rob, I'm sorry I haven't called."

"There's no need of being sorry, you just don't give a damn. Here I've been wondering and worried about you and you finally decide to call after the police done locked your ass up. Again. You don't give a shit about nobody but you."

"Rob, that's not true!"

"Don't cut me off, Rick."

"Okay."

"We've been together since '84, through all that down in Troy and then up here on Cherry Street. You think I enjoyed coming to a prison to see you? I did it for us, thinking that you would turn out alright. And after you got out, things were real good. I felt as if I made a good choice—'til you got back on that shit and now, look at you. What are you down there for anyway."

"Gang banging."

"Nigga, please."

"Speeding?"

"Nope, try again."

"I joined the KKK."

"Boy, are you going to be straight with me or what?"

"Okay, okay. There was a license check as I was coming out of Lakeside…"

"On your way home?"

"No, not really. Well, maybe earlier that night but not this time. When we pulled over, the police said he saw something thrown out of the car.

"Were you alone?"

"Nah, I'd met this dude and he had a little bit of money so, because I had a car, we kind a hung out for a minute. Anyway, they said that gave them probable cause to search the car and when they did, they found a crack pipe so, I got charged with possession, paraphernalia, and maintaining a dwelling for the use of drugs."

"So, now you have another house somewhere."

"What do you mean?"

"You said 'maintaining a dwelling'."

"Oh. No. The law see the car as a dwelling."

"So, they confiscated the car."

"They did. But, I can get it back."

"How's that?"

"After court."

"And when's that."

"In a couple weeks."

"Won't you need some money?"

"Yeah, I guess so." Well, now, it's about time. This thing is starting to get a little better. I was wondering when she was gonna loosen up.

"Then, I don't see how you're going to get your car back since you don't have any money."

"Well, I can work something out after a while."

"Well, you're gonna have to and it better include me."

"I always include you."

"So, is that why you forged my checks?"

Uh-oh. Damn, I forgot all about that shit. An overwhelming silence tiptoed into the phone line. Boy, she set me up pretty. Caught me totally off-guard.

"Huh?" she quizzed angrily. "I can't hear you. I believe I asked you a question!" More silence. "Oh, now you can't talk. But, you sure know how to write don't you, Mr. Moore. Here I trust you with a key and you decided to go rummaging. So, you found my checks and figure you'd go have a freebie. This is how you like to include me, huh?"

"Dag, Rob." I mumbled, real soft and low. She was pissed and had every right to be.

"I can't hear you. Speak up!"

I exhaled. A little too loudly.

"What's that? You blowing your breath at me now or what. Is that it? You tired of me telling you about yourself, huh?"

"No, Rob."

"Well, what is it then? You sound like you're tired of hearing this and we both know that can't be true. Besides, I know in my heart you've got a real good answer for this, don't you?" Even more silence. "You know, I can take you to court for forgery if I want to."

Geez, this wasn't going to be easy. I suppose I could've just sucked it up, apologized and hoped she'd forgive me, but my moral guidance system was off-line. What should have been the simple and forthright thing to do became a monstrosity that I could not get out of my mouth. So, I said the first, most obviously honest, thing that came to my mind.

"I needed some money, Rob."

"So, you lie and steal from me to get it, is that right? Is that how things are done in your world?"

"I didn't want to go rob a bank or a store. I needed a couple hundred dollars right then and there, Rob."

"Oh, you didn't want to do it to a bank or a store, but you didn't mind doing it to me, huh? Something must be really wrong with you. Why'd you need money in such a hurry anyway?"

"Look, I owed some people some money and it was getting serious. What I owed them for is pretty much irrelevant."

I didn't get a chance to finish the sentence before the recorded voice said, "You have one minute remaining."

"Just so you'll know, your Momma has offered to pay me back. I told her no, that it'll have to come from you so if you don't want me to press charges…"

"Thank you for using Pay-Tel!" That same recorded message had now become my new pal.

Shit, I'ma have to deal with all of that later.

ζ ε

Actually, my police record wasn't all that bad. It was 1991, I'd had two prior felonies and a couple of DWIs (back in my Chapel Hill days) so the judge knew, the DA knew, my lawyer knew, everybody knew that my presence there was all about getting high. Sure, I had a top-notch educational background and came from a good family that would support me. But it still looked tacky as hell, a guy with my credentials being messed up this way.

After having talked with my lawyer, I decided to push for trial, right then and there, for the cocaine charge. Since they had no cocaine to present as evidence, I took the chance that, rather than send me back to jail to wait on a case they knew they couldn't win in the first place, they would go for my pleading to both misdemeanors, the judge would run the sentences concurrently, give me six months' probation, a fine and court costs and I would get my car back. Which is exactly what happened.

No real probation, basically just stay out of trouble, and no treatment center. However, the judge did say, "Mr. Moore, it is obvious to this court that you are not dealing with your substance abuse problems. A 30-day treatment center admission is strongly advised. Though this court will not impose this as part of your sentencing, keep in mind that our law-enforcement community will not forget you."

03   80

When I got back to the annex, the few faces I'd met since I'd been there asked me, "Yo man, how'd it go?" "Who was the judge?" "Yo man, was the DA cool?" and on and on. It was clear to them, since I was processing out and had come through the lion's den without being eaten, that I must know something everybody else didn't know. So, I gave them the low-down on what I did while the detention staff processed my exit papers.

"Yo, look, if they ever come at you with a possession charge and you ain't have but a crumb, tell 'em to put 12 in a box, they ain't gone have enough evidence to do shit with! I pled to the misdemeanors because they agreed to drop the felony."

"Why they do that?" A voice shouted out.

"Because they ain't have no cocaine to bring to court as evidence, they got to be able to *produce* what it is they charge you with. They got a positive test reaction from the residue they got out the stem is why they gave me a felony charge in the first place. But, res ain't no coke, so I pushed the issue."

"Daammnnn!" a few voices rang out. "You played they ass!"

"Yeah, well, so don't go for that shit they be tryin' to put down. You gotta have game to know game."

THIRTEEN

I had been in jail over a month. I'd been away from a drink or a drug all this time, so I figured I could build on the bit of clean time I had going.

When I got home, our den/kitchen/living area was as comfy as it was when I left.

"Whatcha got to eat?" I asked as we went inside.

"About the same. If I'd known you were coming, I'd have made something special."

"Aw, Ma, whatever's in the fridge'll be alright. It's just good to be at home." I looked inside and said, " Hold it, look a here, I see you've got some 7-Up cake."

"Yeah, just some."

"And a little ice cream? Let me look in here and see…oooohh, there's some cabbage and some squash casserole plus ice cream in the freezer, so I'm good."

"That cabbage and squash casserole is a couple of days old."

"The better the taste, my dear. All it takes is for me to know those little bacteria done set up shop on that food and have simply added to its goodness. It's just waiting for me to proclaim it!"

"And when you fall out on the floor, don't look at me. I won't even know you. I'll tell the paramedics 'he just some stranger that walked in here. I told him that food was tainted, but he ate it anyway' and hope they take you to the hospital instead of the morgue!"

We got a good laugh out of that.

"Well, Ma, I'm gonna have to take my chances."

And, without fail, her food did produce the most supreme sense of well-being and contentment one could imagine. I hadn't felt this way in weeks. There's no way I'd sacrifice these good vibes for some dope. No way. Regardless of the occasion, Mom's cooking was on the money. I could finally let my hair down, and relax a little. It escapes any sense of rightness why or how I could forfeit the level of peace I was feeling for some dope.

I'd just finished eating when Momma called me to the phone. I guessed it would be Roberta. I had yet to call her.

 Instead, it was a slightly husky, definitely male voice. "What up, man?"

"Yo, what up. Who 'dis?"

"So, this the kind a dude you is, huh? Get a brotha locked up and then forget about him."

"Mike?"

"Yep."

"Boy! How you get my number?"

"Well, you know, after we met and we was talkin' about this and that, I remembered your last name. Then, I looked it up in the phone book and this was the only Moore on Sawyer Drive, so I figured it might be you."

"Damn!"

"Yeah. So, what's up? Whatcha doin'?"

"Yo man, I'm just getting' out."

"When?"

"This morning."

"You lyin'."

"For real, dog. Momma just came and got me a few hours ago."

"Yeah?"

"Yeah. But, hey, look, I'm glad you called 'cause now I get an opportunity to get this off my chest. You know, after I thought back over things, this is all my fault."

"How so?"

"'Cause if I had'n a tripped out like I did, we'd still been back in the cut. We would'n a had to come out 'til all the dope was gone and by then that license check would a been over, so all of what happened is kinda my fault."

"Yeah, well, you shook me up that's for sure, but you one of the few people I met that was straight up and ain't have no game, I appreciate that. So, I was wonderin', you know, if you'd come by and pick me up, maybe we could do something."

"Yeah, man, that'd be cool 'cept they done impounded my car."

"No shit!"

"No shit. So, I gotta get it back somehow."

"You think they gone let you have it back?"

"Well, that's what I'm doing now. I'm helping my Mom out around the house to see if she'll help me get it out, gotta pay the court costs and impound fees. After I do that, then I can get it."

"Well, that's cool then. When do you think y'all gonna do that?"

"Oh, just as soon as possible. Hopefully tomorrow."

"Yeah, hopefully." He rejoined, with such wistfulness in his tone that let me know he was really disappointed. "This ain't your first time, is it?"

"Nah, I been in before. But, I bet it was your first time."

"Yeah and my last."

"So you say. Long as you keep fuckin' around with this shit, they gone always have a bed for you downtown. It's just the way it is."

"Not for me though. I ain't goin' out like that."

"I hear you talking. And, you know what's weird is how, all of a sudden, your situation can change. You'll see. Here I was earlier today, in handcuffs and everything going through the courts and then in a flash, all of a sudden, this afternoon I'm at home. Just like that." I snapped my fingers. "But, you keep on with this shit, you'll see. Your situations will change in split second. This dope thang becomes a part of your life, as close to you as your skin is to your bones. You become it and it becomes you. Watch and see."

"Whatever, man. Well look, call me when you get straightened out, maybe we can turn some corners."

"A'ight dude." Obviously, money was of no immediate concern to this guy, so I didn't bother to ask how all this was going to take place. "That'll be cool. Soon's I get hooked up, I'm a holla at you, a'ight?"

"Bet it up, then. Check you later."

Damn, that was pretty cool. I never expected to hear from that guy. Just goes to show you how your own conduct can affect people. He keepin' it real with me, showin' me love like I showed him.

"Who was that, Ricky?" Mom startled me just a little and I jumped ever so slightly. Apparently, she had overheard portions of the conversation, plus she didn't recognize the voice either.

"Just a guy I met before I got locked up."

"Well, why is he calling here and why did you jump so when I spoke to you?"

I had to pause moment because I really couldn't come up with a reason why he would be calling. There's no way I could say, 'Oh, he just looking for a get-high partner.'

So, taking a cue from my silence, she asked, "Is this about that money?"

Though I hadn't been able to figure out how I was going to broach this subject, she did it for me and the timing couldn't have been better. All I had to do was to embellish this story as it developed.

"Somewhat, Ma."

"What do you mean 'somewhat'?"

"Well, he's not exactly the guy I owe." I paused for a moment, trying to get this part right. "He's calling *for* the guy I owe."

"So, how'd he get this number?"

"Phone book, Ma."

"So, how much do you owe these people?"

"It's a nice little sum, Momma."

"How much, Ricky?"

"About ten-thousand dollars."

"TEN-THOUSAND DOLLARS! Boy, people will kill you for that kind of money. How do you owe so much?"

"Well, I ran short of money a few days ago, before I got locked up, and I borrowed some. So, in order to repay it, I agreed to sell some stuff."

"You mean drugs."

"Yeah. So, when I got the stuff, I couldn't sell it all myself, I figured it was best to let other people sell it and I'd collect the money. I guess it goes without saying that no one came up with their money, so I was left with the ticket."

"Have mercy, Ricky, I don't know what to do with you. How could you be so foolish? You think just because you've had a few laughs here and there that those people are on your side, well they're not. You ought to know by now it ain't no trust in the streets, boy."

"Yeah, well, I'm learning about that. But, right now, I'm in a bit of a bind."

"Well, you're just gonna have to get you a job and repay it, that's all there is to it."

"But, my car is in the 'pound lot, Ma…" I whined, "…and until I pay the court fines and costs and everything, they'll just keep it."

"Lord. Well, I guess I'll have to help you get your car back, but you're gonna have to get a job and pay me back boy, you hear? I don't care if it's at McDonald's, that's all there is to it!"

CB BO

After that conversation, our evening remained quiet. We watched some TV, had some small chit-chat, then went to bed. The next day started with a bang.

"Okay, Ricky. We're going to go downtown and get your car, but as soon as we get back, you're going to cut this grass!"

"Oh, no doubt, Ma. This yard needs a little attention and I'll be glad to do it."

"I guess you would."

After we went downtown and made all of the necessary transactions at the courthouse, I got my car. And, sure enough, just as soon as we got back in the house, she had me change clothes and get right on that grass.

"You puttin' me right to work, aintcha, Ma?"

"And why not, there's things around here that must be done. And while you're out there, you might as well spend some time with Lady. She's been moping around here ever since you've been gone."

Now, Lady was a treat. She came into the family at a time when I was searching for some order, some way out of the cycle of drug use that I was in. As my addiction re-emerged, I thought that it'd be a good thing to get a dog. We'd always had one down at the house on Jackson, so I thought we needed one on Sawyer, too.

One day, I decided to go have a look at the pound, just to see what might be there. As I paced those fences, there were dogs jumping and yapping, dogs curled up and distant, dogs sitting and staring, none of them fitting the profile I had in mind—until I came to a certain pen with three dogs, two larger than the other one. When I stepped toward the fencing, the three of them, tails wagging, made a move to greet me, but the smallest one, this pup, showed her feistiness and spunk when she growled and stomped her front paws at the other two in a real menacing manner, really taking them by surprise. It was clearly this pup's intent to claim this visitor as her own. When the others backed down at her ferocity, she marched proudly to the fence, giving me the prettiest smile and the daintiest tail wag you could imagine. I was hooked.

When we got home, I immediately, as soon as she clambered and scrabbled her way out of the car, walked her around the perimeter of our yard and all around the house, for these would be the limits of her domain. She got the idea quickly and never chased cars or bothered people or other animals that were not on her territory. Just like that, an eight-week old puppy caught on, almost instinctively, to the boundaries of her country.

She was equally bright when it came to house-breaking. A couple of pops with the newspaper then, plopped her down immediately in the yard and she figured out the rest. When it came time to "go" she'd sit by the door and whimper and scratch at it. Real smart, and friendly too, with a good dose of fierceness. Just what I had in mind.

So, when I went outside to get the mower from under the house, there she was on the porch, tail going so furiously she could hardly contain herself. Jumping up and down, she'd dash me with her front paws, drop to the floor, jump up and dash me again. She was a black and brown lab/collie mix with a regal stance, perky ears and a sharp, piercing attentiveness that belied her doubtful pedigree. Maybe she was just a sophisticated-looking mutt. But, when you spoke to her, she would sit on her haunches and look you directly in your eyes with such intelligence that it was as if she were really about to say something. We all knew that at any moment, Lady was actually going to talk!

"Hey, Lady! How ya doin' girl?" I said, as she panted at me with that toothy grin of hers, tail swishing back and forth. "You been a good girl, huh?"

I took her off the chain as she pranced and danced in place, just waiting for a little freedom. She ran off the porch and raced around the yard, sniffing here, sniffing there, tail raised majestically, tracking those trespassers she couldn't get to while she was on the chain. A real gem she was, but as time went on, she became more of Momma's dog than mine.

There was a wooded area, a stand of trees that extended behind all the homes on our side of the street. A healthy population of squirrels living in those trees had, somehow, become her arch enemies, though I'm sure they never knew why it was that she always chased them. Whenever she got off the chain, one of her first areas of investigation and pursuit would be those trees. She'd get to the base of one and stand with one paw on the trunk, peering upwards into those branches as if she were saying, "Where dem squirrels at?"

Once I got the mower out, I'd call, "C'mere girl!" and straight off she'd come bounding out of those trees and up the hill to the storage room under the house where all of the yard equipment was kept. She'd follow me around the yard as I blazed a trail through the grass. Though she didn't seem to be afraid of the mower, she never got in front of it nor ever got too close. She always kept it at a polite distance.

After I finished the yard and cleaned up, I decided to go visiting my brother-in-law.

CB BO

"What up, Rick?"

"What up, Paul?"

"I see you got your car back."

"Yeah, I just got it today. Me and Momma went to pay all my court stuff and they went on and let me have it."

"Well, that's good."

"Yes, it is."

He and Johnetta met in California and had moved to Winston to get married. Paul and I had a cordial relationship. In fact, he gave me the greatest respect even though I had a dope problem.

"So, what you gonna do now? You gonna get a job and work or you just gone run the streets?"

"Looks like I'm a have to get a job and I still have no clue as to how to stay completely out the streets. I'm not like you, Paul, though I wish I was. I've hoped and prayed some sort of deliverance would come my way, but it just ain't happened."

"I guess prayer is part of the answer," he began, "and so is discipline. That's a part of it, too. Once you make your prayer, you've got to put your foot down on your urges and your prayer helps to put your foot down."

Paul was a pretty good dude. He didn't get too upset after he gave me his TellerII card and the BMW to get some money out of the bank. I didn't come back before I spent $500.00 of their money. I only stopped because the car ran out of gas and I couldn't get the gas cap off to put more in. Johnetta was pissed, but Paul seemed to understand.

That episode was a real indication of what powerlessness was all about. I could not believe what I was doing even as I was doing it, spending *their* money on dope. I would shake my head back and forth in horror as I steadily punched in the code of the bank card, totally disregarding the loss of trust and the volume of anger that was bound to ensue.

"So, what you're saying is not once but *twice* you've been involved in world-class medical institutions in a professional capacity, and each time you've fucked it up behind some dope. Is that what you're saying?"

"Well, yeah, that pretty much sums it up. I can say categorically that it went down just about like that."

"You be funny if you want, but that's a helluva record."

"I ain't bein' funny."

"Well, that explains why you ain't gonna ever stop using on your own."

"How's that?"

"Your luck's too good." There was a brief flutter of laughter, but there was real truth in his observation. "Good shit seems to come your way and the people around you don't ride you too hard. I'd say that's a good recipe for keeping your addiction active."

FOURTEEN

One of the challenges of being a new jack on the street scene is how to get money when you're broke. Though I'd been out there for a little while, I had yet to acquire the hustler's acumen of survival in the 'hood, thieving and stealing from others, besides friends and family, being necessary requisites for this survival.

Even though I had come on the set with a few dollars, which was quickly exhausted, I was tired of loaning my car for a bump. I was so tired of being stressed out while waiting for it to come back, I knew I had to try something else. I was scared of the robbery thing or holding up a bank or a store, so all I was left with was small-time shit. That's all I could see myself doing. After I got broke, I went on out to the K-Mart to see what was up.

Just straight-up going into a store and walking out with something was brand-new to me. I couldn't figure out how to not get caught. I just wanted a blast. Bad. So, I went to the appliances section where the vacuums and microwaves were and looked, pondering as though I were a real K-Mart shopper. I went to the electronics section where the TVs, VCRs and such were and looked. I knew I could sell this stuff, I just had to get it out of the store.

I got a shopping cart and put a VCR and a microwave in it. I figured if I went toward the checkout line, the surveillance camera people would think I was going to pay for it. Fortunately, all of the clerks were busy, so it would be my attempt to pass by without being noticed, real casual like.

As I pushed the cart out of the automatic double doors, it was all I could do to not look back. I was just waiting to hear the pounding of feet on the pavement or voices yelling, "Stop! Stop!" But, all I heard was…nothing. There was the silence of the night, the muted chatter of passing shoppers, the distant honking of a horn, and the sound of the cart rolling on the asphalt. I got away!

Now, this was a feeling of unanticipated power and was very intoxicating. I consciously knew this couldn't be true, but if it were this easy to steal, then I didn't ever have to worry about money again. All I had to do was walk into one of these shopping paradises, pick up whatever I wanted and go. Simple.

Getting rid of it was as easy as taking it. Since it was brand-new stuff, I could go to the scene with the confidence of having real money. Hot merchandise was as good as legal tender.

The thing was that I did have a family and even though I loved them very much, I loved crack more. It was just a fact. All I wanted to do was to hang out and smoke crack all day, every day. But at some point, I knew I had to go home.

Once I got out there and on that shit, I'd forget about how I'd told Mom that I'd be sure to get a job to pay her back for getting my car out, I'd forget about how she stood by me regardless of my circumstances, I'd forget everything. I just took it all for granted as though this is how things were supposed to be, how I should expect to be treated…like I could do no wrong.

There was no small amount of anguish associated with this dilemma. It was the principal cause of my not calling Mom. Feelings of guilt, shame and remorse always surfacing because I knew I was doing wrong…but could not stop.

I could ignore this triad of anxiety while I was out and about doing my thing. The dope, the street, the lifestyle, insulating me from feeling any real emotion, the feelings normal people have to lead a good life, but that wouldn't stop me from doing the things that caused the anxiety in the first place. Eventually, I still had to go home.

03 &0

"Ricky, my God! Where have you been?"

It had been a couple of days since I'd left the house to go visiting. Honestly, my intent was to just hang out for a little bit, then go back to the crib. Mom kept such a nice, loving and comfortable home that it should not have been so difficult for me to come home. Seemed like I'd turn my back on the comforts of home and the security of family every time. All I had to do when it came time to head home was lie a little bit to kinda straighten things out.

"Well, Ma, while I was out visiting with Paul and Johnetta, I was on my way home and ran into the people I owed the money to when I was at the gas station."

"And what happened?"

"They just wanted to know when was I gonna start gettin' them straightened out." My thinking was that if I could turn this deception into a smooth enough lie, I might be able to con Mom into giving me money.

"Have you been looking for a job? You know you're going to need money to deal with these people."

"Yeah, Ma, I went to Debbie's Temps. They said they'd give me a call. I plan to call them back tomorrow."

"Well, that's a start. But, son, this late night staying out and not calling when you do stay out is getting on my nerves. Somehow you've got to have more concern for your mother than you do."

"Okay, Ma."

愉 愈

I stayed around the house all that day and most of the next mainly because I was broke. However, I did call the temp service to see what was up. They told me that the job would be stacking boxes at a local warehouse. Lentz Warehouse kept much of the inventory for Sara Lee and Hanes textiles. Warm-ups, thermal underwear, undershirts and shorts, all in large cardboard boxes, were handled by hand, stacked on pallets and loaded onto 18-wheelers. It was relentlessly boring, but it was work.

I was able to drive there and back but I was doing it just to get high. The pay wasn't great and it didn't take long to spend those few pennies in the 'hood, then I was right back at that most crucial of questions: Where was I going to get some more money?

I did recall how easy it was for me to go into the store and walk out with a couple hundred dollars' worth of electronics so maybe that would be the next move. Because stealing was new to me, I had not caught on to the nuances required to be a good thief. From seeing the floorwalkers to knowing when to walk out before getting caught to knowing what the smaller, more concealable items might be that people would want.

As I was waiting for my loaned-out car to be returned, deciding whether or not to go out and greet those wares waiting for me, a guy I'd known since early in life interrupted my decision-making. He had that certain look in his eye, a look like an opportunity might be here. Maybe something would happen here that could help me get some dope.

"Yo, Rick. Wha's up. You got to be somewhere in a minute or two?" The lateness of the hour seemed to press upon the conversation.

"I ain't figured it out yet. Why, wha's up? I'm tryin' to wait for my car to get back."

"If you game, I got a little hustle where we can make a few dollars."

"What's that?"

Now, June was a guy I'd met back during grade school, before all of this drug/jail shit. He was a couple years older, rather tall with impressive basketball skills and had been a local phenom on the high school scene before he, too, succumbed. I'd become reacquainted with him, years later, on Cherry Street. This would be one of those spontaneous hook-ups.

"My girl has an apartment on Third St. and she's away 'til 7:00 in the morning. I figured you had a car and we need a car to do this."

"To do what?"

"Go down there when your car comes and get that 19-inch, cable-ready, color TV that's there. I know a dopeboy up on Liberty who just moved into one a them rooming houses who ain't got no TV. Said he'd give top dollar to the first one to come back with a TV like that." He was a handsome fellow with a smooth face that belied his 40-some years. Those boyish good looks had charmed many a girl. Even the ones he'd plot against.

"How you know for sure ain't nobody coming while we there? I know you said she ain't comin' back 'til in the morning, but it's 1:00 already and my car still ain't got back."

Here I was, on pins and needles, not knowing if my car would come back. I had an opportunity staring me in the face and couldn't take advantage of it.

"Nah, ain't nobody gonna be there, she at work. This I know." He paused, looking over my shoulder. "Hey, check it out, ain't this your ride?"

I jerked my head around, startled and sure enough, there was my little hoopty coming down the road just as charming as you please. It felt good to see my car, to have that small, but really vital portion of control returned to me.

June was in the passenger seat before I could get under the wheel good and while we drove to his spot, I had a moment to reflect on a few things. As he prattled on about what we should do after this was over and where we should hang out, I was wondering whether to call Momma. I'd told her that I would call, but it didn't look like I was going to show her that simple respect after all.

I wondered what that said about my character and my morals, about my make up as a man. Being male is a matter of birth, but being a man is a matter of choice. You had to choose to exercise sound judgment, strong integrity, and complete responsibility. I was becoming more and more out of the will of God, more and more into the will of my flesh. I wondered if I should continue to expect God's favor as I expected it when I was doing the right and honorable things in life. Or, should I expect Him to turn His back on me in the midst of my most egregious offenses? Would He still be there for me as I knowingly and willfully sought to do this thing I was about to do? Or, would He abandon me as I had abandoned Him? Was there any Karmic value in doing right by the folks I dealt with in my errant lifestyle? Was living like this—doing wrong, but treating folks right—an equalizer?

"Yo, this the street right here." June's words snapped me out of my reverie.

"Turn here and park. Her place is right there on the bottom, left side door."

I had traveled by these apartments on Fourth and Highland all the time, but never stopped. He got out and went around the other side while I waited. A couple of minutes later, he tapped on the trunk of the car signaling me to follow him. We went through the sliding glass door off the terrace that opened directly into the living room. And there the TV sat, perched on its stand. We unhooked it, loaded it in the car and left. A clean get-away.

At that moment, I had an epiphany. It struck me that I could make a go of this street-living, crack-smoking lifestyle and not be tied to the ho-hum drabness of going to work every day. I could make a living doing shit like this. The rigamarole of getting up when they say, doing what they say, paying your bills like they say, was no longer for me. I was unwilling to be a part of.

We took the TV to its new home and the deal was done. And just like that, I had some crack.

Since it was 4:00 in the morning, we could travel the streets in my car and smoke without too much concern about being noticed, provided we stayed off the major thoroughfares.

The trick to smoking crack while driving is to find that comfort spot where the steering wheel can be guided by one's bended knee, leaving the hands free to load the pipe and light it.

Now, this is where it gets risky. If the occasional passer-by or the local neighborhood crime-watch citizen who just happened to be up at that hour would see a car moving slowly down the street with the flame of a lighter burning way longer than it would take to light a cigarette, that meant only one thing. They might say, "Check that out, they drivin' down the street smoking' dope!"

Given my tendency to paranoia, I'd always think, "Somebody done seen me an' they fixin' to call the po-lice!"

Not a good thought to entertain when you're doing dirt.

Still, it was worth the risk. It was easier than going all the way to somebody's house and then have to give them some, especially since we could use the darkness to hide from being discovered—smoking crack ought not and should not be done publicly.

One thing you're not likely to see is somebody standing on the corner lighting a crack pipe. Not likely at all.

As we got to the end of our supply, June directed me to a house on 24th and Dunleith, where he got out.

"Yo man, that was like real solid. If you wanna do somethin' else, come by here and holla, I should be here. We can hang out again."

"A'ight, June. That's cool, I'll try to holla at you later."

We gave some dap through the car window and I drove off.

It was getting to the crack of day, just as the lights of the horizon began to give their faint glow, letting everybody know that daylight and sunrise were not too far behind. Though the streets were mostly empty, people were beginning to stir and traffic would begin its inexorable swell to the morning rush.

So glad I was free of all that shit. Such silly people. If they only knew how much fun they could have doing it like I do.

"Yeah," I whispered softly to myself. "This is how we do it."

FIFTEEN

I was down to my last hit and I knew that the jonses would be coming fast if I didn't find a way to get some money. What could I do to get some quick cash?

I'd been back to the stores, but it scared me so bad, I just turned around, put those items down and walked out. Maybe no one was watching through the surveillance cameras, but it sure felt like somebody was watching. I guess it was part of being new to the shoplifting scene. I'd taken a lawnmower out of a driveway, walked into an open garage for their weed eater, had reached inside an open car window and gotten a purse, but it was broad daylight now, so that type thing wasn't going to work.

Still, there had to be something else I could do right then and there.

Oh! My mind rang out. Yeah, that's what I'll do. All I needed was a quarter to use the phone. I pulled into the Wilco on New Walkertown where everybody was coming and going, getting gas, cigarettes, and sandwiches. Somebody had to have some change.

"Yo, bruh. Uh, I need to make a call real bad, can you let me have a quarter?"

"Nah, bruh, ain't got it. Catch me later."

Damn. I know that nigga had some change; I could hear it in his pocket. Niggas ain't shit. It ain't nothin' but a fuckin' quarter, don't they know this a call I got to make? While people were moving in and

169

out, conducting their mornings' business, I was out begging and panhandling.

"Yo, bruh. Uh, I need to make a phone call really bad, but I'm short. Can you help me out with a quarter? I'd really 'preciate it."

"Sure. No problem. Here you go."

See, now how hard was that? That's the way it's supposed to work. Don't be giving a brother no drama when he trying to get his hustle on. I went to the phone and punched the numbers.

"Hey, Ma. Sorry I didn't call last night."

"And, as usual, I didn't get much sleep either. I just wish you could do this one thing that I ask of you. Just this one thing."

"I will, Ma. I promise I will. It's just that I feel so guilty when I haven't called by a certain time, I get stuck and can't call."

"But now, you just have to call. At this moment. Right now, at 7:15 in the morning. Is that what you're telling me?"

"Uh, yeah, Ma. That's about it."

"What is it then?" She said rather curtly. "I'm going over to Carver this morning, I got to sub there today, so speak up."

"Well, you know I've been trying to get up some money to cover this debt…"

"Uh-huh."

"…and last night I was told I needed to come up with some real money today."

"What does 'real money' mean? I don't understand."

"It means a couple hundred bucks, at least."

"Boy, I declare." A brief pause. "So, what do you expect me to do about it?"

"I was hoping you would loan it to me until I get my check from Debbies' and I'll give it back."

"Son, you better be sure you give me that check. I'll be looking for it, too. You come on here and I'll write you a check so you can get started cleaning this mess up. The bank opens at 9:00 and you can cash it then."

"Thanks, Ma. I'll be there in a minute."

BAM!! Just like that, I was paid. Damn, looks like this little thing is going to work, at least for a little while. I've just got to figure out what to say to keep it going because that check from Debbies' was already spent. I'll come up with something, though.

ଓ ଣ

Getting money from Mom seemed a legitimate way to be illegitimate. I mean, so what, I was fabricating the whole thing. So what? At least, in my mind, it was saving me from committing more drastic types of crime, this rationale being the result of the mysteriously convoluted logic of my thinking. I was too scared to go into a bank and I knew I could only push Ma but so far, so my options would quickly become limited.

ଓ ଣ

After that money was gone, I remembered Mike had called and asked if I could come get him. Well, that was rather recent, so what did I have to lose? I'd have to give it a try. This time I had a quarter, so I punched the numbers.

"Damn, boy. Ain't you ever gone get out the house?"

"Who 'dis?"

"You, mean, you just give your number out to anybody, huh? Don't have no idea who's calling. I'm surprised you don't know who this is."

"Word up. Who dis?"

"This Rick, man. Wha's up? You told me to call when I got my wheels."

"Rick! Yo, what up, man!! Man, I was just headed out. I been in and out over the last few days and was just out the door when the phone rang. So, wha's up with you? What you into?"

"Oh, I'm just out and about. Wanted to know if you wanted to do anything."

"Oh, hell yeah! You just come get me."

"Well, where you at?"

"You know where that Amoco station is on Pine Hall Road?"

"Yeah."

"Well, I'll be standing there in 15 minutes."

"Okay, cool. I'm headed your way."

Going to Walkertown was no big deal, maybe 10 or 12 miles east of Winston. I checked the gas and maybe I could make it. And maybe I couldn't. What choice did I have? I'd just have to chance it.

He was as good as his word and was walking up to the station as I was pulling in, goofy grin and all.

"What up, boy!"

He gets in, gives me some dap and we ride off.

"You got any money?" I ask.

"I got a little bit."

"Well, at least we can get started." I didn't mention the gas even though I was on "E;" I figured I'd just let it slide 'til I got me a hit.

He looked over a bit and asked, "You got any gas?"

"I mean, just a little bit. I mean, you can see where it is, but it's got a few miles in it before it runs out."

"Well, whyn't you say something when we was at the Amoco?"

"Hey, you know, just wanted to get going."

"Well, next station you come to, let's get some. Ain't nothin' worse than runnin' outta gas and you got money in your pocket. That's some retarded shit, right there."

"Yeah, that is pretty dumb, huh."

After I pumped, we headed to the local stop-n-cop. All the fellas hanging out noticed us but we didn't really pay them any attention. We had our eyes for someone in particular. The last time we were here, there was some really good dope around, but where is that dude? Oh, look. Right over there. He saw us coming and met us halfway.

"Yo, Mike. What, up? You lookin'?"

"Yeah man, I might be. Whatcha got?"

They went to the side of a building where he pulled out a plastic baggie and let Mike choose the pieces he wanted. They finished their negotiations and Mike motioned for me to follow him to the nearest smokehouse.

These apartments had always been low-income dwellings, so there were several choices we could make. We chose Pookie's place mainly because it was close, but also because I figured we'd be comfortable there.

Pookie kept a respectable place. Far from the stereotypical, roach-infested, candle-lit scary place, hers was decently well-kept. And, in fact, this was typical of places to smoke. For sure, there were those places right out of a horror story, no electricity, no running water, stinking and repulsive, but they were more the exception than the rule. You went to one of those when there were just no other options.

We went to the rear, knocked and Pookie invited us in. The door opened directly into the kitchen. There was a TV in the background and voices drifting in from another room. The place had a respectable living room with the couch, armchair and coffee table situated just so. In the kitchen, the dishes were washed and drying under the curtains that hung at the window over the sink. The refrigerator was relatively new with magnets on the front that held a child's artwork. There was a smaller bedroom for the kids, but they were away at the time. We sat at the kitchen table and asked for a razor, which she provided and sat with us. Idle chit-chat took place as she and I waited for Mike to pass out hits.

She got hers and put it on her pipe. I was in the process of doing the same when Mike said, "Yo, Rick. Let me use your gizmo."

This caught me quite off-guard. It had been a while since my last hit and I was really ready for one. But, as I thought about it, what the hell. I could've made a big deal about it, but stood down.

"Sure, dude, go 'head."

He put his on, flamed the pipe and inhaled. Slowly, his eyes began to sparkle and here we go again. I had to get my pipe from him because he goes stone-still, nearly catatonic when he gets a good hit. The differences in the way people act when they get a good hit range from the comical to the downright scary. Especially me, I should know.

Pookie got up and looked out the window—apparently, that was a pretty good hit to her—and came back to the kitchen. "Hey, fellas. That was a pretty good hit. Where'd y'all get that?"

"Right around here, Pookie. Just outside in the parking lot. Why, you gon' buy some?"

"Nah. I ain't got my check yet. But, you know, if something comes up, I'd get me a piece."

"Something like what?" I asked, tuning in on the possibilities implied in this statement. That blast had me horny as hell and this conversation could go right down my alley. This could become one of those beautiful things and I wouldn't have to find a girl. Pookie just might be the one.

"Boy, you know I don't get down like that! What is you sayin'?"

"What you mean?" I said defensively.

"I ain't one a them trick ho's out on the street. I might want another hit, but I can wait! I got a check comin' and I ain't got nothin' to do but wait."

"Well, that's all good, Pookie. But sometimes things can happen, you know, kind a spur of the moment, you know, with no bad feelin's on nobody's part."

"Well, ain't nothin' like that's jumpin' off in here. Besides, somebody else is s'posed to come by here in a little while, so if y'all ain't gon' do nothin' else then I'll just catch y'all later."

Throughout this exchange, Mike just sat there. Stupefied.

"Oh, it's like that, huh. Just put us out 'cause you think all the smoke's gone. That how it is?"

"Nah, it ain't like that, not really. But, I am hoping these people will stop by like they said they would. They usually do, that's all."

"Yeah, I bet. See how she do, Mike? Just gon' throw us out."

Mike, ponderously stone-faced, sitting there glazed and silent, could say nothing. Well, at least, I had my car.

"C'mon man. We got wheels. Let's get outta here."

❧ ☙

As I went into the house, Mom was in the kitchen being her usual domestic self. I tried to be cool, asked about her day at school, but my stomach was churning for 'just one more.' Somehow I had to play it off, so I got the remote and clicked on the TV while she went on about kids with no respect for authority, using profanity.

After what seemed like hours of small talk, with me looking for an angle to work, Momma said, "Now, the big question is when are you going to get straightened out with Roberta? She called here today a little while ago looking for you, talking about you having left in a huff and hadn't called or stopped by since. What's that all about?"

"I mean, Ma, as soon as I come by, she starts right in on me. I mean we can't even chill for second without her bringing up what I owe her. So, I got outta there and ain't called back."

"Well, Ricky, she's hurt and frustrated and unsure about what's in store for the future; you can only imagine how she feels."

"So. That ain't no reason for her to ride me and ride me; that ain't right. I can't just make the money appear."

"And so, because of all of that, I went on and gave her the money and told her it was from you."

"Ma! Why you do that? She knows it's not from me."

Now, I was obligated to go by there and kiss her ass like everything was all right. And I loathe ass-kissing. Except when I'm trying to get some money.

Before I could decide what I wanted to do about that, the doorbell rang and Momma went to answer it. I heard a male voice asking for me in my full and proper name. This can't be good.

"Ricky, this detective is here to see you."

I went into the foyer where Mom was standing with a tall, brown-haired, unfamiliar white man in a white shirt and tie.

"Are you Frederick Moore?" he asked.

"Yes."

"I have a warrant for your arrest. Please turn around and place your hands behind your back. You have the right to remain silent..." as he put the cuffs on me. "...anything you say can be used against you in a court of law; you have the right to an attorney..." as we walked out the door to the car. "If you cannot afford one, one will be appointed to you. Do you understand these rights?"

I was in shock; Mom was grim.

"Yes."

"Mrs. Moore, we'll be taking him down to the Public Safety Center first and, from there, to the jail. If you wish, you can make bond arrangements at that time."

Shit! This was so-o-o embarrassing. Leaving my house in handcuffs in broad daylight with the police. I glanced up and down the street and didn't see any neighbors, but the slight movement I noticed in the curtains across the street extinguished any momentary relief I felt. I guess everybody was looking out their windows. In this neighborhood, this type thing didn't happen. This was a quiet, crime-free, middle class area whose residents did not break the law.

The drive to the Public Safety Center was muted, quiet; yet my mind was racing away at how I might be able to get out of this. When we arrived, I was put into a sparsely furnished waiting room. Shortly, the detective came and the interview began.

"Mr. Moore, do you know Debra Johnson?"

"Yeah."

"Were you at her place last night about 2:00 a.m.?"

"No."

"Can you explain why we found two clearly defined fingerprints belonging to you at her place? It would really help us out if you could." He sneered.

Damn. I'm floored, shocked beyond clear thinking. I mean, they got right on this thing and I'm caught totally off guard. How do I explain my prints being there? I know I didn't wear gloves so they could be all over the place. All I remembered touching was the TV and it went with us. Damn.

"Sir, I'm waiting for your answer."

"Well, I don't have one."

"I suspected as much. Just so you'll know, you will be placed in the county jail until you post bond or go to court."

He left the room and I was crushed. I could only hope Mom would come and get me when I got there. He escorted me to the car and drove me to the jail where I was placed under $25,000 bond. And just like that, I was locked up on another journey into the bowels of the justice system. Didn't even get a chance to get the joneses off my back. Now, I got to call Ma and tell her the deal.

"Hey, Ma."

"Hey, son. What happened?"

"Well, they're saying that I broke into this girl's apartment a couple nights ago."

"Did you?"

"No, Ma."

"Why would they accuse you of it? The police usually don't make accusations like that unless they've got a good reason."

"Yeah, well, I don't know what it could be, but my bond is $25,000…"

"And…"

"…and I'm hoping you'll consider getting me out."

"Son, this might be one you're going to have to deal with yourself. I'll never understand you squandering two promising careers, a young man with your talent would rather waste it on the streets than do what God has provided for you to do. So, just deal with this thing the best you can."

"You mean, you're gonna leave me down here?"

"Well, at least, now I can get some sleep! Your poor old Mother can finally get some rest now that she knows where her youngest one is tonight."

"Gol-lee, Ma. Why you doin' this? Why? I can't believe you'd leave me down here like this."

"I think it's for the best. So, you do your best and I'll write you soon, okay. And you be sure to write back, you hear?"

"Ma!"

"This is tough love, son. Now say bye-bye."

Fuck. Here I was again. Back down in the county. I'd been coming down to this place for a good while now. I knew what I was here for, but didn't know if I could get out of it. A 37-year-old grown man in 1994 ought to be able to handle his own legal affairs.

By and by, I found out that those fingerprints that incriminated me came from the terrace entrance—on the outside. None were found inside. Hmmm. Maybe there's some daylight here.

The Public Defender informed me the DA was offering a plea bargain. Considering my felony background and the misdemeanors I had accumulated, he offered 3-5 years instead of the 8-10 year maximum. This is a sweetheart deal, the lawyer insisted. Heck, you'll be out in 18 months, he went on.

But man, fuck that shit. Something else has got to give. I'd had an epiphany the day before where I could see the light in this thing. I told him it'd have to be a better deal than that or we'd go to trial. He said that's the only deal. I said let's pick a jury.

So, after a while, on a certain day, I was given a court date. I didn't tell Mom or anybody else because I didn't know if the ploy I'd constructed would work. It would be the ultimate in embarrassment, not to mention considerable jail time, if the thing blew up in my face and this marvelous insight would turn out to be just misguided opportunism.

The prosecution is saying that the fingerprint it has is clearly, undeniably, categorically mine and nobody else's. Okay, cool, that's their evidence. No witnesses. No recovered property. Nothing else other than this perfectly intact fingerprint was taken from the outer entrance on the terrace. Well, that can't be enough. I mean, they've got to have more than that. All I've got to do is come up with a perfectly reasonable explanation for why my print was there and I can do that.

The Public Defender said that if I get on the stand in my own defense, it gives the DA the right to bring up my prior record which did have some length, but that could be to my advantage because I had no history of breaking into people's houses.

CB   BD

The jury selection was a long and tedious process. After they were seated, the State presented its case.

The DA called two witnesses. One would testify to having actually lifted the print. The other would testify that the print, through the intricacies and complexities of forensic science, did, in fact, belong to Frederick Patton Moore. Though I was never seen going to or from the apartment, the evidence stated that I was there.

The defense stated that my prints were there for a simple, perfectly innocent reason that would be described shortly as I would be the only witness in my defense. After I was sworn to tell the truth, the whole truth and nothing but the truth, I proceeded to tell one of my better lies.

That, yes, I was at the apartment earlier that evening, ostensibly to visit her boyfriend who had told me would be there; just stopping by to say hello. As I walked up to knock, I noticed that the sliding glass door leading from the terrace into the living room was ajar. Well, this was spooky enough. All I could do was kind of lean on the doorway and call out "hello" and when I didn't get an answer, I backed away. I never went inside, I never went back by to check and, no, I did not steal a 19-inch cable ready color TV.

After this, the case went to the jury, where the judge charged that they could find me guilty of 1st Degree Trespassing or Not Guilty. They exited the courtroom and I was taken to a holding cell. But not for long, they were back within the hour.

When they were being selected, I told the lawyer I wanted all white people, thinking that I might be able to curry some favor as a result of white guilt, doing what they could to reverse the stigma of Darryl Hunt, an African American man from Winston-Salem who served 19 years in prison for raping and murdering a young, white female newspaper editor and was finally exonerated by DNA evidence.

He did his best and got 10 whites and 2 Blacks. I figured if they could be given enough reason to find me Not Guilty, they would. A majority Black jury might not have needed any reason just to prove that they could lock up one of their own.

As it turned out, my instincts were right. Not Guilty by unanimous vote.

Some would say, "But, did you really get away with it?" and I would answer,"Damn, right!" because I felt no guilt, shame, or remorse about it at all. Quite the contrary, I felt proud about how I played the system.

Although I perjured myself, no one knew but me.

Hah. Only in America!

SIXTEEN

The games started as soon as Mom brought me home.

I'd been without dope for right at six months while I was waiting for my trial, but the desire to use had not abated. I was clean, but I wasn't sober. The worm to get high crawled menacingly in my gut.

Being found not guilty of a crime for which I was truly guilty was good fortune. But, in no way could I make being a junkie good fortune, as this was what caused me to do the crime in the first place. An inconsistency for sure.

Natural Law dictates that wrong action begets wrong consequences and right action begets right consequences. So, would the wrong action of going into that woman's apartment, being a part of taking and selling her TV, result in a fair and just consequence? Doesn't seem so. Here, I've done wrong in my heart and my deeds, lied about it to man and society and got away with it.

What I told myself was that the "Not Guilty" verdict was tacit acknowledgement by the Powers of Life and Living that I was to keep on smoking. An agreement by the Unseen Forces that it was okay for me to carry on. Otherwise, I would have been found guilty, right?

But what was I going to do with my life?

My first setback came when we pulled into the driveway at the house and I noticed something quite out of kilter.

"Ma, what happened to my car?"

"I didn't think you were coming out of there any time soon, so I sold it."

"Ma! You sold my car?"

"Now, look boy. Just because you had a good day in court don't mean you're going to use that tone of voice with me."

"No, Ma, it's not like that. It's just that I was caught so off-guard, I kind a raised my voice out of surprise more than anything else."

"No need to be. You didn't buy it, I did. And it was an eyesore, with that windshield broken out like that, I just had to do something."

I could kind of understand how that car looked in this driveway, that cracked-up windshield adding a ghetto-type atmosphere to our side of the street. Never could figure out why it happened, just one of those crazy situations when I dropped off two dopeboys and one of the local 'hood rats ran up on the car and slammed a cinder block through the glass. But I drove that car anyway 'til I went to jail. Could hardly see to drive, but I went on anyway, had to do what I was doing. It was a mess, for sure.

Dope should have been the farthest thing from my mind. Yet, there it was. Large and bright and shiny.

I played with Lady, watched a little TV, and answered Mom's questions about when I was going to call Roberta as evasively as possible. But my mind was elsewhere. I knew I couldn't just get up and walk out, even though that was hard to resist.

Sure, I thought about dope a lot while I was in jail, but because I had no access, those thoughts were manageable. Now that I was out, my mind was completely awash in the problem of getting that first blast. As time passed, call it epiphany, call it inspiration, call it whatever, the thought hit me: What if I could get a phone call? What if I could control that phone call? That way, it could be from whomever I said.

So, I went to the phone while Mom sat dozing and punched "0." When the operator answered, I asked if she would call back to check my line to see if the phone was ringing properly. She did and the phone rang.

"Hello." I said. "Yeah, it's okay."

"Yo, man, what's up?"

"Nah, I ain't got none, I just got outta jail."

I paused. "Maybe tomorrow."

Paused again. "What, you mean tonight? Man, I don't know, let me see. If so, I'll see you at the corner. Yeah, you know, same place."

I hung up.

"Who was that, Ricky?"

"Nobody, Ma."

"Don't tell me nobody when I heard you talking."

"I thought you were sleep."

"Well, I wasn't. So, who was it?"

"Nobody, Ma. For real."

"Boy, if you lie to me one more time, I'm gonna get out of this chair and you won't like it when I do."

"It's the people I owe, Ma."

"So. What do they want?"

"Money."

"And what did you say."

"I said maybe tomorrow, but they insisted on tonight, said I'm lucky they're giving me a break."

"And what's that supposed to mean?"

"Well, Ma, I really wouldn't want to speculate."

"So, what are you going to do?"

"What can I do, Ma? I ain't got no money." I pause for a second. "Is there any way you could let me have some money tonight, Ma? I'd really appreciate it if you could."

"Ricky! Lord have mercy son, I don't have that kind of money."

"I know, Ma, but whatever you could spare would help."

"Lord have mercy, boy. Let me go see."

 C8 &O

And it went this way on many, many occasions. I'd run out of money in the street, come home and fake a phone call. I'd put on an Oscar-winning performance which rarely failed and, if it did, only until the bank opened.

Because I didn't have a car, Mom would drive me, day and night, into some of the most dangerous, drug-infested crack zones in the city. And wait for me. All at my suggestion. Usually, I'd come right back but, occasionally, when I couldn't find the right dope or nobody I wanted to cop from, I'd leave her sitting there…waiting…and waiting…and waiting.

Sometimes, when I did cop, I'd have to get a hit in some strange, litter-strewn backyard or local abandoned house before I got in the car. More often though, I'd get my dope, come back to the car and we'd go to the house.

"Did you see who you needed to see?" she'd ask.

"Yeah, Ma. They told me to just keep it up and it'll be all over in a minute."

"Well, I sure hope so, Ricky. It's so dangerous out here, all those crazy-looking people come walking by the car, looking like they're from another planet. Scares me to death. This'd better be over soon because I can't take too much more of this. Now, how much else do you have to pay?"

"I'm not sure, Ma, we don't keep receipts, but I'm thinking another few hundred and that'll be that."

"Well, thank God."

ಚ ಬ

When we'd get home, I'd tell Mom my stomach was a little nervous from dealing with all this and I needed to go to the bathroom. And there I'd be. I would hear the phone ring and it would be Johnetta or Roberta and I'd hear Mom say, "He's in the bathroom," as I'd put another piece of crack on the pipe.

Although the door was closed and the window was high above the neighbor's driveway, once I'd get that blast and the euphoria would begin its delicious frenzy, I'd look around and peek about, hovering around that window, feeling completely sure, beyond a shadow of a doubt that not only the neighbors could see in and know what I was doing, so could Johnetta and Roberta. Paranoia and a guilty conscience made excellent partners for a weirdly confusing get high experience.

Sometimes when I'd be jonesing so bad for a hit and couldn't go to Mom right then, I'd take Roberta's car while she was asleep. Going out on a short mission. She ended up calling the police and I just didn't care. I needed a hit.

My biggest challenge was transportation so either I'd find something to steal within walking distance or I'd catch a ride out to the Lowe's or the K-Mart or the Wal-Mart. Late night is when they would really be on the lookout for creeps like me. When I came in the store, the staff would become really alert, but I was so dim-witted, I'd try them anyway. I just didn't care.

I'd pick up an item or two and march out of there just like I'd paid for it. A lot of times, I'd get away with it; a lot more times, I'd get caught. I'd hear footsteps coming up behind me, then, "Sir, Stop!" and I'd keep going. "Stop, sir. Stop!" I never thought to drop the shit. I'd run as hard and fast as I could but, because I waited so long to run, they were right up on me.

They'd get their shit back, march me right back inside, call the law and off to jail I'd go. Again.

I wouldn't call Mom until the next day or so and she'd scold me for having left her out in those streets or for not having called her sooner and how much all of this was really worrying her. In my heart, I prayed that all this worriment wouldn't be too stressful, but I didn't have a clue on how to stop it.

As I continued my downward spiral, I wasn't even above stealing directly from my own mother. After she returned from a weekend in South Carolina visiting her sisters and found the floor model TV gone, she took my key. I left her no choice.

ᥬ ᥬ

My presence in Mom's house should have been for her care and concern. That's certainly the way it was going when I was at Bowman Gray, but I was too far gone this time.

Which begs a profound question: What had she done to deserve, first, an alcoholic husband and, second, a drug-addicted son?

If good acts are requisite for good outcomes, when had Mom ever done anybody wrong? She had done only good for her family, her friends and her community. She did right by folk, but got done wrong by her husband and her son.

On one of the occasions when I was home with Mom, the phone rang and I answered. It was Roberta.

Ever since I had walked out behind her bitching about the money I owed her, things hadn't been the same. Oh, we talked while I was in jail, she even came to see me. I half-heartedly promised that things would be better once I got the case behind me, but I was a poor actor in that play. I just couldn't pull it off.

I mean, how could I chase some dope instead of being with a beautiful, well-rounded woman who gave me chance after chance, and came from a terrific family of well-respected educators? How I could give her up over some dope was beyond even my own thinking, but that's what I did. And I finally reached the point where I couldn't see bringing both of us down.

This night she started in, like she always did, on why I couldn't just quit so we could go on from here.

"I don't know, Rob. Looks like I ain't gonna be no good to nobody if I keep this up. And I don't see this ending no time soon."

"You telling me that this dope is stronger than you, is that what you're saying?"

"What can I tell you, Rob? I just don't see this thing changin' any time soon. It's some strong shit, that's for sure."

There was a long silence. Maybe she was pulling herself together. Maybe she was figuring out how to kill my sorry ass. What she said next was the last thing I expected.

"Well…listen, I've been talking to your sister a lot lately and she's really concerned about how you're handling your Mom."

"What you mean 'how I'm handling Mom?'"

"C'mon, Rick, don't play me. All I'm saying is just let your Mom have some peace, okay?"

"Yeah, Rob. I mean, you're right, but what can I do? I owe money. But after a while this whole episode will just be a bad memory."

"So you say. If you owe money, you need to get your ass a job instead of sponging off her."

⊂⅁ ⅋⊃

Maybe that conversation and all the other ways I'd tormented my mother were on my mind the time Mom said, "Ricky, I think you need to go to another treatment center."

"Why do you say that, Ma?"

"Because, son, you're in and out of jail stealing and carrying on, using drugs and staying out in the streets like some kind of hoodlum. You weren't raised this way and it's almost like I don't even know you. Surely, you can't be my child."

"Yeah, well, Ma, that's just fine. You want me to go to a treatment center, then I'll go to one. But, I've been to three so far and they really don't make you better. You have to want to get better. And, right now, I don't know how to want to get better."

"Son, I've been told about this place in Butner. It comes very well recommended."

"You mean, the crazy house in Butner?"

"No, that's not my understanding. It is on the same property as the asylum, but it's not the asylum. It is a different building altogether. Look at how well this 12-step program has done by Johnny Boy. He's been clean some years now and swears by it."

"Well, Ma, I suppose it might do some good. At the couple of meetings I've been to, I heard them say, 'If you can't get clean for yourself, get clean for somebody else.' I sure can't claim to want to get clean for me. But I'm willing."

"That's good enough for me!"

I could feel her pain. Some of the shit I'd done was so fucking derelict of any kind of civility or decency, I couldn't see how my own Mom stuck by me the way she did. Never any violence, just plain ol' manipulation and deceit. Many times, that could be worse than physical abuse.

So, the idea of another treatment center was probably more of a well-deserved rest for her than it was for me to get clean. She agreed to take me if I agreed to try. But, my heart wasn't in it. My heart was in the streets. I did the 28 days, participated in all of the activities and was a good in-house client, but took none of their advice after I got out.

CB   BO

Change your playgrounds (the places you hang out), change your playmates (the people you hang out with), do 90 in 90 (90 12-step meetings in 90 days), and get a sponsor (somebody in a recovery program who you can admit to when you feel like getting high), they told me.

I cooperated with the staff, listened to the lectures and asked questions. I even listened to those sad, bitch-ass stories everybody told because no one was willing to be straight-up like me and admit, "Hey, I ain't through. I love that shit and I still got some get-high left in me!" I'm sure there were those who were earnestly trying to get a grip, but I just laid it on the line.

Oh, the wide-eyed gasps of disbelief that were heard around the facility. "Did you hear what he said?" "I can't believe he said that!" and so on. It was like an Ultimate Truth had finally been revealed and true Enlightenment had descended on all listeners. Because I wasn't there by court order nor was I under any legal obligation to stay, I didn't have a role to play. I could be straightforward. Because I was there by family order, my dope-infested life had not reached rock bottom. I had no job, no money, no car, and no prospects, but I was all right…in *my* mind.

So, when I came back to Winston, I did make it to a couple of 12-step meetings where I said all the correct 12-step-type shit. "Hello, my name is Rick and I'm an addict." and I'd "share" in those meetings, many times with dope in my pocket. But none of that got to the core of why I was getting high. And it couldn't. I got high because I liked it. Period. I was hooked on the lifestyle of the whole thing and I wasn't ready to let it go. I mean, I did good for a little while, looked for jobs and everything, but the same ol' became the same ol' and I ended up right back in the streets.

SEVENTEEN

I'd never forgotten how Mike dissed me that time when I dropped him off over on First Street and I'd been praying for any opportunity to get him back. My old haunt at Teddy's proved to be just the place for subterfuge. Regardless of the time or place, Teddy's was the place for heads to gather.

After I had copped, I went over there for just a short while. When I walked in, lo and behold, there's Mike sitting at the table with that stupid-ass look he gets after he takes a blast. Hallelujah, there is a God! I recognized that car in the driveway and I knew it wasn't his, so I played it off like everything was cool.

"Yo, son, what up? Ain't seen you in a minute."

"What up, Rick?" he said rather flatly, his eyes glazed and vacuous, a look on his face as though he'd lost or forgotten something, but couldn't quite remember what he'd lost or forgotten.

"Long time no see, 'specially since I thought I would've heard from you since our last outing."

No raised voices, no cause for concern, he didn't have a clue. Besides, tension around the crack table is a most unwelcome guest. The ambience for a smooth get-high experience is dependent upon camaraderie at the table and things being cool; it was nerve-wracking enough just being in a crack house. With dope all over the place and paraphernalia everywhere, the possibilities of law enforcement showing up were enormous, so coolness was necessary. Still, we were just talking.

"Yeah, man, I kinda got tied up and everything, you know how I do. But, uh, you wanna hit?"

"Yeah, man, that'll be cool."

He broke off a piece and passed it to me.

"I noticed your new car. When'd you get that?"

"Oh, it ain't mine. It belong to a friend a mine, a family member. They just let me use it for a while."

"Oh, yeah. That's real cool you got people lookin' out for you like that. That's real cool."

A pensive reverie descended as I smoked. I looked out, through the haze of that hit, surveying my surroundings and the people in it. A couple of them just looking around, painfully lost, not sure of their next move.

The table, the kitchen itself, needing the attention of somebody that gave a damn. Teddy sure didn't. There he sat, quietly humming to himself, fiddling with his pipe, waiting for somebody to give him another hit. It was all so sad. But, my thinking did not let me down. It gave me a plan to take advantage of this gift so generously presented to me.

"Hey y'all, I gotta go. I'll catch y'all later. Mike, thanks for the hit. Teddy, y'all be cool and I'll holla atcha after while."

As I left walking to the nearest telephone, I was organizing an approach to this conversation. I knew Mike's benefactor's name was Watson and I knew she lived on Maryland Avenue, even the address. But, what would be the chances her number would be listed? I got to the phone and scanned the listings of Watsons; there was one Watson on Maryland Avenue. I dug out a quarter and dialed.

"Is this Mrs. Watson?"

"Yes, it is."

"Well, uh, I think I got some information you might be interested in."

"Oh, really. What might that be?"

"Are you missing your car?"

"Oh, yes! Do you know where it is? Do you know how I can get it?"

189

"Well, yeah. I'm looking at it right now, as we speak. It's a yellow Chrysler right?"

"Right."

"So, what do you want me to do?"

"Well, this is just wonderful. I've been waiting on Michael since last week. He said he needed to use my car for just a little while and I said okay, mainly because I'm a friend of his grandmother. I'm so mad I could scream. I called her and everything, but she hadn't seen him either. I didn't want to call the police since we're all friends but, if you could just tell me where it is, I'd really appreciate it."

I just bet you would. I gave her directions and she said, "I'm on my way!"

In this type of underhanded, backstabbing, sell-out scenario, I had no real clue of the outcome. I could only hope that it turned out my way. Maybe she'd give me some money, maybe she wouldn't, but I knew I would ask. The bigger point about stabbing Mike in his back and, maybe, turning this resource of his into a resource of mine was well worth the risk. Revenge was quite tasty when served cold.

I went by Teddy's a little later on and was told what had happened. That this lady showed up looking for Mike because he had her car and she had a police escort. I could only imagine the shock and panic that came when somebody looked out the window and would say in a loud whisper, "It's the po-lice!"

Fortunately, they weren't there to make a bust, only to help the lady get her car back. Well, goody. I figured I'd go by her house after a while and see if there were benefits I could reap.

Ca ʞ

Mrs. Watson turned out to be a congenial senior citizen who had a full-time job as a hairdresser in her stylishly remodeled home. She told me that the majority of her customers had been with her many years and enabled her to live quite a comfortable lifestyle. Since she never had children, her financial status was intact.

She had been in her home and that neighborhood for 40 years and was a well-respected member of that community. It had been a quiet, peaceful place until the last few years, she said, because of all those drugs and things. "Look over there." She pointed. "That young fellow right there I've known all his life, been living off his Momma for years and worries her constantly. All these strange people coming and going, walking up and down by her house all the time. But, she loves him and he still lives there. It's just a shame," she said.

I nodded my head in mute agreement.

"Well, let me give you a little something to show my appreciation for calling me. I don't know if or when that boy would've brought my car back. He's another one I never thought would do such a thing." As she talks, she goes to her pocketbook and pulls out money, my bones began their familiar dance.

"Well, I don't know, Mrs. Watson. I'd been over here a couple of times with him and I was just uncomfortable with seeing your car in that neighborhood. Now, don't get me wrong, I really appreciate what you're doing for me here, this is real thoughtful of you. But, it just seemed so wrong to see your car out of place like that. If you ever need me to do anything or if you hear from Mike and he becomes a problem, you just let me know."

"Okay, Rick, I sure will. And I appreciate that, too."

As we say these things, I'm moving toward the door.

"Okay, Mrs. Watson. You take it easy and we'll see you later."

But, now, the question became how do I return to see her now that the money she gave me is gone? Under what pretense? I couldn't just turn around and go right back and ask her for more money; she didn't really know me like that anyway. I'd have to come up with a reason.

Meeting her proved to be a singularly important event in my life. It had become useless to ask Mom for money. Johnetta and Paul had moved in after it became apparent that I'd never get out of debt and didn't seem to mind that Mom was getting increasingly in debt. Since they were building a new home, they "conveniently" decided to move in with Mom while their house was being built.

I'd given up any pretense of living a normal life. My life had become dedicated to the streets. Either I would find myself and stop this madness. Or I would die.

I did a lot of walking and bumming rides since I didn't have a car because when that urge to use reared its ugly head, I could only do what it told me to do. Once the euphoria wore off, you were left with a muscular desire to get more. If satisfying that desire meant walking, you walked; if it meant cheating, you cheated; if it meant stealing, you stole. Just get that dope!

It was nothing for me to walk behind a house to see what was lying around or to pry out a window and go inside. Not only did these events put me in harm's way, they also gave me an opportunity to really think about finding a better way.

On one such occasion, I had a flash of insight. I'd learned that Mike had been flim-flamming Mrs. Watson by masquerading as her faith-healer, oracle and prophet. I figured if I could insinuate myself by duplicating or imitating the role he played and get him out of the way at the same time, my coup would be complete. This way, I wouldn't really have to lie to her face. I could parlay our recent acquaintance into bounty for me.

So, I began to create and cultivate this other persona who would manifest only on the phone. His voice would be strange and other-worldly and his story would be believable to her. It would be a relevant narrative that would have meaning in her quest to be free of the many insecurities that haunted her. The telephone persona would relate the storyline, Rick would be the go-between.

To say that she was gullible misses the point. Because she was a deserving, unselfish person, she had every intention of using the resources that were promised to come her way for the betterment of her church, her family and friends. She wanted to believe so badly that there could be a person who could intervene in natural events and cause manna in the form of money to rain down on her. But those proceeds would never materialize.

捹 掀

One day I found myself at Momma's side door. Lady was there, dancing and prancing as usual; if no one else was glad to see me, I could count on her to be. I knocked and Mom peeped out, pulling the curtain aside. And there I was, in all of my raggedy, unkempt, poorly sanitized splendor. What a sight.

"Hello, Ricky."

"Hi, Ma." She opened the door, let me in and went to the

kitchen. Since Johnetta and Paul weren't there, I was fiendishly, frantically trying to come up with a reasonable lie to get some money. I sat at the table and fiddled with the remote. "I'm surprised you're here. You're usually at the school."

"Well, with Johnetta and Paul here, I don't have to work so hard. I can go more at my own pace. They're really a big help."

"Well, I'm glad. That's good."

She gazed at me with a look of consternation and sorrow. This is my child, I imagined her saying, and I love him, but I don't know what I've done for him to turnout this way.

"You know, Ma, you've been a real friend through all this and there is really no way I can repay you."

"Oh, yes there is. You can straighten out your life, come into this house clean and sober and get off those streets, that's what you can do. And I wish you would before I leave this earth."

"Ma, don't talk like that!" Now, there's a thought I truly didn't want to consider. If something were to happen to her, what would I do then?

"Son, I'm 74 years old and the Lord says you do good to get three score and ten so, I'm already over my limit and I'd like to see you straightened out before I close my eyes."

"Geez, Ma, that sounds so final."

"Well, death is final, but this life you're leading isn't and it shouldn't have to be. It's one you can change, if you want to."

"So far, Ma, my efforts have come up short. I'd love to see me change so you could see it too, but listen, here's something I hope we can work out. For the last little while, I've been doing my best to get rid of this debt I owe and I'm at the point where I need just a little bit of help to…"

She exploded. "BOY, DON'T YOU COME IN HERE ASKING ME FOR NO MONEY!!" Her eyes glaring and waving her hands menacingly toward me. "I used to have a few pennies I could put my hands on, but you have run me to ruin. I trusted you, but now I know better. And here you come in here looking like a zombie—I mean, just like them people in front of the soup kitchen—and got the nerve to ask me for *more* money. Oh, I just don't know…"

And she started crying. And crying.

Now, look what I've done. Suppose Johnetta and Paul come home while all this is going on, I'd never hear the end of it.

"Aw, Ma…" I go over and try to console her.

She jerked away from my touch. "GET AWAY FROM ME BOY! You don't mean it no way. And go take a shower, you stink. Gonna try to pretend like you really care. You don't care about me, you just want some money."

A morose disquietude descended on the room, neither of us looking at the other.

"Johnetta said this would happen. She said you'd be coming around here looking for some money," she said between sobs. "I'll never forget how you snuck into my room while I was sleep and stole out my pocketbook. Never have forgot that. She says I'm your number one enabler, that you use me to get drugs and I let you. Like I couldn't help myself. And I couldn't."

I suppose I had it coming. I just wasn't expecting it with so much vehemence.

"You think you fooled me when you'd stay in that bathroom for hours and hours," she said. "But, I knew. I knew all along. I just said to myself, I just rationalized the whole sorry situation and said, 'Well, at least he's at home.' I'm just glad somebody talked some sense into me. But I loved you the only way I knew how."

I really was unprepared for the display of disappointment Momma showed me. I couldn't take no more of this. I had to make a discreet get-away. The enormity of my failings was evident in her dreadful pleadings.

"Well, Ma, I'm a take a shower, okay."

"Go ahead, son. Just be gone when they get back."

Through the closed door of the bathroom, I undressed for the shower and listened as she continued to talk about her disappointment in me, her youngest, the one with so much promise.

As hard as her attack hit me, in my head I was still searching for a way I could get her to give me some money.

If there was ever any doubt about the spiritual teaching about reaping what we sow, there was much less now. Here, I had sowed great amounts of misery and anguish into the life of my mother and family and here I was, reaping a life utterly filled with misery and anguish.

CŞ ȘO

It turned out, as I began to frequent Mrs. Watson's neighborhood, that her streets were more drug-infested than appearances would suggest. Well-maintained lawns on those tree-lined streets gave the impression that all was well. But, along with her neighbor who had the troublesome son, there were four or five houses in a two-block radius where smokers would gather.

How fortunate that I could smoke in an area near the money.

Satisfying this obsession was a relentless, time-consuming endeavor that led me to coerce and manipulate this kind and graceful woman. The control was so thorough that I could call at 2 or 3 a.m. and she would meet me at her door, and sometimes come to another house, with money. This money would be for The Prophet I was representing, for the work he was doing for her. I was two people: on the phone, I was The Prophet, who gave all manner of advice, counsel and guidance; the other, myself, who was the go-between, the financial conduit from her to him.

Certificates of Deposit, bankcards, checks, cash, church money all came through my hands. The beauty of it was that Mike could never figure out how he got blocked out of her good graces. He couldn't even figure out how she found out where her car was! I saw him from time to time and he never indicated otherwise. A helluva coup.

At those times when Mrs. Watson was not able to get away from the shop or had an errand to run, I was left to do what I could, either break into somebody's house or car or get up with one of my several crime-partners. On one of these occasions, I'd met Steve, a younger white guy, over at Teddy's and here he was coming down the street, driving just as pretty as you please, as though I'd called him to meet me.

"What up, boy! When you get this?"

"My aunt let me use it for a little while…"

"Your aunt? Shit, you lyin' aintcha?"

"Naw, for real. She let me use it for a little while."

"A'ight then. What we gone do? You got some dope?"

"I got a little hit, you want some?"

"Nah, if all you got is a little hit, I can wait 'til we get some money. Since we got a car, getting' some money ain't gonna be too hard."

We drove that car like it was ours for nearly a month and I began to gather that it wasn't his aunt's. I became a little more aware of how and where I drove it, where we used it to steal, and where we smoked crack in it. But, as luck would have it, our time had run out.

I took the car, as was routine, one morning on my usual routes and picked up a local dopeboy who needed a ride. While I was driving around, the police pulled up, blue light flashing. Goddamn! Here these mother fuckers are. I got dope, paraphernalia, a stolen car, no license, all kinds of shit and he had dope on him. Damn!!

"Yo, young blood, just be cool."

"Man, what? What you mean 'be cool'?"

"The law's behind us. They getting' out an' comin' to the window, so chill." I rolled the window down.

"Good afternoon, sir."

"Afternoon, officer."

"Let me see your license and registration."

"I don't have either one, sir."

"Alright, stay in your car and let me call this in. What's your name, sir?"

"John Lee Moore."

"Address."

"3711 Sawyer Drive."

"...and date of birth."

"2-27-53."

"Alright, Mr. Moore, I'll be right back."

So, we sat there for several tense minutes. I didn't know what the outcome would be, but something just didn't feel right. I began to fidget and look around for some of the dope I had in the car, but it would look too outrageous for me to take a blast with the police right there. But, what the hell, it felt like I was going to jail anyway, so why not? Nah, I'd survived other scares like this so, let me just sit tight.

A few more seconds passed and the cop had not come back to give his report. I look in the mirror and there seemed to be a squadron, a whole fleet, of blue and whites descending on our location.

"Oh, no." I said dejectedly. This would be the end.

They came to my side and got me out, then to the other side to get the young boy. A couple of them had their guns drawn and it was a rather intense moment. Looked like I should've took that blast anyway.

Wasn't a whole lot of conversation; they just put us in cars and took us downtown. When we got there, they let the young boy go (he was able to hide his stash on him, somewhere) because he had no warrants and the car wasn't under his care and control. I was charged with all that.

Well, here I go again. Wasn't no way for me to even think about asking anybody to bail me out so, I figured I'd better tell Mom, let her know where I was. When I called, she was rather detached about the whole thing, almost indifferent. Said she'd see me whenever I got out. Johnetta and Paul didn't even want to talk, so it was no use in trying to tell them it'd be better or different this time.

I didn't stay in jail too long. I pleaded my sentence from 35 months to 9-11 months with the help of a court-appointed lawyer and got to the DOC about three months later. This was my third felony and I'd be eligible for "The Bitch" if I came back for any others.

Habitual Felon is a status that Structured Sentencing provided, allowing prosecutors to enhance an offenders' sentence due to his history of felonious infractions. Even though I had way more than three felonies in my past, many of these multiple charges were consolidated into one charge, as was the standard. In other words, if my behavior didn't change, I could look forward to lengthy prison stay in the future. This was made quite clear in court.

The DA began, "Your Honor, if it please the Court, the State calls Frederick Moore."

The bailiff called out, "Frederick Moore!"

I stood, in my blue jumper with Forsyth County Detention Center stenciled on the back, and met the lawyer at the table designated for defendants.

"Your Honor, Mr. Moore has agreed to a plea agreement and the State recommends the minimum 9 to 11 months active."

The judge said, "Very well, I see that the paperwork is in order. Mr. Moore, are you stating here, in open court, that you have not been coerced or threatened into making this agreement?"

"Yes, I am."

"And that you are not under the influence of drugs or alcohol."

"That's correct, sir."

"Very well, I will consolidate these charges for judgment and sentence you to 9 to 11 months in the Department of Corrections."

"Thank you, sir." I sure hoped he didn't change his mind. It was a damn good sentence especially for all the shit I'd been doing. Besides, I needed the rest.

"Your Honor, if I may." the DA interjected. "I'd like to make the record clear. Mr. Moore has a serious drug problem He is considered a 'person of interest' by the police and this is his third felony. I am telling him and this Court that if he doesn't address his addiction in a meaningful way and comes back here with another felony, the State of North Carolina will have a very stern response."

"It is so noted, Mr. DA."

EIGHTEEN

Oh, sure, I heard what the DA was talking about, but I knew I wasn't through with the streets. The drive to do drugs was idling, just waiting for the end of my jail time.

Because I had a short sentence, I was transferred to the minimum custody unit in Lenoir County, a laid-back place where there was no violence, no crazy-acting guys and no overt homosexual behavior, rather like a summer camp with dormitory-style accommodations and an everybody-eats-the-same-thing menu in the chow hall. Lines to eat, lines for the canteen, lines to change clothes, lines to get your weekly draw were all part of being on state.

I passed my time on the road construction crew. We put in drainage pipes, filled in potholes and graded unpaved roads. Being on the road squad was neither hard nor unfriendly. You were able to be out and about in the community, which was a good thing, and go about your daily activities without too much scrutiny. This bit of freedom allowed you to come into contact with people in the community and, as a result, I got myself into a bit of trouble.

My cravings, though diminished, were not absent. So, I substituted weed which is a pretty cool high in prison. Things seemed so much more agreeable and everything was funny. It didn't cost much, about $2.00 a joint, but it was still illegal, especially in prison.

So, when the CO happened to observe me and another guy sitting rather suspiciously close, he came over before I was able to hide it.

I was taken to the local jail and charged with Possession of a Controlled Substance in Prison. A felony. Had there been an overzealous prosecutor in Lenoir County, this infraction could have been used to habitualize me. However, the county simply found me guilty of this offense, sentenced to me to 6 to 8 months and ran that concurrent with the 9 to 11 months I was serving.

I stayed in seg four months before going to court and when I got out after this sentencing, I was sent back to the Caldwell unit. No sooner than getting my bags in the dorm was I called to the sergeant's office. Damn. What could it be, now?

"Fred Moore?"

"Yeah."

"You need to call home." A lump of lead, formed in the pit of my stomach. This could only be bad news.

"Hey, Johnetta. I just got a message. What's up?" A slight, unnerving pause.

"Mom's been diagnosed with liver disease."

"What!"

"Yeah, and it's already spread. Looks like it's terminal."

"Geez, is that what the doc says?"

"Yeah, they're recommending hospice care, but we're going to keep her here for as long as…uh, until it's, uh…well, as long as we can."

"How long have you known?"

"Just recently, last month or so. She didn't tell anybody right away."

"How long do they think she has?"

"They don't say precisely. A few weeks, a month, maybe. It's not too hopeful."

"So, what do you think I should do?"

"We've already sent the paperwork to the DOC from the doctors to see if you can get an emergency release. Whenever they let you out, just come on home and spend some time. But I'm telling you, she's lost a lot of weight. She doesn't look the same so don't be surprised."

Damn, ain't this something. The very thing I thought wouldn't happen for a while is now about to take place. I knew Johnetta or Johnny Boy or somebody would have something to say about the likelihood that stress causes cancer and that, ultimately, I was responsible for her untimely demise. But, that's all so inconclusive. Hopefully, I could duck and dodge the issue long enough for it to lose its steam.

CB   BO

A few days later, I got a call from the sergeant's office and was told to pack it up, I'd been released. I collected my belongings and was driven to Winston-Salem where I was dropped off in the parking lot of Mt. Zion. I found my way home from there by catching a ride with a church member who happened to be headed that way and knew about my circumstances and Mom's illness.

Johnetta's greeting was brief and to the point. "Hey, Ricky. I sure hope you can stay out of those streets for a while and stay here with Momma. The least we can do is be here for her."

I carried my jailhouse belongings inside, in a white plastic bag with my name and DOC number printed on the side, and put them on the floor next to the lounger.

And there was Momma. Sitting at the kitchen table. Her eyes were clear, but her body was…nearly skeletal. I inadvertently made a small gasp. My goodness, what kind of cancer could eat you up in two months' time?

"Hi, Ma," I said cheerfully. I could only hope shock and disbelief were not apparent on my face. This was not the Momma I left eight months ago, who was healthy and active. This was a person in a death grip and it looked like death would have its way.

She gave me a slight smile, but didn't say anything. She recognized me and knew who I was, but her vivacity, long the hallmark of her personality, was absent.

Johnetta said, "She won't speak because she's too weak. At least, that's what the doctors think. I mean, she can speak, but it takes too much effort."

I looked at her and thought, Jee-zus, this is terrible. Momma had always been extremely independent and I knew she didn't want to go out like this. One of God's most beautiful flowers reduced to nearly nothing. Why couldn't she go out in her sleep without having to suffer this way? Where's the fairness here? She'd done nothing to deserve an end like this. Given all that she'd been through in her life, it's the least that could have happened, to come to a quiet and peaceful end.

She gazed at me as though she might never see me again.

I sat at the table with her, just to be there. Didn't try to make any conversation or coax her into saying anything, just pretty much talked with Johnetta, said hello to Paul and met the 24-hour hospice caretaker. With her independence and ability to do for herself gone, the cornerstone of her character was wiped out.

After a while, Johnetta and the caretaker suggested Mom ought to rest for the night. Since she sat in a wheelchair, it was simple for them to roll her away from the table down the hallway to her bedroom.

I took this as a cue to get settled in my room and get organized for the days to come.

With Mom's passing imminent, there was now a real urgency to get my shit together. Get a job, get a car, pay some bills, all of that. To make her proud in these final days had to take precedence before anything else. Surely, I could do these few simple things.

I knew that this would go a long way to helping Johnetta and Paul overcome their nearly reflexive mistrust of me. I could show them that they didn't have to keep their room under lock and key, which Paul had installed it as soon as they moved in. I thought it was a tremendous insult; everybody else thought it was a necessary precaution. Just because I stole from folks every now and then was no reason for them to think I'd steal from them. Like I couldn't be trusted or something.

I slept calmly that night and, in the morning, I got up to see how Mom was faring.

The caretaker was there and Ma, oh Momma, how could life be so unfair. There she was, hardly able to move. Just lying there. Waiting. In that same room I used to sneak into and steal money out of her pocketbook while she slept. Waiting. Fully cognizant of her surroundings and conditions, yet able to do nothing except wait.

Jeez, I just couldn't stand it.

I left the room and went up front. It was the weekend and everybody was home. I sat down to watch a little TV and shortly the mail came. I wasn't expecting anything, but went to get it anyway. Lo and behold, the DOC, in its wisdom, saw fit to look out for a brother when a brother needed a look out. They sent me a check for $135.00 out of my trust fund account that I knew for sure was less than that, maybe $13.50. Definitely not $135.00. But, hey, who was I to argue?

To this point, my urges had kept themselves at a low hum, mainly because I was broke. But, with this unexpected reversal of fortunes, that low hum rocketed to a high-pitched scream. My stomach began to churn, my fingers and toes became all tingly and I began to contrive an easy exit. What to do next. Shit, I had to go!

"Johnetta, I'm going out for a while, okay?"

When she heard this, she looked at me warily. "How long will you be gone?"

"Oh, just a little while. I kinda need to stretch my legs."

And off I went, on foot. It felt good to be back on the scene with a little change in my pockets and a little rest under my belt. I missed those streets and believed they missed me. We were made for each other.

ა   ფ

I made it back to the house that evening before it got too late. All the while I was gone, not once did I think of my responsibilities at home. I figured they were holding it down well enough.

I knocked and, thankfully, was let inside with an ominous glare from Johnetta to accompany me. I went to my room and slowly, the tentacles of that maddening desire began to subside and I could stop tossing and turning and get to that place a cocaine high won't let you. A place called sleep.

Mother was weakening by the day and I felt so helpless and out of place. I wanted to get out in the streets so I didn't have to deal with any of this, but I didn't have any money. I knew I couldn't go back down to Lakeside, I'd never make it back and in that way, I'm glad I couldn't go out. So, it came as a complete surprise that the

DOC, during a period of mistake-prone activity, sent another check in the same amount. Now, what was I supposed to do?

The honorable thing would be to hold on to those few pennies and stay around the house, to just *be* there. But, another voice was talking, another issue was at hand. It should've been my dying Mother and family who loved me through it all, in spite of myself. But, it wasn't. I told everybody, I even spoke in Mom's ear, as she lay there helpless and mute, that I was going job hunting, that I'd be back.

I didn't come back.

Ↄ ⁊

When the money ran out I returned to Mrs. Watson's place. I'd already called ahead, so she was waiting at the door. She seemed to have an inexhaustible supply of cash and I just hoped my little scam would last. If I could avoid jail, I might be able to really enjoy myself this time. Then I could, somehow, get enough of this shit and come out of these streets. This was my silent prayer.

She hit me off pretty good. Not only was I able to cop, I was able to buy an old second-hand car that had been lurking about in those neighborhoods. It was in a driveway and I just walked up and asked if it was for sale. No license, no tags, no insurance. I just stole the tags off another car, I didn't know whose, and went on my merry way.

Now the fun could really begin. I went to dope spots all over Winston. Running the streets, smoking crack, stealing when I had to, having just a good ol' time. Not once during all of this did I call home. It crossed my mind, but I just didn't take the time to do it.

Finally, after a couple of weeks, I decided to get in touch.

"Ricky? You need to come home, boy. Now. Momma passed last night."

"Damn. For real?" It seemed so eerie, so surreal that this point in time we knew would come, actually did.

"Yeah, for real. She passed in her sleep and now she's in a better place. No more suffering for her in this world."

So, now I've got to get home. I've got to go deal with all the people, all the sorrow, all the sad faces and all the detail that surround such an event. Because she fought the good fight, lived a good life, was passionate about giving aid and comfort to those less fortunate, her absence would be noticed by many and her passing a hard reminder of everyone's destiny. She was a stellar, incomparable example of how one ought to live.

This was my Mother. The one who gave birth to me and loved me unconditionally, even when I didn't deserve to be. And yet, I just couldn't get home right then. I was going to get there, I just had to get one more blast. Besides, I had a little time. Winston had to come in from California and Johnny Boy from Washington, D.C., so it was no big-time rush, not really.

In a way, Momma's passing was a gift to me. It freed me from much of the guilt and shame I'd go through when I lied to her or stole from her or saw her woeful downcast expressions whenever I did come home. All of that remorse was no longer. In a real sense, her death set me free.

γ∝ ∝γ

I made it to the house a couple of days later. My brothers had arrived and there was a solemn gravity about the place. I suppose that was to be expected, but it seemed to be directed towards me. Nothing overt, just sideways looks and barely discernible frowns. A smoldering anger.

The decision was for us to view her body that day at Caldwell's Funeral Home. When we got there, it proved to be a quiet and reserved time. Respectful, as a gathering of this nature ought to be. My thinking wasn't grossly preoccupied and I was able to enjoy a few moments of community with my brothers and sister.

While Winston and Johnetta were tall and graceful, full of dignity and wisdom, Johnny Boy, saddened and teary-eyed, tried his best, but was overcome, he just couldn't help it. I, on the other hand, felt comfortably remote about it all. Momma's passing had quite an emotional tone to it, yet I was removed from it all, maybe for good reason. Death and the finality of life had been topics she and I discussed openly. She felt that it was as much a part of life and living as was eating and breathing. It was a natural consequence of life; we ought to embrace it, not be alarmed by it. Folks ought not get so anxious about this final moment because, the secret is, it isn't so final.

We commented on how good a job they did on Mom, how natural and life-like she looked, don't you think? We lingered for a few moments more and chatted about the service to be at Mt. Zion the next day and the burial to be at her home church, Mountain View, in Anderson County, SC. On our way back to the house, the mood was low and I figured I could get up, out and back before any of the preparations to leave took place.

The urge to use was never too far away.

So, the first thing was to go get the car. I'd left it in Cleveland Projects and I could only hope that it would still be where I'd left it. It wasn't.

I walked a couple blocks in each direction, hoping to spot it. And there it was, a burned out hulk, just waiting for the junkyard. Oh, well, easy come, easy go.

I had just enough, maybe twelve or thirteen bucks, to get me a hit and, so, I did. I could either waste my time trying to figure out who handled my car and what to do about it or I could pursue an abbreviated mission, some short, quick moves to get high. Since I was on a tight leash and the clock was ticking, I had to get in all my smoking before everything kicked into high gear.

When that hit was done, I just couldn't stop even when it made sense to. And so it went and so it would go, from Mrs. Watson's house to one dope spot after the other.

And still, I had issues at home to contend with. What was I going to do about that? As time would pass, I knew I had to show up or something. So, I called Johnetta.

"Ricky! Where you been? We've been waiting and waiting since yesterday for you to come. The funeral is today and we're going on to South Carolina afterwards for the burial. Are you coming?"

"Yeah, Johnetta, I'm on my way."

Damn, here we go again. Right between these get-high episodes, right when somebody is going to cop, I gotta go. I mean, how could I leave right when shit is about to jump off? I knew it was momma's funeral day, but I just couldn't, not right then. A couple of hours pass and a little more crack is smoked. There's still more coming but I'm preoccupied with this funeral thing over my head so I called again. I really couldn't enjoy myself because of it.

Next, my ex-sister-in-law Paulette would be sent for me.

Shit. Now what? Maybe when they get here, they can give me a couple a dollars. Damn, this is really fucked up. I can't believe I'm actually out here in these streets on the day of Momma's funeral, acting like a fool. Shortly, no more than 30 minutes, I see a familiar Cressida coming up the street, with my nephew L'il Calvin and my niece Warrenetta. Paulette rolled down the window.

"Ricky, what you gonna do?" Paulette was Big Calvin's ex-wife and she had seen the destructive effects of drugs and alcohol up close, which resulted in her divorce from him. "Are you getting in or what? We might have time to run by the house so you can get a quick shower and change, but we've got to go right now."

I did my best to come up with a fast one. "Yeah, I'm ready, but you see them people right there." A rag-tag bunch for sure. Real losers. "I need to give them just a few bucks of what I owe them."

"You mean, you want me to give you some money? No, Ricky. I'm sorry you're in this situation, but I can't give you any money."

L'il Calvin said from the back, "C'mon, Uncle Ricky, let's go."

"Yeah, well, it would be unwise for me to just get in and leave," I said. "I think I'd be putting myself in a bit of jeopardy."

"Well, if you don't come with us you're gonna be in a lot more jeopardy than you can imagine," Paulette said. "Your brothers and sister won't like it too much at all."

"See, I can dig that, but I gotta hang around 'til I come up with some cash or somethin'. Y'all go 'head on, I'll be there before you know it."

My niece and nephew, witnessing this whole sad parade of desperate unhappiness, just watched their favorite, most fun uncle crash and burn.

I watched the car fade in the distance, silently acknowledged that I was committing an act of extreme contempt and dishonor. They came in an effort to help me avoid doing this unholy thing. They threw me a life-line.

And I threw it back.

NINETEEN

"Hey, Mrs. Watson."

"Hey, Rick. What are you doing here? You really should be at home."

"I know, Mrs. Watson, but I already missed my ride to the funeral and I was wonderin' if you could spare me a few bucks so I could catch a bus to South Carolina."

"How could you miss the funeral?" she asked, incredulously.

"Yeah, well, I know, but I want to try to make the burial at the old home church cemetery where everybody is gonna gather at. I can get there, but I'm a need a little bit a help."

"Well, I can get you a bus ticket, but you're going to have to find your own way to the bus station."

"That'll help out a lot. I can get a way to the bus station."

"Okay, then. But, there is something I've been meaning to tell you."

"I'm listening."

Then she told me about a woman in a blue Buick who pulled up in front of her house a few months earlier.

"Rick, a few months ago, your Momma came by here and asked me to look out for you. She didn't look sick or anything so I never thought about it until I learned that it was she who died last week." Her tone of voice and the look in her eyes revealed no suspicion or distrust. "So, you've got her to thank. There's no way I could turn my back on a dying woman's last request for her son."

Oh my. That's just like mom, always on the lookout, even from her front row seat in heaven. Maybe there was some divine redemption tied to all of this somewhere, but I sure didn't see it.

As my crack habit continued to blossom, I took Mrs. Watson's money and went straight to the dopeman. Didn't call back home, didn't even try to make it to the church, just said fuck it and didn't go. And why should it be so important for me to be there, anyway? I knew that Momma'd be cool with it. She knew what I was going through with this dope thing. She'd understand.

I had freed myself of any kind of guilt or remorse. Eventually, I tried to call my brothers and sister, but the conversations were brimming with anger and disgust.

Even though I wasn't there, it was like I could see the whole scene at the old home place where Mom grew up. Friends and family were sure to ask, "Well, where's Ricky?" Johnetta or somebody would be forced to answer, "He out in them streets, somewhere."

☙ ❧

After this, my life really fell apart. I was on foot, going from one place to the next, my waking hours dedicated to hustling up crack money. Because of my unswerving devotion to crack, I would go for great periods of time, a week, 10 days, and not comb my hair, brush my teeth or change my clothes. I might wash up in a bathroom somewhere, but good personal hygiene was out of fashion for a while.

I'd actually had one of the locals to tell me, "Boy, you stink. You need to go take care a that before you come back here!" My feelings were hurt, but they were right. So, I ended up at Teddy's where I had free roam of the premises and, at least, I could take a shower.

☙ ❧

The crack scene is not all hostility and violence. For sure, you could find yourself in hostile situations, but for smokers sitting around the table, it tended to be a rather sociable and hospitable setting, pleasant and friendly.

Teddy let me in and I walked through the dimly lit living room to the kitchen where, around the table, sat four or five familiar faces. I'd come across a piece on my way over, so I wasn't begging right off the bat.

That had to be the most lazy, aggravating, petty way to get high I had ever seen: sitting around the table or just waiting inside the house to beg somebody for a hit rather than going out and hustling up your own. Jeez, I couldn't stand that and I just didn't do it. There were one or two who would look out for each other. When one had it and the other didn't, the favor was returned when they got straightened out, that was something I could deal with. But to not go out and get yours and yet, sit around begging others for theirs was just trifling. Not me, I was a go-getter.

Even girls, who used sex as their hustle, would find themselves on the short end when a guy wanted to smoke more than he wanted to fuck. Happened all the time. They were quite willing to trade a favor or two for a blast, but when the supply was short, that sex shit was put on hold.

Fortunately, I didn't have a problem telling anybody, man or woman, "Nah, dog, not this time." I had mine when I sat down so they knew not to try that.

"Yo, fellas. What up." I said, greeting everyone.

"What up, Rick." They all said, not in unison.

To the lone female at the table with whom I was somewhat familiar, "What up, Neicy."

"Nothin' much. Wha's up with you?"

"Nothin', just fixin' to take this little hit. You doin' anythang?"

"Depends. What you talkin' about."

"I don't know right this second. Let me get a blast and we'll see."

"Shit, nigga. You'd rather smoke, anyway."

"Uh-huh, right now, yeah. But, gimme a minute." As I lit up and took my hit, I watched those white clouds of smoke roiling and curling, racing through the barrel of the pipe, to do what only they can do. And I held my breath. A great chest full of narcotic announced its glorious arrival as I go away…and away…and away.

Alrighty, it's a brand new day! All of that turmoil and grief I'd been going through with the funeral and my family was just a bad dream.

"Damn, tha's a helluva hit," I stated dreamily, barely able to get the words out.

All the heads at the table were begging with desire in their eyes.

"You know who got that truck out there?" I asked. See, my mind was already ahead of the game. I knew if I wanted to get high with Neicy, I had to get some more dope.

"Uh, that would be me." This white boy. I noticed him when I came in, but didn't think much of it. White boys in the 'hood weren't plentiful, but they did come through now and then. Wasn't nothing strange about it. Usually, when they ended up like this, hanging at the crack house, no money, no dope, no way to get either, they couldn't go home because they'd catch hell for being a fuck-up. They, like everybody else, were trying to get just one more.

"You, uh, wanna make a hustle?"

"Depends."

"You need some gas, some cigarettes?" I didn't have any money, but he didn't know that. I did come in with some dope and had a piece left, so I must have something going on. Didn't take no genius to figure that out.

"It'd help."

"You wanna hit?" All the others envious as hell, but that's the way it goes. He had something I needed. They knew the drill.

"Damn right. First time a stranger ever offered me any. I usually have to go somewhere or drive somebody or do something to get a hit."

"You're likely gonna have to do the same thing here, but at least, you'll have your head on tight. It's always more fun that way, to me."

I load the pipe and pass it to him. He lit it and inhaled and I began to see a smile make its slow, upward curl at the corners of his mouth. "Yeah, this is pretty good," the timbre in his voice having mellowed decidedly. "Uh, where was it you was wantin' to go?"

"Not too far. Up Patterson, out there by Motel 6. You know where that's at?"

"Uh-huh."

"Up by there. I got your gas and everything, a'ight?"

"Okay, so. Then, whenever you're ready…" I got up and head to the door. Since he was already standing, he just follows. "A'ight, Teddy, fellas, we'll catch y'all later. Neicy, I hope you'll be here when we get back."

"I'm a try, okay."

Bullshit. She knew good and well she wasn't going nowhere. Unless Scarface himself came through with a bunch of dope, she'd be there right along with the rest of them.

We go on to the truck and pull off. I give him the directions and ask about the gas again, this being a real crucial detail when you're out stealing, but he said he had enough.

I look at him on the sly, just to see if there was any character in his face. And he was there alright, eyes all big, still juiced up from that hit I gave him. He might work out after all.

"Yo, dude. What's your name or what do you go by?"

"Oh, just Jim is all. My real name's James, but Jim'll be fine.

"Okay, Jim. My name's Rick."

Everybody knew where Motel 6 was. A lot of transactions went down there and, accordingly, there was a regular police presence. North Patterson was an area of town where several mobile home dealerships were located. I had visited a couple of those dealerships, just browsing, recently and had a good idea of their layout. Those furnishings and appliances could be an easy late-night lick if I had a truck with the right driver.

We get to the light at Germanton and Patterson and go to the first driveway that led to an area behind one of the dealerships. I told him to kill the lights and we rolled to a slow stop in the shadows of one of the buildings. I got out, looked around and briskly walked out of the shadows across the gravel parking lot, as quietly as possible. There was a soft crunching underfoot, but it was tolerable. Because it was late-night, there was very little street traffic. I got to the trailer I had been to earlier and tried the door. Locked.

Not to worry, there were lots of make-shift keys all over the ground. I found a sturdy brick and smashed it through the window.

So much for quiet. With great risk come great rewards. I scrambled through the window and looked around in the dim lighting. There was the side-by-side refrigerator and matching stove, both brand-new, both Kenmore. Name brands always had more value.

No need to worry about selling these items at 3 o'clock in the morning, I knew exactly where to go, if only I could get them away from here. I look out the door and motion for him to bring the truck, being ever so thankful that it had a quiet motor. He backed it to the door, came inside and we loaded the appliances. Wasn't no need for conversation as nervousness and tension were at critical levels.

We got in and began to leave the way we came with the lights still out. All total, from Teddy's house to that point, took about 45 minutes.

"Gol-lee, Rick, that was pretty damn easy."

"Yeah, well, gettin' it is one thing. Gettin' away with it is somethin' totally else."

He had a startled look on his face, "What do you mean? We can't get caught. This my Dad's company truck, no way we can get caught!"

"Well, I'm just tellin' you the reality of all this. You wanna get high, you wanna smoke, you ain't got no money, well fuck it, you gotta take a risk. Period. Now, when we go out this driveway, we better pray we don't see no car lights 'cause it just might be the police."

"Shit."

"For real. It's possible. Hadn't happened yet, but I never overlook the possibility. Besides, with this stuff on the back of this truck, we could be legitimately moving somebody as anything else, so don't get your shirt all wrinkled."

As we get to the street, we look left, then right…and there were car lights in the distance. Shit. The likelihood that it would be the police was slim, but a likelihood nonetheless. And, yep, they were coming up the road. There was nothing we could do, we were already at the exit. We're going to have to take a chance. I just don't tell him.

"Okay, turn your lights on." He does so and as he entered the street, he noticed the approaching glare of the car headed our way.

"What do you suppose that is?"

"Probably nothin'. If it is the law, just be cool. You got your license?"

"Naw."

"Goddamn, man, whyn't you say somethin'? Fuck." Sure enough, it was a cruiser, but he didn't seem to notice us. We just held our breath, looking straight ahead, watching the mirrors, as those red taillights receded into the darkness.

"Boy, did you see that!" Jim exclaimed.

"Yeah, boy, that was pretty close."

"I'll say." A mixture of joy and relief on his face.

The mood lightened greatly, having narrowly escaped what surely would have been a nightmare had he paid us any attention. Lucky us.

Headed toward the 'hood, we stayed on Patterson and went to 14th Street, not too far from the areas I frequented. Though there were regular people who lived in this 'hood, it was rife with the movement of drug sales and dopeboys. People on the street 24/7, in and out of certain doors, standing around watching. Folk doing what they do. All night long.

The foot traffic and the car traffic, though not tumultuous, was steady. It never really stopped, but it did fall off. This is where "hot" merchandise could be bought, sold or traded. We had something that would go in a flash, you just had to know who to go to. Even Jim, with his conspicuous white ass, could've done it had he been a regular. Once the fellas got accustomed to you, once they became comfortable with your presence, you were accepted. Race became unimportant.

"Yo, pull over here." It was a Saturday night, so things were humming right along. Heads were on the sidewalk, over here by this tree, across the street on that porch, as though it was broad daylight, trying to see what they could see.

I picked all this up in a quick scan of the area. One of these niggas gone try to make a move, I thought. Since I knew most by face and vice-versa, they could see from where I parked and the load I had, who I was going to see. This helped me to relax a bit, but my nerves were still jumpy. Jim was the x-factor. I didn't know him or his whereabouts or his background. He might've pissed off one of these people in the past and they never forgot about it, just waiting for the time to see him again. Fuck it.

"Yo," I say to the look out. "Where Dave at?"

"He inside."

I say to Jim, "Wait here and whatever you do, don't look around. Just chill like you belong here. Ain't nobody gone bother you. You ever been on this street before?"

"Nah."

"Well, just be cool. I'll be back shortly." I went to the door of a white, A-frame house where you could look through the front door straight out the back. It was on a splotch of land with a rickety fence and a sparse topping of grass.

I knocked. "Come on in." And stepped inside.

"What up, fella. Ain't seen you in a couple a days." He knew my face, not my name. I'd copped from him a time or two, even sold him something once or twice, but that was about it.

"Yeah, well, I've been doin' what I do. Look, I got somethin' out here you might wanna take a look at."

"Okay, lessee whatcha got." He came to the truck, didn't seem to notice Jim, and said, "Alright, what you want for this."

"Well, the fridge retails for about 900 and the stove about 600 and half of 1500 is 750 so, let me get 600."

"Yeah, that's a good deal. I'd sure like to Jew you down some, but you took all the bargaining power right out from under me. You got a winner here. You gonna take it to where it got to go?"

"You gone show me?"

"Well, follow me, then." And, just like that, it was sold. He said something to the lookout, handed him something, gets in the car and I get back in the truck.

"What about the gas, dude?" I ask.

"We might make it, depending on how far it is."

"Okay. Flash your lights and when he pulls over, park behind him." This happens and I get out and go to Dave's window.

"Okay, check it out. We on fumes, we got to get to the BP." He didn't say a word, just grunted, nodded his head and handed me a twenty. "A'ight, go straight to the nearest gas station."

After the store, we off-load at Dave's. I tell Jim that he gets half of whatever I get, I just never told him exactly how much I got. I asked him if half was cool, he said, hell yeah, that this was the easiest lick he ever made.

The deal turned out to be $580 in cash and dope—$250 in dope (about a quarter-ounce) and $330 in cash. I looked at that dope and said, "Is this that homicide that's 'cross town? Sure looks like it." It had a glow about it, kind of like a swagger, the dope did. This looked like that same ass-kicking shit.

"I really don't know how good it is or it ain't, I just sell it. Look, you come across any more deals like this, you come see me. Period. Here's my pager number and here's your code." He says, while writing. "I won't answer for nobody unless I see a code that way I'll know it's you and I'll call you back."

"A'ight, Dave. But, you know I made you a helluva deal on this shit so, next time, we gonna try to be more in line with the prices and everything, okay."

"Yeah, fella, I hear what you're sayin', but here's what I'm sayin'. It is 3:30 in the morning and you do got that white boy with you, which I ain't complainin' about; he with you, he cool. But, ain't too many other places you can go to this time a day especially draggin' that shit behind you on the back of a company truck. So, you keep that in mind." He said with a sly smile.

I grin and wave to him as I get in the truck. We pull off and I don't say one word. Nothing. I know Jim wants to know what's up, so I wait another little bit.

"So, where we at? What's up?" He asked nervously. I couldn't blame him, I'd want to know, too.

"We straight. I got a good deal." He smiled broadly.

"For real? What'd we get?"

"We got $200 cash and a quarter ounce…"

"No shit?"

"…and half is yours." While he's driving, I peel off five twenties and hand them to him. He's all smiles now, for real. "Now, as far as the dope goes, we'll divide that at Teddy's, okay. But, in the meantime, I know you want a blast, right?"

"Damn right."

"So, I'm gonna break a piece off. Can you smoke and drive…"

"Yeah, did it plenty times."

"…or do you want me to drive?"

"Nah, I'm cool. I got it."

"Okay, then. This shit is pretty good, so here we go." I get my stem out and put a good size piece up. "Now, you see this a pretty nice size piece." He nods his head. "I'm a melt this down and give it to you, then I'm a hold the wheel while you hit it, a'ight."

"Yeah, man, that's cool." As I put flame to the rock, the sweetish aroma of its perfume engulfs us, letting us know this is the real deal. "Damn, that shit smells good, don't it."

"Yeah, it do." I respond. I pass him the pipe and the lighter. "Now, turn on this street, let off the gas and just cruise. I got the wheel." As I guide the truck, he lights the pipe and begins to inhale, a full, full, chestbuster of a hit. "Now, Jim, hold that shit in. It's that same homicide I had at Teddy's, so watch out."

He smiled crookedly and replied with a muffled, "Okay," his mouth choked with smoke. At this hour, there was no traffic so I could watch him, then the road, watch him, then the road, and as the narcotic began its cerebral parade, his eyes grew wider and wider and wider still. He started looking around, left and right, back and forth, as we rolled down the street.

As his unrest continued, I regretted giving him such a heavy dose. It was too much and I should've known better. Because I still had the wheel and he was in no condition to drive, I was glad that he didn't accidentally step on the gas or brake pedal. But, he was trippin'. Hard. Looking at his eyes and his face, there was a jumble of bewilderment, panic and determination in his expression. I could only imagine what was going through his head.

"So, Jim, check this out. You think you can drive now?"

"Mm-hmm." He mumbled stupidly, looking all around like he was being chased by something, a veneer of dread cast all about him. Maybe he did need something to do to close the floodgate of colliding thoughts he was dealing with.

"Okay, check it out. Here's the wheel. I'm lettin' go so you can take over." He took the wheel, staring straight ahead, looking really fucked up, and began driving as though it was the most relaxing thing to do. He passed me the lighter and pipe and seemed a bit more focused, but still a little scary. It was better than before and good enough to get by, as long as we didn't see the police. As slow as we were driving, a white guy in a Black neighborhood with a Black passenger was sure to draw attention.

We needed to get off the streets. We needed to get to Teddy's house. "You know how to get to Teddy's house from here?" I said quietly.

"Mm-hmm."

"Okay, let's go there." I wanted to hit that stem bad, but with this situation borderline out-of-control, I'd have to wait. It was all my fault, anyway, giving him all that dope. He did make all the proper traffic moves though, signals and signs, and I calmed a bit as we approached the corner to Teddy's.

And there it was. Whew! Glad we made it. As we pulled into the drive, I looked at him and he gave me a confused grin, "What the hell was that?"

I laughed, "Boy, that's that good shit, ain't it?

"No shit. I didn't even know where I was for a minute or two."

"You damn sure had me more than a little scared, I ain't gone lie about it. That was one ride I don't wanna repeat." We had a quiet chuckle and, right there in the driveway, I hit that stem. It didn't need no dope on it, it was fully loaded. And I got good and fucked up.

"Yeah, boy, this that good shit. I didn't even put nothin' else on it and it's still rollin'."

"Hell, yeah. That shit still got my ass, right now," he whispered. I nodded my head in agreement. I got out, he followed and we knocked, but the door was unlocked, so we walked right in.

"What up, fellas?" I state amicably. "Teddy, y'all come on in here."

A dopefiend's dream come true. For those that remained after we left or came in while we were gone, we were like angels, heaven-sent, bringing much needed relief. And here they come, lining up, just waiting to be treated. What the hell, they've looked out for me when I was low, so turnabout was fair play. It's just how things go.

"Hey, Neicy. Thought you'd be gone by now."

"Nah, I ain't have nothin' else to do, so I stayed around, see if y'all was comin' back. Wayne asked me to go with him, but I told him no." I just bet you did.

"Anybody else been through, Teddy?" I asked.

"Couple guys just left, said they'd be back after while."

"Well, if anybody wanna buy somethin', let me know. Okay, y'all?" You try to sell what you can, keep the cash flowing as long as you can because you know, sooner or later, you're going to run out.

As I take my seat, everybody kind of drifts in gradually. They're all standing, about three of them, with four sitting at the table.

Those that sat at the table were Royal Members of the Court, temporary though it might be. Jim and I, of course, being kings for a moment, were seated, then Teddy, as always since it was his house, then Neicy, being the lone female. Undoubtedly, some attentions had to come her way. Everybody else just stood around.

I didn't call out names, wasn't no need. There was a respectful decorum when freebies were being passed out, all you did was look at whomever the piece was for and that's who it went to. Because I had kept a portion before I left Dave's, I could bring out what was left as though it were all I had. I took a razor, cut off a few pieces, gave Teddy the biggest as respect for the house (Rule #2: always look out for the house), and gave the rest to Jim.

"All that?" he exclaimed, rather shocked by the amount. Plus, he had a hundred dollars. Seemed more than fair to him, all this good fortune.

"Well Jim, part of your duties will be to take care of these gentlemen here."

"I can do that."

"And, just to say, I'm real proud of the way you handled yourself. You did real good. Hey, y'all, he scared the shit outta me on the way in. We was takin' a hit and I put a big one on and that shit fucked him up bad, but he held it in the road as good as any one of us would've done, for real. I was impressed."

"Naw, man, you took care of everything. I just drove."

"And a helluva job at that you did." As long as he was satisfied, as long as nobody was disgruntled, the game was going smoothly. But, I had to get out of that kitchen. All that begging was about to start. Besides, I had something else on my mind.

"Teddy?"

"Yeah, man."

"Lemme use your room."

"Go 'head." His old ass. Stopped drinking to smoke crack, said drinking made him a mad man, crazy as hell. I'd heard stories about how he used to stand out in the middle of the street and yell at passing cars when he got drunk. Said he'd never quit smoking, that he'd smoke til he went to his grave. From the looks of things, that wouldn't be too long from now.

He looked completely comfortable, glass pipe in hand, legs crossed at the knee, humming some indistinct, off-key melody. Got two grand a month retirement from RJ Reynolds Tobacco Company, paid the utilities, bought a little food, spent the rest on crack, and broke by the middle of the month. He had been doing it like this for 10 years or better, was in his element and was content with his lot.

"C'mon, Neicy." We go to the back and I closed the door. Never could figure out why I got so horny when I smoked, but the shit was a real aphrodisiac and brought the freak out in me. "So, wha's up?"

She smiled that smile, like everything was cool. "Lemme see your stem." I said. She gave it to me and I put a nice hit up, but not nearly as big a Jim's. No way, I saw what that shit could do.

"You got a lighter?" She shook her head, so I gave her mine. While she did hers, I loaded mine up.

"Damn, Rick, tha's that same good-ass shit you just had."

"Damn right."

"Uh-hmm, sure is," she purred.

"So…" as I looked at her, I begin to feel the quickening excitement, the juicy glow that comes with anticipation. "…what we gone do?"

"What you talkin' about?" Her attempt at being coy.

"You know, just some head. Can you give good head?" I'd never been with her nor talked to anybody who had, so it was a fair question.

"I don't know, I ain't never did it before."

Now I know this is a lie.

"Neicy, for real, you ain't gotta play me," I said flatly.

"I ain't playin' you. For real, I ain't."

See, this is the real bullshit that makes these situations unfriendly sometimes. Here it is, 5:00 in the morning, she's the only girl in a known crackhouse and it's full of men. She knows, and so does everybody else, what the deal is and now she wants to play games. Shit, I been played enough in my career. Back when I was new to all this, I'd pull a girl to the side, treat her with respect, she'd end up smoking all my dope and I'd end up with nothing. No touchy, no feely, nothing. Just got played because I was green. Not no more. These days, I knew what was up, what was to be expected and when I was about to get played.

You had to be really straight up with these hard-headed ones, thinking they're going to get over. You can't treat them with no real respect or they'd try to take advantage. Now, there were those who were cooperative and didn't make a hassle of things. They knew what was expected and they delivered. This way of doing business made everything so much more pleasant. But, this shit right here. Hell, no!

"Okay, look, check this out. Either we gonna do this or we ain't. All this conversation about you ain't never is just game to me…" My attitude rising a little.

"But, I ain't…really."

"…or I'm outta here. Word up."

As I head to the door, she says, "Wait a minute, Rick. Why you actin' like that? I mean, that don't mean I can't try or somethin'."

Now she wants to try.

"What you mean 'try'? Either you gonna give me some head or you ain't smokin'. It's that simple. I'll fuck this whole package up in there with my boys before I fuck it up with that bullshit of yours." And I reach for the door.

"Okay, wait a minute…"

"Wait a minute? What is you talkin' about?"

"I mean, can't you chill out back here for a minute, it's all good."

"See, and I hear that. I ain't no hard ass dude, but you can't play me unless I let you and, right now, I ain't about to let you. I'm tryin' to get my swerve on and since you don't do head…"

"I mean, we can have sex, can't we?" she asked.

"We could, but that ain't what *I* wanna do. See, it ain't about whether you have or you haven't or whether you will or you won't, that's not the point. The point is how much fun can we have? That's what this is all about. It's why I go out and risk my freedom to hustle up some dope and why you hung around 'til I got back. Not that it's me you're interested in, it's just the dope. Hell, we all know that. But, if a whole lotta drama got to be involved, then it ain't worth it."

"Nah, Rick, ain't gone be no drama."

"Alrighty then, we'll see. But like I said, I want some head. Just like it's all about you from your point of view, it's all about me from mine. Besides, I got the dope. But, hey, what the hell. Fuck all this conversation, let's just go ahead and call it quits 'cause this ain't workin'." And I reach for the door again.

"Okay, okay. Just let me hit this again." She said.

"Then what."

"Then, I'll do you. No drama. For real."

"A'ight, then. Let's see what you workin' with." She got a thin piece of metal, usually a section of clotheshanger, and pushed the screen in the pipe to the opposite end. When you smoke, the heat vaporizes the crack into an oil. As it is inhaled, that oil is being pulled through the screen away from the heat and the oil begins to solidify onto the screen at the opposite end. It crystallizes onto the inner wall of the pipe as well, so that after the screen is pushed, the oil and its' crystals are on the end to be fired and it's like a fresh hit. Then she got the lighter and took another smoke. I joined her as soon as she gave me the lighter.

"That shit is good, ain't it?" I said.

"Mm-Hmm…"

"So, look. Since we got a understanding, let me get a sample so I can tell if you workin' with somethin' or not," I said softly. She gave me a glassy-eyed nod, nearly imperceptible she was so buzzed, but it was a good enough signal for me.

I unbuckled my belt, unzipped my jeans and stood in front of her while she sat on the edge of the bed. "Go 'head."

She took it out and started, and goddamn, that shit was cor-r-rect. I mean, I could tell she knew exactly what she was doing, real slow and easy, she was. Oh God, this was glorious! I knew it, I just knew it. She had to be lying about not ever having done this. She was too good to be a rookie.

And look at her, got her eyes closed, getting into it because she knows it's something she really likes to do. With a steady, constant rhythm, that shit was good. When a blowjob is this good, it can lead to one of the most fantastic sexual experiences I have ever known, which is to take a big hit at the moment of climax. But, it had to be timed just right.

As she made me more and more of a believer, I could feel myself stiffen to its hardest, a glistening shaft of steel, and I could feel my climax begin to rise and rise. I had to clinch, I had to clamp down hard, to hold on. But she knew I was coming, so she started going faster and faster and just as I was about to release, I took a hit. And Oh…My…God. The explosion was nothing short of nuclear, an atomic bomb that blew all of me into another realm entirely.

This combination is off-the-charts intense. Magnitude 10, at least, on the volcanic scale. The euphoria of the climax collides with the euphoria of the dope and it is an experience like none other. It makes you scream out loud, "Oh shit, OH SHIT!! Ah-h-h!!!" It is a visceral, primal yell. You try to keep quiet, but it's impossible.

And it is complete and total bliss.

TWENTY

As the early morning proceeded toward midday, the dope was smoked and everybody began to go their own way, I just chilled out in the back while Teddy stayed on the couch. Neicy and I had come to a reckoning of sorts. We knew this was just a crack thing, but that we should make the best out of it while we could. There is nothing more impermanent than a crack affair and to think otherwise is just plain silly. It lasts only as long as the money and the dope.

No one knew of the money I had left. I ended up smoking the rest of the dope back with Neicy because she made it so very worthwhile. I was able to sell a couple of pieces as other patrons would stop by, so my cash was in good shape, but I was really tired. I hadn't had any sleep in two days and I was ready to crash, but the urgency of keeping it going and the presence of money in my pockets kept me wanting to go out and get more.

Still, I had to get some sleep. And I did. For 24 straight hours, without even getting up to pee. But, not before hiding the money. I don't care who you are or how cool you may be with the locals, when you're sleep hard like that and dead to the world, people would try your pockets. I'd learned the hard way, which brings Rule #1: Ain't no friends in the dope game.

When I finally woke up, Teddy was still on the couch, but Sam had come in. The first thing though was to get something to eat then, get some dope. I got Sam to drive me to the Bojangles then, to the 'hood, then back to Teddy's. During the course of that day and part of the next, we'd make that run, to the 'hood and back, 'til the money ran out. Fortunately, Sam was there and I could count on him.

"Yo, man. I'm a need a ride to go do somethin' in a little while."

"Okay, man. Just give me a minute here." He had a piece and it was only right for him to enjoy it.

I'd met Sam down in the county during those six months I was in for that B&E in which I was found Not Guilty. We swapped stories and shared a few laughs making the most out of a difficult situation and we'd been true friends since, sharing everything fair and square. He got out before I did, but we exchanged addresses and promised to stay in touch after we got out. And we did. He and I were of similar age, similar upbringing and similar in our approach on how to handle ourselves on the street. Neither of us had any business being out there. We weren't 'hood rats, but we liked that 'hood rhythm, the hustle and grind of the streets.

Whenever I got arrested for the various crimes I would commit, he was the only one out of all the folks I smoked and hung out with who came to visit. Now, that's a true friend. We shared dope, money, girls, everything and whenever we got together, it was always hassle-free. Never any cross words or hurt feelings.

When he was ready, we headed to the Wal-Mart. He and I had done this tag team more than once. I'd go in and get something then, because he had valid ID and Wal-Mart didn't ask for a receipt, he'd take it back in for a refund. Other times, we'd take whatever I'd get and sell it.

When we got there, I kind of knew better than to try them; they'd given me "never to return" warnings on a couple of occasions so, it would be dumb of me to try it. But, against my better judgment and listening to the incessant bleatings in my gut for another blast, I went in anyway.

It was no surprise that I picked up surveillance shortly after I entered. I knew the overhead cameras were on, that there was somebody probably watching, but I'd slid in and slid out on other occasions. I was taking the chance that they'd miss me now, but every aisle I turned down, somebody was shadowing me on the parallel aisle so, fuck that, I headed to the door.

On my way out—either I was struck by a seizure of kleptomania or I had a psychotic hallucination that I was David Copperfield—I picked an item right off the shelf, knowing they were following me but thinking, absurdly, it wouldn't be noticed.

As I went out the door, I could see their reflections in the glass, but not once did I look back. Sam was pulling up at the precise moment I heard, "Excuse me, sir." I made a move toward the car, but it was too late. They were on me like iron on a magnet. I was heartily wrestled to the ground, gashing my head nicely in the process and was immobilized with my hands cuffed behind my back. Watching sadly, Sam rolled on out of the parking lot. Wasn't a thing he could do.

When I got downtown, I was greeted by the magistrate with, "Hello Mr. Moore, would you like your same suite?"

Smart ass.

As they searched me, they found the crack. I wish I'd known it was there, I'd've gotten smoked that long time ago. But, to have this in jail is a felony itself. I remembered what I had been told the last time. I just hoped I had one more shot at getting straightened out before they really sent me away.

At court, I was able to cop a plea for 6 to 8 months and what would have been a simple misdemeanor was boosted because those fragments were felonious contraband (like I was really trying to sneak some in, they should've let me smoke it). I got out in 5 to 6 months, was assigned to probation, but never went. I was too busy getting my groove on.

While I was in, I was able to come up with a nice story for Mrs. Watson and she responded generously. A deposit was made into my account that took care of me until my release, which happened on a warm day that spring. This made getting out of the joint a rather joyous occasion, especially for an unrepentant crackhead with a fist full of dollars.

Mr. Wright, a genuine fellow who did no drugs or alcohol, went to church regularly and led an otherwise clean life, came to get me. I met him during my comings and goings about Teddy's neighborhood and found that we had friends in common. He took to me because, so it seemed to him, I had "no business out in them streets." Since I never burned all of my bridges, I had him as a welcome resource. He knew that I was basically a decent guy caught up in a ruthless, unforgiving syndrome who didn't, in a mean-spirited or vicious way, ever mistreat anyone. This gave our relationship buoyancy.

First thing was to give him some of the money to hold for me and to take a portion for his troubles in coming to pick me up. I told him I needed a car and, sure enough, he took me to the auction where I bought one in his name. Though I was illegitimate, the car wasn't. Taxes, tags and insurance were in his name.

For three hundred dollars, it wasn't a substantial car so, it lasted about 3 months. During this time, all the deeds I'd done, all the moves I'd made, all the places I went, not once did I get stopped. I wonder what that says about reaping and sowing? Finally, it gave its last gasp and died. Accordingly, I was a pedestrian once again and I found myself at Teddy's. I was smoked out with no dope, no money and no way of getting either. I did have a stem and a lighter and I could recall many times when my smoke gear would be my most valued possessions. As long as I had a stem and a lighter, as long as I had my gear, there was purpose in life.

Leaving Teddy's on foot, I walked the neighborhood, not for the exercise, but because I didn't have a goddamned thing. I didn't have shit. I was hungry, I was broke, I was fiending for a hit so-o-o badly and the world had turned against me. These were dark moments indeed, when psychological and spiritual collapse was imminent, when you really took stock of the situation and asked, "What the fuck am I doing?"

A moment of clarity hovering, but not fully descending.

Sometimes you up, but most times you down. Most times are spent trying to get up, doing all kinds of crime just to get back on the mission and, whether you admitted it or not, you were just miserable. Walking and just walking. Looking and just looking…on the ground for anything, just something of value. Begging myself and begging the Invisible Forces to please, please, oh, please let me find some money or a house to break in or a car to steal or a weed-eater to pawn or something so I can get a hit. I got my stem and a lighter and I wanna smoke, goddammit!

As I walked up Manchester, a street I had walked a hundred times, a well-kept, middle-class neighborhood around the corner from Teddy's, I noticed a car idling in front of one of the homes. There were two people talking at the door of the house, just chatting away. No big deal, two friends talking, right there watching the car. Nothing to worry about.

I said to myself, if she's not at that car by the time my feet get me there, I'm getting it and gone.

I was a desperado, for sure, up to no good and as I came up on that car, I hopped in and drove off like it was my car. While they stood right there in the doorway.

I didn't stop at the corner, just went right on around it. I had to get away. And boy, oh, boy, the joy at having some wheels! This was just what I needed. And nice, too. A new Escort wagon. I went straight to the dope corner where I figured somebody might want to rent a car. They didn't know it was hot and they didn't need to know. I got out.

"Yo, what up, fellas?"

"What up, Rick. What you doin'?"

"Nothin', just chillin'. "

"Who car that is? You tryin' to rent that out?"

"Yeah, maybe. Belongs to my aunt. She lets me use it from time to time so, if you get it, you got to come back on time. I mean, you got to."

As this conversation takes place, a car pulls up behind the one I was driving. That driver got out and said, "Who's driving this car?"

My dumb ass spoke right up, "I am!"

"You know the police lookin' for this car right now, so you best be on your way. You know it ain't yours."

"Of course it ain't," as I got in and started it up, "it's my aunt's!" and sped off.

I took that hot-ass car over to the nearest 24-hour Kroger and relieved them of two bottles of Moet; that would get me 25 or 30 bucks. Not wanting to go back to my side of town, I recalled a spot on this side where I could sell the Moet and cop. Though I had smoked here only a time or two, I wasn't real familiar with these 'hood rats. So, it came as a surprise when a recognizable face came through the door.

"Boy, what you doin' over here?"

"Hey A.K. Just hangin' out. Whassup?" I inquired.

"Nothin', man. That you out front? I don't see no other cars."

"Yeah, that's me. Still, whassup? You wanna do somethin'?"

"Nigga, I'm on a mission, what you think? You oughta know I'm down."

"Well, then, let's go to Charlotte."

"When?"

"Right now."

"A'ight. But, what is we doin'? Why we goin' to the Queen City?"

"Just because."

"That's a whole lot clearer now. I mean, for real. What's the deal down there?"

"It'll be all good, you'll see."

"So let's go!"

We go to the car and get right on the highway. Who knew what adventures lay before us? For me, it could only get better than it was.

We went down I-85 toward Charlotte.

Since he knew his way around once we got to Charlotte, he directed me to a home off South Tryon Street where he went in, stayed for a minute or two and came right out. This is working out pretty good, this coming to Charlotte, I thought to myself. We divide the dope and pull off, going to find a buyer for leaf blower we had acquired along the way.

Being the experienced heads that we were, smoking and driving was the norm. And there we were in a different city, nobody had license, the car was stolen, hot goods in the back, paraphernalia in our hands, narcotics in our pockets, driving and smoking crack on a busy street. That's just the way we rolled.

We tried valiantly to sell that leaf blower. Maybe it was too early, maybe we didn't have the right look, but it didn't sell. Consequently, we ran out of cash and dope, so back to the K-Mart we went.

While I was waiting for him to make further procurements, I had this great insight of invincibility. So I went inside to get something else to add to our inventory of valuables. I picked up a chain saw and walked out, just like I had paid for it, thinking it was so busy no one would notice. As I got near the car, I was totally unprepared to hear, "Stop, sir!" Which I did. "Put down the box…" I did that, too. "…and come with us." Damn.

Shortly, the police showed up and took me downtown. I saw A.K. as I was being escorted from the building, but what could I say. He was on his own. He had some money and was on familiar turf so, he'd be alright. My circumstances, however, were much more unsure.

Now I was on my way to jail in Charlotte with no money and not a friend in sight. They booked me for petty larceny and dressed me out for my stay. Their jail attire was hospital gear, not jumpsuits. The type with a V-neck top and baggy bottom with a drawstring, all in orange. Rather comfortable. We were transported from the downtown facility out to the satellite complex for non-violent crimes. Bond was set at $1,000 and first appearance was the next morning.

ଔ ଞ

In Charlotte, first appearance was unlike any I'd ever seen. It was all by video remote and none of us ever left the facility. The TV screen was divided into 4 sections: the judge, the DA, the stenographer and myself. I was led into the video room and sat in front of the monitor with its camera on top.

The DA spoke. "State vs. Frederick Moore. Mr. Moore, are you there?"

"Yes."

"Your Honor, Mr. Moore is charged with petty larceny. He was caught coming out of K-Mart with a chain saw valued at $120.00. Charlotte PD picked him up yesterday and that's why he's here. He's under $1,000.00 secured bond."

The judge, "Anything to say, Mr. Moore."

"Yes, Your Honor. I really don't do this sort of thing. I'm visiting from Winston-Salem and would have no problem in returning to Court whenever it's docketed. I want to apologize for any inconvenience I may have caused your city and it would really

help if you could see your way clear to unsecure my bond. I will
return to answer this charge."

"Mr. DA, do you have his record?"

Oh, shit.

"No, Your Honor."

Whew!

"Well then, Mr. Moore, I will unsecure your bond. Come back
to Court June 15th."

"I will and thank you, sir."

"Next case!"

And just like that, I was out. All I had to do was give a little
impromptu speech, bullshit 'em a little bit and it was a wrap. I
couldn't believe it. One minute, you're locked up, guilty as hell, the
next minute, you're free, still guilty as hell. They must've been
pressed for space or something. I'm so glad they didn't print my
record.

They processed me out and gave me a ride to the downtown
facility where they released me to…what? I didn't have any money
or any way to get any money. I needed to get back to Winston, but
how? Mrs. Watson told me it would be a couple of days before she
could send me some and I knew better than to try my sister or my
brothers. In a town of unfamiliar places and unfamiliar faces, I could
only do what I did to get down here.

I began walking in the direction of where I thought I-85 was
and, yep, there's a sign saying it's straight ahead. I'm looking at every
possible car, those in driveways and at service stations. I did see a
couple with their keys in them but people were close by. I walked
further and came to a self-serve Exxon and, lo and behold, there it
was. Somebody had gone inside to attend to their bill and left the
keys in a new Bronco. Well, hallelujah, here's my ride home!

I hopped in and tried to start it, but it wouldn't start because the
clutch pedal was too far from the floor. The seat had to be adjusted
quickly because the owner was sure to show up any second. As I
tried again, I heard in the short distance, "Hey, get the fuck outta my
car!"

I didn't need to see who it was and as soon as it started, this guy jumps onto the running board and grabs the steering wheel, hooking his arm in it. I didn't think to roll up the windows and lock the doors as soon as I got in the car, now look at this shit.

"Get outta my car, motherfucker!" he screamed.

I guess he was too polite to call me nigger.

"No sir, I can't. I gotta go!" I responded.

I struggled with the gear shift and the brake release but, because I had the clutch pedal depressed, it began to drift down the incline the station was built on.

As we picked up a little momentum, we were headed toward the street exit and that whole line of traffic that was in commute. He still had the wheel hooked and it's canted to the left. We drifted in a wide semi-circle at a pretty good clip back into the service area where I slammed onto a service island knocking over two gas pumps, jumping that island and crashing into a minivan being fueled in between. Lucky for that driver the gas port was on the other side or I'd've nailed his ass, too. The owner of the Bronco was no longer hanging onto the steering wheel as he bailed when he saw we were headed for disaster.

When everything came to a rest (what took 15 or 20 seconds seemed to take much longer), I jumped out and ran. Didn't know where I was running to, I was just running, trying to get away from what was surely a frightful moment. It was surreal.

"Somebody get 'im!" I heard over the sound of the wind whistling past my ear. And I caught a blur out of the corner of my eye. Apparently, somebody had taken on this request and was going to summon me to the offended person. They were in pretty good shape, too. I had a head start and they still got me.

Whoever it was caught me by the collar and slammed me face first into the asphalt. "Goddamn nigga!! You coulda killed me and hurt my family, boy!"

A swath of angry pain clouded my thoughts. My nose was split, a front tooth was sheared off and I was numbed by the shock of it all. He had me by the scruff and marched me back to the theatre of war.

"Look. Look what you did! It's niggas like you that give us a bad name." Shoving me down onto the curb. "And stay there!"

He really wanted to fight, to do some kind of bodily harm, but the onlookers restrained him.

I suppose it was a bit disquieting to be filling your tank peacefully and calmly, a routine chore, and out of nowhere get broadsided by an SUV. With the wife and kids inside their recently purchased minivan (the 20-day tags were still on it), anybody would've been pissed.

As I looked around that strange combat zone, it was so dreamlike. There was the Bronco, its face all bashed in, the loser in a brief, but powerful prizefight; there were the gas pumps, two dead soldiers lying in state, side by side. There was broken glass strewn about, steam rising from the grille of the truck and all those glaring and unforgiving faces. Total and complete bedlam.

In the background you could hear sirens approaching, louder and louder. An odd source of comfort for me right then.

When they pulled up, their first question was, "Now, who's responsible for this mess?" Everybody pointed at me, seemingly in unison.

"Alright buddy, get on up. Those look like pretty bad cuts on your lip and nose there. An' lemme see. Lost your tooth, huh? You're a mess, but we'll get you to the hospital in a minute. Did you thank the nice man for giving you a paper towel?"

A muffled "Thanks" came out.

"That's good. Come on over here and sit in the back of the car. I ain't gonna cuff you just yet, you need to hold that to your bleeding. So, what's your name?"

I couldn't talk, didn't want to talk, didn't feel like talking. My face was all fucked up behind this foolishness and I just wanted to go lay down. Me, Mr. Big Time Criminal, couldn't even steal a car; just got out of jail two, maybe three, hours ago. I held my arm up in a pathetic gesture of surrender, showing him my wrist ID band from the jail. Hell, I hadn't even taken the time to cut it off.

"You mean you just got out? Damn man, you didn't waste no time, didja?"

TWENTY-ONE

Yeah, this time I really fucked up.

Given my record in Winston plus these people letting me out on good faith and then come down here tearing some shit up was not going to look good. On the ride, I wondered how much time would I get, how long could I look forward to being locked up. Wouldn't be no six or eight months this time, no sir-ee.

I'd be gone for a while and it's probably for the best. I'd been fucking up, fucking around, just fucking crazy, for way too long, anyway. A guy with my talents and abilities. What a waste. Seems like I'd taken all of God's gifts for granted. A guy who could do all things domestic, who could play an instrument and sing decently, who could think and debate with the best, who could teach and had a way with words and people, but was squandering it all. On what, some bullshit?

They got my lip stitched up, bandaged my nose, then took me to the downtown jail.

"Didn't we just let you out?" one of the staff commented.

I didn't have anything to say, just hung my head morosely, as though looking sad would make things better. They set my bond at $15,000 and back out to the satellite facility I went. This was a collection of double-wide trailers outfitted in barracks style that houses about 45 men in each trailer. There were about 10 of them, each with its own fenced-in exercise yard. Hadn't noticed any of this as my last stay was rather brief.

I called everybody to let them know I wasn't dead and that maybe I might get some real time on this one. I could detect in their voices a smug satisfaction, a triumphal I-told-you-that-nigga-was-gone-fuck-up tone that comes when you know you've been proven right.

On my first appearance, the public defender did get my bond reduced to $5,000 but what good would that do? Might as well have been $500,000. Still, one of the more efficient things this system did was to allow defendants to talk to their public defenders at will. There was a direct, dedicated phone line to that office in each trailer. I saw the advantage in this and used it liberally. I talked to Mr. Johnson two or three times, told him exactly what happened, wasn't no need lying about it. He told me to hang in there, that he'd see me in the holding cell on court day.

Jail, being the boringly unhurried dance that it is, compels you to shout with great joy when your court day comes. Regardless of the outcome, you want to just get the hell out of there! All I wanted to know was how much did I have to do.

We were called out name by slow name, feet dragging and sliding, and loaded into buses for the ride downtown. Wasn't no videoconference this day. Today, you came to see The Man, face-to-face.

After a relatively brief wait, I heard my name. I went to the holding cell door and there was this tallish, blonde-haired guy who said, "Fred Moore?"

"Yeah."

"I'm Mr. Johnson, your public defender."

"Oh, cool. We talked on the phone."

"Yes. Look, when we go in there, I want you to take a careful look around and see if you notice any familiar faces from the day this happened. Faces that might have been there or witnesses that you might remember. Can you remember any of those people?"

"Yeah, I think so."

"Good man. If you do see somebody, let me know. I'll keep my eye on you."

"Okay."

We go into the courtroom, about five of us, and are seated in the jury box. Because this is a preliminary hearing, no trials are being held, only motions being made by the prosecution and the defense. One guy is called, goes forward and gets a date, another one is called and gets a continuance. I'm hoping to waive all of this tap-dancing and get my time.

All the while, I had been scanning the room, looking for any of those faces indelibly carved on the walls of my memory. I couldn't imagine what difference it would've made anyway. What possible way out could come to pass by me *not* seeing anyone from the scene was beyond me. I was guilty as hell and ready to fall on my knees in front of the judge and beg his mercy. It was the drugs, Your Honor. It was the drugs! Please have mercy, Mr. Judge, sir.

I caught Mr. Johnson's eye and shook my head slightly as he spoke to the DA.

"Your Honor, next up is Frederick Moore vs State of NC and K-Mart. Come around, Mr. Moore."

I walked slowly and carefully, in a pathetic attempt to inspire some kind of empathy, to the area between the defense and prosecutor's table, directly in front of the judge.

"Your Honor, Mr. Moore is charged with destruction of private property, larceny of a motor vehicle, driving while license permanently revoked and, from District Court, petty larceny at K-Mart."

All that? Boy, this shit is fixin' to be crucial. This was trouble indeed, so I kept my eyes glued to the floor, hoping to look like a poor wretched soul who needed—and maybe deserved—some mercy.

"Any evidence, Mr. DA?"

Who went on to describe the events of three weeks ago.

"Mr. Johnson, anything your client wants to say?"

I looked up imploringly, wanting to purge myself, to admit in open court the guilt and shame of my actions only to hear, with great alarm, Mr. Johnson say, "Your Honor, my client would like to move ahead with trial. Right now."

Trial? I don't want no trial.

"We are ready to proceed."

Proceed? Proceed to where?

Now, if this was some kind of scare tactic, it sure was working, especially on me. It had to show on my face because my bewilderment and confusion were on full display. Still, I kept my peace.

"Mr. DA, the defense says they are ready. What say you?"

"Uh, Your Honor, the State would ask two weeks to prepare."

"Alright then, seeing as I have no choice, the defense being ready, the State not, I'm going to dismiss this to the grand jury though I'm sure Mr. Moore will be picked up again by then. Next case!"

I went to my seat not really sure of what had just happened. I tried to get the lawyer's attention, but he put up one finger, telling me to wait. On our way back to the holding cell, he walked up and said, "That's what you wanted, right?" Not sure of what he meant, I asked, "What did I get?"

"You get to go home, Fred. 'Dismissing to the grand jury' is a technical formality that can happen in the right circumstances and yours happened to be one. You'll be indicted later on, but for now, you're free to go."

And he walked off.

What? I was utterly dumbfounded. Totally surprised. Trying, with great effort, to wrap my mind around this, this, this… "You mean, I'm getting out?"

But by then, he was already around the corner. Shit. I had to ask somebody who would really know, this couldn't possibly be true. So, as we were loading for the ride back, I asked the jailer for the disposition in my case. He said, "You'll be released when we get back."

Well, goddamn then. Let me the fuck up outta here! I couldn't believe it! One minute you're locked up, guilty as hell. The next minute, you're free, still guilty as hell. Only in America!

Charlotte was now my new best friend. I couldn't believe those fools would actually let me go, knowing full well they had an airtight case. But, sure enough, not too long after we got back, they called my name to pack it up. Even as I walked out, I had to pinch myself. Goddamn, this is a good feeling.

It was late evening, around 11 p.m., when they opened the doors. The night was calm and the air was comfortable. I had just a few bucks and I decided it would be better spent trying to get a ride back to Winston.

But first, I had to celebrate.

It's never too far from the surface, thinking about a blast and how to get one. But, being in a strange town with virtually no money or other resources meant I'd have to wait until I got back to Winston before I tried anything.

The thing is that wherever they sell Wild Irish Rose or Thunderbird or MD 20/20, there's bound to be some dope nearby. So I found a store, had a few swallows and began to get a little mellow, then I looked around and saw a homeboy. No matter where you are, you can always tell a 'hood rat.

"Hey, yo. Homeboy!"

"What up."

"You doin' somethin'?"

"What you talkin' about?"

"I got a dime."

"Nah, but go over to that house right there. They'll serve you."

"Solid."

A stranger in a strange land. Still, if you were fluent in street you could fit right in. And there I was, doing the same old insane. Spending my last money, knowing I had no other possibilities of getting home, and still a slave to that shit.

ᑕᔑ ᔑᑐ

Next thing I knew, I was waking up in a phone booth. I tried to call Mrs. Watson, but no luck.

Daylight had arrived, traffic was moving, buses were running.

I started walking again and noticed a woman start her car, then go inside while it idled. Hallelujah! This would be my ride home.

I checked the gas and there was a quarter tank, probably not enough to get me there. There was a bag phone plugged into the lighter and I figured I could use that as collateral if things got tight. I just held it steady, hoped for the best and made it to Winston…on fumes.

C/3 &

A serious head like me could only go so long without a hit, so I put my hustle game in full force. I started making moves to generate income, mostly through a nice supply of stolen checks, so Teddy gave me complete run of his spare bedroom to use as I saw fit. It became my home.

One evening while I was walking, I came across a squad of police cars at the corner. Uh-oh, something was up. I just walked right on by. Good evening officers, I said, nodding my head in their direction. Just your average citizen going about his lawful business.

In passing, I overheard one say, "That does look like him, doesn't it?" And then, "Hey you. Stop right there!"

Damn.

"Put your hands up!"

Two came around and one handcuffed me against my futile protestations, "I din't do nothin'!"

"No, Mr. Moore, you've done everything. We've been looking for you for a while now. All the squad cars in this northeast quadrant have had a BOLO alert on you for weeks. You've been pretty slippery. We all got your picture in all the cars assigned to this zone, you and a few others. You should've gone to your probation, sir."

Probation. What probation?

And just like that, I was locked up.

How unlucky could I be? Just as I was at a point where I could see this lifestyle working for me, where I was beginning to make ends meet, this happens.

Call it Supernatural Intervention or Divine Appointment, God was demonstrating His love and Power for one of His lost sheep. Though I didn't see it at the time, the Hand of The Almighty interceded on my behalf and got me started on a process of redemption and healing that I could not have done on my own.

I didn't know what got those police to stop me, but I did know that this arrest was most untimely and it got in my way. I had a program going on and I wasn't ready for it to be over.

I was taken downtown, put under $42,000 bond and charged with 14 felonies: Forgery (eight counts); B&E (three counts); Credit Card Fraud (three counts). As usual, no introductions were needed at the jail and since there was no need to think I could make bond, I tried to settle in. Yet, I was sure there was a way out.

I figured it might be a good idea to call Johnetta since I'd probably be off the streets for a little while. Though I'd hardly talked to any of my family since Momma died—feelings were still a bit vinegary—she had never denied any of my calls from jail and they were always collect.

"Hey Ricky. I see you're back home."

"Well, it ain't really my home, but it has been a place of refuge from time to time."

"Whatever."

"So, how's everybody? How you doin'? Everything good?" Routine questions, just making conversation, trying to break the ice. And it was icy.

"No, Ricky. Everything's not okay."

"What you mean." A brief pause.

"Paul died last week."

"What! Quit lyin', Johnetta." And to think I almost didn't call. I couldn't believe it. I was shocked. "Paul's dead? From what? How?"

"I guess it was just natural causes, I don't know. We were getting ready for work, going through our routine. It was my turn to get the coffee and when I came back, there he was, laid back on the bed. Just died."

"Aw, Johnetta, that's terrible. So, now what?"

"I've told his family and all of ours. I wish you could be here with us, but you've got your own problems."

Uh-oh. Could she be persuaded of the value of bonding me out, being with family during troubled times and all that? "Yeah, but my problems are small compared to what you must be going through."

"Not all that small. You've got a lot of reconciling to do."

"Yeah, and I was thinking this could be an opportunity for me to do that since everybody is going to be around."

"How would you do that? You're in there."

"I was thinking you might help me get out."

"How much is your bond?"

"42,000."

"Boy, you know I don't have money like that…"

"But, you could…"

"Don't you even say it."

"Say what?"

"Do you actually think I'm going to put my house up?"

"But, Johnetta, where am I going?"

"Boy, them must be some mighty strong drugs you been taking for you to even let such a thing come out of your mouth!"

"But…"

"Why are you still trying to talk. You're just pissing me off. You got yourself in it, now get yourself out of it!"

I did talk with my brothers over the phone when they got there for Paul's arrangements. I could sense the anger and resentment just under the surface as we meandered through the necessary polite questions of how you doing, when you getting out, what you gonna do with your life and all that. It had been a couple of years since Momma died and those wounds simply had not healed. What I did was nearly unforgivable and the only thing that could set things right would be the simple, healing balm of time. From the way things were looking, I'd have plenty of that.

This time, more than any other, jail was just miserable. I knew I had to be there, I knew I deserved to be there, I just didn't want to be there. Not just yet, not when I was just getting it together. Thinking about the streets, the beautiful freedom that had been so righteously snatched from me, the groove that I had gotten to, the strides that I had been making, was so frustrating. I played it over and over in my mind and I just couldn't get over how such coincidence and happenstance could get me off the streets so easily.

But maybe, it wasn't coincidence. Maybe the Hand of God did come down and scoop me up. Maybe, this was the beginning of the answer to my secret prayer: Lord, help me be free. This had been the plea from the depths of my being. Ever since spiraling out of control after Bowman Gray, this was my silent prayer. Lord, help me be free.

But, the timing…the timing was just all wrong.

☙ ❧

I stayed in jail six months waiting for a reasonable plea deal. The news was not good. Because of that well-publicized change in the law known as Structured Sentencing, my past record, everybody's past record, was organized into categories of points and levels of infractions. The lower your level of crime, the lower your points, the less time you could get. My points and levels were off the charts—literally.

This new law used a grid chart to connect various classes of crime, like murder or larceny, with its respective point value. The number of points you had was determined by your personal history of convictions. Put your finger on the square with your points, the other finger on the square with your crime, let them meet and that's your time. Since my points were beyond the upper limit, I would get an upper limit of time. Turned out to be 101 to 135 months. Incredible! Eight to ten years for some checks and some credit cards? No way.

Because of my never-ending skirmishes with the law and my repetitious, seemingly interminable presences in court, I was classified as a Habitual Felon. A loathsome designation with an attendant ominous aura. This classification enhanced your time from a little bit to a lot. And, yeah, I had to admit, I was habitually committing felonies. If nothing else, the term fit me.

I tried, through my court-appointed attorney, to get the DA to see the merit in letting me repay the banks for those checks and credit cards; that it would be to the benefit of all involved to give me a little prison time with some structured probation to follow. Oh no, Mr. Moore, the DA countered, we don't want your money. It seems to us it would be to everyone's benefit to get you off the streets. We warned you, gave you a fair warning, that if you didn't straighten up, we would come after you. Well, we keep our word.

I stood my ground until jury selection when my lawyer told me, Fred, if you want another chance at life, take this deal. With each charge tried separately, he said, they could find you guilty as a Habitual 14 times and each sentence, by law, would be run consecutively. You'd never get out. The math was rather compelling. With that bit of insight, I took the deal.

It was time for my career in the streets to be over.

TWENTY-TWO

From my questions as a teenager, through college and beyond, I had marched to the beat of a different drummer and at 42 years old with all the tumult I had set upon myself, I still had a sound mind and a family that cared, though its rends and tears were yet mending. I even had one or two good friends remaining. I would be taking a long hiatus, using this time to count my many blessings. I would also use this stay as a time to get clear about how my life had answered all the many questions that had set me on such a different pathway.

As a result of Court and of processing through the system, I was assigned to Craven Correctional Institution near New Bern. It was in an air-conditioned, single-cell dorm which came with a kitchen job assignment. Each man had his own room and his own toilet, plus cable TV in the day area. For prison life, that's real luxury. I didn't want for a thing. Considering it all, I was truly blessed.

Craven housed 600-700 men at any given time and was set on 20 acres of a dirt-filled swamp. Each housing area had its own weight pile, basketball court, volleyball net and horseshoe pit. The facility also had the full array of medical, dental, psychological, educational and religious services.

It is ironic, yet completely predictable, that when a guy gets locked up, one of the first places he runs *to* is the church, but when he was free to come and go as he pleased, that was the place he ran *from*. And so it was for me. Now back in prison, I took to the band and choir like water to Kool-Aid. It was no accident, it seemed to me, that of all the prisons I could have been sent to, I got sent to one that would nurture my special musical needs. More to the point, there were a couple of guys who were professionals before they got in trouble. They had tremendous musical skill and were willing to help anyone who wanted to learn.

The Divine Mind knew what I needed despite anything I might have done or any place I had been. Despite all the skeletons in my closet or all the injustice I might have caused, the Divine Presence would still provide.

Now, I had begun to have a small, inspiring vision, a rousing, moving thought of coming home, being at the camp on Cherry Street, with a newfound musical ability and an exciting repertoire at my disposal. To put my talents to use, displaying what could happen when you allow God to have His way in your life, would bring my life full circle. This vision was magnified as I basked in the truth that the Divine had put me at this place so that I could be about the work for which I was being prepared. I would be a living testimony. Of course, for that to happen, I had to be alive. Being back behind bars took care of that part of the equation, too.

Another blessing of imprisonment was receiving a full and complete physical, which revealed an enlarged heart—the result of that bout of pneumonia I had back in the day. For sure, if I'd stayed on the street much longer in that condition, it could have taken me out long before my time. Instead, I received the treatment I needed to save my life and restore my health.

CR   RQ

The next big step I took might seem merely symbolic, but I think it was a way to say goodbye to my old street persona.

I'd grown up as Ricky, which changed to Rick as I tried— unsuccessfully—to step into manhood.

I knew that prison, for me, had been in the past an environment that encouraged positive change. If I were going to change, it would be from the ground up, piece by piece. And the first thing that would change was my name. I decided to leave behind all the drama and chaos associated with the name Rick. Since the only name being heard on the intercom was "Frederick Moore report to…" everybody came to know me as Fred.

I decided to let Rick go and just be Fred.

And Fred, I decided, would not be at the mercy of those never-ending cravings that continued to speak to me. I'd heard there was some dope around at Craven and I had money to get it, but I turned it down. It just wouldn't be enough. Besides, I'd be even more miserable behind those fences all cracked up, trapped, with nothing to do. Nah, not in prison, not while I was caged up.

The DOC does nothing to make you drug-free, does nothing to rid you of your irritating ways nor does it do anything to make you a better person. What it does is provide an environment, relatively free of distractions, that is reasonably safe and healthy, where change can occur. Without these structured surroundings, change, especially sobriety, is elusive indeed.

Permanent, concrete change does not occur from the outside of oneself, it does not occur because some else thinks it's a good idea. Real change, long-lasting change, comes from within and only when *you* want it. The earnest desire to be relieved of the burden of self-destruction is the beginning.

I'd been in and out of institutions, in and out of police custody, in and out of trouble, my entire adult life, but there was never enough effort on my part to get myself back together again. This new reality established the beginnings of a good and sustainable recovery.

Slowly, on my own, without prompting from my family, friends or the DOC, I began to face up. I started going to Narcotics Anonymous meetings and began to share these real demons of desire that haunted me. I wanted relief. I wanted this thing to be over, to be free of its constant nagging which meant reacquainting myself with the awesome truth contained in those 12 steps.

For one, I was surely powerless over that shit. Once I touched it, everything else became a distant second and my life was completely unmanageable. Second, I'd always believed in a Power greater than myself and it was my hope that this Power could restore me to some sense of sanity. This awareness could only happen for me in the reasonably safe, mostly non-toxic, relatively calm environment of incarceration. Third, the decision of turning my life over to God's care had already been done. In fact, it was this principle that had kept me alive over the years. So, with the renewal of these first three steps, I re-established a philosophy to live by.

I was told that thoughts of using and getting high were normal, that I could expect to have them regularly, that they would diminish in intensity, but never end. More importantly, having these thought is one thing, but acting on them is something entirely different. Having these thoughts might make me miserable, but acting on them would send me back into the abyss. Over time, I'd learn to deal with that. I didn't get strung out overnight, so don't expect to get better overnight. There are very few miracles in this business. Just hang in there and don't use.

☧ ☙

Being in the system also gave me time to dispose of any outstanding charges, and I set to work facing everything the authorities had on me, especially from those events in Charlotte. On the day that I learned all pending charges against me had been dismissed, the officer said to me, "You know, the change can happen in here, but the challenge is out there."

"Yeah, you said that right. I think about it all the time, the things I must do to stay clean. 'Cause, for me, stayin' outta prison means stayin' away from drugs. Simple as that."

"Well, if that's the case, you know you're gonna have to face this thing at some point. What's the deal gonna be then?"

"Don't get me wrong, I think about dope every single day. Don't a day go by and I don't think about dope. But, now I finally see how weed and alcohol are gateway drugs. Even though my drug of choice is cocaine, if I smoke some weed or drink some beer, if I get high in any recreational way, eventually, in a week or a month, I'm gonna get me some cocaine. And there I go, off to the races, once again. If I want to stay outta prison, I can't get high. Period. And that's real progress, for me to finally get it."

"Well, you talk that shit now while you're locked up, but this ain't the test. The real test is when you get you some passes or go on work release with money in your pocket and easy access. That's the test."

"That's right. And I've thought about it like, what if I get some and do it at work or what if I get some and do it on a pass. I play that scenario all the way out and the results are not pretty. That feeling of wanting just one more, that dope hunger of just wanting some more so bad, I never want to feel that again. It carries a emptiness in your soul so terrible, so dreadful, you do not want to go near it."

The officer nodded.

"And if I use on a pass or at work, you might as well look for me on America's Most Wanted somewhere. Just by gettin' that shit in my system and not be able to turn it off, not be able to bring it on in, would keep me out there chasin' it. These things I know today."

⚬ ⚬

The evidence throughout my incarceration, indeed throughout my life, spoke volumes of a Power at work, a Divine Principle, an Almighty Force that was in control. Things had truly come full circle. The spiritual miasma that swirled in my past had been overcome and replaced by a more profound spiritual maturity that provided purpose and resolve in my daily activities.

Along with the return of confidence there was also a quickening of the can-do-anything attitude, which I had longed for. This was the tell-tale sign that the old me was returning and was an indication of how one could change given time and the inclination. But, because it was true for me, did that make it true for anyone? For everyone? Probably. Given time away from negative influences with the predisposition and the desire, anyone could change.

All this reinforced an observation I had long noticed: there was a natural illogic and asymmetry to the way life's favors were bestowed on some folk or withheld from other folk.

None of us can predict, control, or influence everything that will or won't happen to us with any accuracy, but we can predict, control and influence our response to everything that happens to us. Even those things we do to ourselves. Living this life has very little to do with what happens to us, but more about how we deal with and how we respond to what happens to us.

Although "just one more" seemed to be my mantra for decades, there seemed to be an Influence that affected my continued participation in life. This Presence was beyond mere religion. It was something more real, something more tangible.

Had I come through my difficulties declaring that I had prayed for deliverance and salvation and had made it through, my liberation would be recognized as God answering prayer. If I had diligently read the Bible and pursued religious doctrine with zeal, my life would be a shining example of what God would do if you asked Him and just believed. But, I did little of this. Of course, some would say, others did that for me. Maybe my final escape from the life I had created for myself was the direct result of their prayers and not mine.

Whatever the case, it's clear to me that Something was looking out for me, even when I couldn't look out for myself.

What I did do was maintain a constant, ceaseless, never-ending conversation and dialogue with what I believed to be the Divine Mind. Not only did this do much for my spiritual health, it gave me reason to believe my living and my life would not be in vain and gave me hope for a promise-filled future. It was my feeling that if prayer was talking to God and meditation was listening, then each should be done continually, not just on certain prescribed, predefined occasions.

ରଷ ଅଷ

One of the stages leading to my final release was to transfer out of Craven back to minimum security near Winston-Salem, where I could look for work and finish rebuilding my family relationships.

About 4:00 one Thursday morning I heard those magic words, "Go ahead and pack it up."

I experienced a wisp of nostalgia, a passing moment of melancholy, even a pleasant droplet of gratitude for this place that had allowed me to grow, personally and spiritually. And now I was actually leaving.

I packed up my things, glad to be moving on, glad to be going home. We got on the bus about 6:00 and made it to Winston that afternoon. Riding into Winston, I saw streets I hadn't seen in years and a slow grin spread broadly on my face. The view evoked memories of a time when I was truly in a crucible, when terms of life and living were dictated by the availability of dope. We even rolled past First Street where Mrs. Watson lived and all I could do is sadly shake my head, glad that it was all over. The recall of it was forbiddingly intense.

One of my first connections was with Roderick Caldwell, who had been a new chaplain back when we made our acquaintances in the mid-80's on my first sentence. He was now senior chaplain with Forsyth Jail and Prison Ministries, the whole thing funded and equipped by community donations. I made a commitment then and there to get involved with the choir.

Then, I gave Johnetta a call to let her know I'd arrived. She, like everybody else, had done a marvelous job of standing by me. Much of the enmity and animosity had dissipated and hostilities were at a minimum. Our conversations had softened to the pleasant give-and-take of healthy relationships. My sister was still solid as a rock. Her steadfastness, consistency and sense of humor were a real inspiration to me. It was wonderful to simply be able to appreciate her qualities fully. I had similar praises for my brothers. They, too, had been solid and dependable, but it was Johnetta who had been there.

The other issue was my job assignment, which could impact my release date. It was a high-profile job, in prison terms, the chaplain's assistant, as this person interacted with the public, the chaplaincy staff, and made preparations for all events.

I didn't do a whole lot of praying and begging and pleading with God to open this door. I believed I would receive blessings independent of any petitioning I might do of the Divine Spirit and likewise I would receive misfortunes independent of any similar prayerfulness. My life experiences seemed to be inexorably headed to the mighty conclusion that one's blessings or misfortunes have little to do with one's spirituality.

I got the job in the spring of '04, but got reassigned and went to vocational school. About this time, I became eligible for work release and I found a job at a local car dealership. I made this journey every day via public transportation with another inmate, who happened to be a friend from the streets, named John Green.

We did this routine for 16 months without incident, which gave us plenty of time to chit-chat away from the camp. During that time, Green came up with question after question about my beliefs and my philosophy of life. I was able to get a lot of my ideas straightened out from those talks during our 20-minute ride from Winston to Kernersville.

"Yo, Freddy?"

"What now, Green? You forgot your money?"

"Nah, I got money. But, I was just wonderin'...what's your idea about God?"

"Where this come from man?"

"I don't know Freddy. It's just somethin' that's been on my mind lately."

"Word up, bro, you don't want my opinion on this. My ideas don't really answer questions nor go along with the standard party line."

"What you mean 'standard party line'?

"You know, 'the let's-get-you-saved, Jesus-is-the-only-way', line. What is this being saved anyway? If you don't believe the way its taught in church, you're going to hell? Does this include all the Jews, all the Muslims, anybody that's Hindu or Buddhist, even Native Americans who don't agree with that point of view? Is it true that Christianity is the only true way to God and everything else is wrong?"

"Well, what's wrong with that?"

"God, as I've come to understand God, or whatever it is that's operating in the world, is one of inclusion, not exclusion, one who unites and not divides. Because this entire world, this entire universe is divine creation, no one is outright excluded from Heaven or Salvation or Oneness with the Creator."

"So, you don't believe that?"

"I'll put it this way. When others think for you or tell you what to think, then you can no longer think for yourself. Just because Momma and Daddy and the Preacher said it's so, don't mean it is so."

"I don't know, Freddy. This really ain't what I had in mind. I mean, I ain't never thought about none a this quite like that," he said.

"I don't hardly think about much of anything else. I mean, it's like I've been told part of the story, but not the whole story. So, what I decided to do is to look at my life to test the things I've been taught about church and the Bible."

"And so, what you find out?"

"Well, looking back over everything, I don't see that my beliefs have protected me from any harm that has come my way or exposed me, in any noticeable way, to any of the blessings I have received. I mean, I was leading a pretty much clean life 'til I tried cocaine. Now look where I am and the shit I went through to get here. Religion didn't help me out there because I prayed earnestly and cried real tears to have Jesus save me from my sin. On the other hand, look at my physical and mental health since I been off dope, look at how I've been coming up even while I'm in prison. My doing wrong in the past hasn't prevented me from getting blessed now. So, what you think?"

"I don't know, Freddy. I mean, if you do the right things and treat people right, you'll make it into heaven, right?"

"See, and that's just what I'm talking about. Is there a heaven? Is there a hell? If I kill you intentionally, rape your momma, steal all your money and then ask forgiveness, do I avoid hell? If I give to the poor, volunteer my time, never say bad things about people, but happen to be Jewish or anything else, do I make it in to heaven? You can't say one way of approaching God is more right or wrong than another way, so you can't be left out of heaven or put into hell because your approach is different from mine."

It was my suspicion, and had been all along, that there is a unifying philosophy of life and living, which would include all forms of religion, from Christianity, Islam, and Judaism to Bhuddism, Hinduism, Taoism, and Native and Latin American religions. There had to be a philosophy that governed our everyday interactions and I was looking for it. But I could tell Green was having enough trouble digesting what I'd already said. I was going to give him all the space he needed to work through this.

"Okay, but Freddy, what's the deal with right and wrong or good and bad?"

"I'm not sure there is a deal. I mean, just because you do something you know is wrong, do you automatically get punished for it? How 'bout if you do something you know is right, do you automatically get a blessing for it?"

"That's the way it 'sposed to go."

"But, that's not the way it goes. Just because a man beats his wife and molests his children doesn't prohibit his promotion at work or avoiding the car wreck that happened right in front of him," I said.

"We like to think that evil behavior gets punished and good behavior gets rewarded, but it just doesn't happen that way."

"Nah, it don't seem to. You know, I come from the projects and I seen a lot of stuff jump off and folks really do seem to get away with it."

"Maybe they do, maybe they don't. Who knows?"

"I don't know, Freddy. It's hard thing to try an' figure out."

"We're too busy looking at things from an Earth-oriented point of view. But, there is a great, vast universe out there where these principles do apply. Or so it seems to me."

"How's all this fit in with religion and goin' to church and all that?"

"I didn't say nothin' about no church or religion fittin' in together, Green. Just because you go to church don't mean you understand your relationship with the Divine Power. Christianity defines this relationship through Jesus, who brought the idea that the Divine could be available to all people. But, it's not limited to Christianity. Hinduism, Bhuddism, Islam, Judaism all make the effort to have the Divine available to everybody. So, church is set up with rituals to pursue this understanding by the singing of songs, the sharing of communion, baptism, personal and group prayer and so on."

"Yeah, that's right."

"So, after I grew up and went to the streets and since I been gettin' locked up, even though I was baptized, sang the songs and took communion, I recognized that these practices do not give you a relationship with the Divine. In my personal, quiet times, I have found that closeness, but not by a whole lotta prayin' or beggin' for God to forgive me, down on my knees, please, Mr. God, save me from my sins and all that. None a that."

"So you sayin' you don't pray?"

"You know, like on your knees before bed or head bowed before you eat? Nah, I don't do none a that. I just believe in maintaining a prayerful attitude *at all times*. It's kinda like celebrating Christmas or Thanksgiving every day, not just during the season. My prayers are constant, purposeful and never-ending."

"That's all, Freddy? You just pray all the time, that it?"

"Pretty much. And here I am today, doin' just fine. Weird, ain't it? Some would say it's God's grace and mercy that brought me through…"

"That's what I would say."

"…and I would say that if the consequence of sin is grace and mercy, then there is no sin. I think the Divine Spirit is stranger than we know and stranger than we *can* know. We can guess, which is what we're doing with all the different religions and everything, but that's all we can do is guess. Bottom line is, we really don't know."

As we pulled into the terminal, I looked at him and shook my head, grinning. I didn't have a clue that he was interested in the deeper, philosophical questions of life. But he had questions and concerns about religious concepts like anybody else and I was somebody he felt comfortable discussing them with.

"You gotta understand, these are just my opinions. It's not like I've even discussed them with any religious experts, preachers or whatever. In fact, I got into a conversation with a guy the other day who said something that really got my attention."

"What he say?"

"He described to me a situation about Jesus and the Resurrection that was…I don't know, it just made me think."

"Okay, what he say."

"He said something like 'Since Jesus was a fully transcendent being, the highest of spiritual beings. Since He was truly God in the flesh who could walk on water, raise people from the dead, give sight to the blind and perform all manner of miraculous healings. Since he could operate inside and outside the laws governing the Universe, could come and go at a thought and was not bound by the constraints of the physical world, why then, on His resurrection, did the stone have to be rolled away?' "

There was a noticeable pause as he looked at me, the implication of the question not having hit just yet.

"He went on to say, 'Look. Here is a God-man, fully human and fully Divine, who could appear or disappear at will, who had all power given to Him, who could do anything, like he was Chris Angel or David Blaine or somebody. Why then, would He have to be *let* out of the tomb? I mean, here He'd been dead or at least in suspended animation for three days. He re-animates Himself and comes back to life…

"That's a helluva question, Fred."

"…and you're telling me that the power of Almighty God, Maker of Heaven and Earth, who had dominion and total authority over all of Creation, was held in place…" I paused. "…by a rock?' I mean with the way he put it and the suggestion of it all, it really caught me off-guard."

"Boy, I don't know. I ain't never really thought about it, but that's a helluva idea? What's your best guess about what he sayin'" he asked.

"I think he tryin' to say that maybe the Resurrection didn't happen at all and that the evidence for it is right there in the Bible. In John 20: 19 and 26, when the doors and windows were shut and Jesus appeared out of nowhere, right in their midst, said that He had to be God.

Look, this what else he said. He said, 'if you wanted to make an iron-clad, rock-solid case for the Resurrection, the stone would've been left in place, the guard would not have fled or fallen asleep and the seal on the tomb would not have been broken. So, when the Pharisee went to Pilate with this information about Jesus having been seen, here and there, three days after he was entombed, there would have been no doubts when the authorities showed up and saw that everything was in place as it was supposed to have been. They'd figure those guys were just trippin' or something because they forcefully and emphatically declared He was seen out of the tomb.

'Then, when they broke the seal, opened the tomb, looked inside and saw He wasn't there, all doubt would have been eliminated about Him being God because the evidence for the prophesied Resurrection would have been overwhelming. Even this idea of the Jews having taken His body would have no credibility because the evidence of an empty, unopened tomb would have testified louder than anything else'."

Green added, "I mean, for real. If Jesus was truly all that, everything woulda been just like it was when He went in and since

He was spose to be a spirit, wouldna been no need to roll the stone away, right?"

Sounded like he understood more than I gave him credit for. "Well, I mean, it makes me want to inquire more. I have a lotta questions too, but I told him he needed a biblical historian or a theologian or somebody like that. I just wish I could be there when they try to give him an answer!"

☙ ❧

Although those bus-ride discussions with Green helped me get clear about my philosophy of life, they did not resolve the dilemma that I was faced with once again: the reality of being on the streets with a degree of freedom and autonomy.

It had been four years since I left the street and had a drink or a drug. Scarily, those situations and the places where they occurred still waited for me. I was just a moment of weakness away from repeating that tragic and bizarre behavior which was so destructive to me and anyone else involved with me. With the demons of relapse repeating their whispers, I would have to be vigilant.

Because he had been a real presence during my very worst times, I had a desire to stop by and see Teddy, just to say hello. Would that be dangerous? Would a visit to the epicenter of my drug use imperil my sobriety? Was I tempting fate by wanting to stop by?

About that time, Mike was approved as a Community Volunteer or CV sponsor. This was a real coup because as a sponsor, he was allowed to take guys to a restaurant or church or to his home.

Interestingly, Mike lived right around the corner from Teddy so, going to his house was like going through the 'hood all over again, memories of which evoked a parade of images across my mind. Memories of walking down that street right there with somebody's lawnmower in tow, of marching to and fro from one corner to the other looking for some dope, of always trying to find something to steal to satisfy that need, that real stomach-grinding hunger for another hit. And here I was this day in June, 2005, hanging out with my very good pal, not on drugs and feeling pretty good about myself

Riding this day with him through these streets, I felt the magnitude of the blessing of sobriety, of not being strung out or being a slave to that shit anymore. What a wonderful thing!

"So, Mike…"

"Alright."

"Let's stop by Ted's."

A marked and abrupt pause. He peered at me intently. "You sure you want to do that?"

A real good question.

"Well I'm never sure, but I have to. The man was a rock when I had nowhere to go. Many times, I'd've had to sleep on a porch or under a tree somewhere. Maybe it's not a good idea. Hell, I thought he'd be dead by now, but I got to go see."

"Alone?"

"I mean, don't just drop me off. I think I can make it in and out of there without a problem."

"Even if they're doing something in there?"

"Especially if it's going on. I just got to go see."

His concern was justified. Teddy's held great nostalgic value and the memories of all that I did there could easily spark a re-ignition of those flames of desire. Suppose they were smoking. Would I actually take a toke? I had to see.

As we rounded the corner, the neighborhood was just as I had left it 7 years ago. The houses were right where I remembered, all the driveways and trees just like before. And there was Teddy's house, just like I'd never left. The scene was vivid, clear and resonant. As we pulled curbside, I gave Mike a glance and got out. I knew this was shaky, maybe even dangerous, but I wanted to give Teddy my regards. And, truthfully, I wanted to give my sobriety a test-drive.

I knocked.

"Yeah, who is it?"

I said, "Hey, boy. Open the door!"

The door opened and there he was, in all of his under-nourished, dusty-skinned splendor.

"Hey, son. What it is!" I stepped inside. Didn't seem like nothing was going on, the kitchen table being unoccupied.

"Boy, where you been? You out already?"

"Nah. I'm still up on Cherry Street. Mike's out in the car and I asked him to drop by so I could holla at you."

"Well, that's mighty nice."

Jeez, he looked bad. Like he'd shrunk and withered. To see him, his loss of vigor was startling, but that wasn't the thing. It was the place. Those walls, the carpeting, the furniture, all those things seemed to speak to me. And the memories, it all bombarded me too fast. It was the cacophony of images that unnerved me and it seemed like the house was waiting…for me. Knowing all the hell that was right there, just under the surface, was bizarre. I had to get out of there, that shit was too creepy.

"A'ight, Ted. I just wanted stop by and see what's up. Looks like ain't too much changed."

"Naw, everything still the same."

"Okey-dokey, then. I'll holla at you another time, okay?"

"Okay, see ya later."

Mike was curious, in a quiet sort of way, about what had happened inside. I hadn't been gone over 10 minutes, but that's quite enough time for some real problems to occur.

"Boy, I bet I'll never go back in there again!" I declared.

"Why is that?"

"Oh, man…It's like the walls and the carpet and the furniture and everything were all welcoming me back. Like they had been waiting…just for me. Ain't no way in hell I'm ever going back in there. No way."

"Spooked you, huh?"

"That's putting it lightly."

"Well, I guess that says a lot about how far you've come, doesn't it?"

"I guess it does."

"Was it goin' on in there?"

"Nah, he was alone. Wasn't nobody there and, really, that's not what would bother me. What bothers me would be down the road, after I get out, and I start thinking I'm okay, that really, my dope experiences weren't all that bad. I would say to myself, see, you went by Teddy's and didn't nothin' happen, so you must be okay. That kind of delusional thinking, that's what bothers me. As long as I know I'm weak for that shit and that as much as I might want that blast, the ends are gonna always be the same, then I might make it."

We spent a little time that night at Mike's, but not engaging in one of the things that had been foremost in my mind when we had headed out earlier in the day—which was to try to hook up with a woman. The experience at Teddy's had shifted me into a different mindset, had helped me see just how different I had become.

"C'mon, Mike. Just take me back to the camp."

"You sure?"

"Yeah, man. I'm just gonna go 'head and chill out and get ready for church tomorrow."

"Well, you know, we still got some time left."

"Yeah, I know. Maybe we'll do something different next time."

"Okay, man, let's take it on in."

On our way back, passing by those corners where I used to cop, going by those houses I'd once broken into, I was filled with such a sense of relief. Much of the scene hadn't changed, yet it all seemed so different. Maybe it was because *I* was different, maybe *I* had changed. And this was a good thing. I could actually ride by a dope corner with money in my pocket and not cop. The urge was not there. Being in those areas clean and sober was new to me. Maybe that was what made things seem so different. I was able to be out *in* this element and not be *of* it. I was finally free.

Hallelujah!

TWENTY-THREE

As we continued to ride the transit system and go about our activities in a responsible manner, Green wasn't quite finished with our conversations.

"You know Freddy, I been givin' a little thought to what you been sayin'. And I got a question."

"Go ahead."

"Does God punish us for doing wrong or reward us for doing right? Or how does that work?"

"Boy, that's the nail that holds it all together, ain't it. I mean, both of us have done whatever the hell we wanted to and our punishment has been what, prison? Please. Ain't gotta find nothin' to eat or nothin' to wear or no place to wash your ass or no place to sleep, none a that, and this is punishment? Our friends and family, they still here ain't they? We still got our health and our clear thinking, ain't we, so what's been the real punishment? Goin' to prison?"

Green nodded in agreement—who wouldn't see it that way?

But I shook my ahead. "Nah, it seems like that's been a reward, at least to me, because without it I never would a been able to get outta that hell I was in. Seems to me the correct punishment for all the shit I did was to leave me an unrecovered addict, to leave me in the streets, as payment for the way I treated mom and my girl and my friends. That would have been fair. You'd think life would be a little less dramatic, not so many hassles, if we're keepin' the commandments and treatin' folk right and payin' our tithes in church. But, it ain't like that, is it?"

As Green's expression began to relax, I could tell he got the paradox I was pointing out.

"In fact, regardless of what you do or what is done to you, the *real* Natural Law is what operates, which is: if you want some peace in your life, sow peace into somebody else's life. If you want joy in your life, sow joy into somebody else's life. This won't keep bad shit from happening to you. But by your unselfish giving, by your looking to do something for somebody else, you establish a relationship with the Divine. This is the true meaning of 'you reap what you sow.'"

"How's that?"

"Well, look at the other side of that coin: If you want anger in your life, sow anger into somebody else's life. If you want unhappiness in your life, sow that into somebody else's life. You reap what you sow. But, if you do this thing of unselfish giving, then you will receive blessings in ways you could not imagine. You have to give something to receive something and that something you're giving is your most precious resource."

"And what's that?"

"You, my friend. The giving of yourself."

☙ ❧

Every day, it seemed, I felt a little more blessed, a little more uplifted by the way things had turned out. There were many times when I'd be alone and I'd just weep. Out of nowhere, the tears would come. Joyful tears, a silent acknowledgement that although everything hadn't gone my way, most things had. Any bit of injustice that I may have experienced was far outweighed by the many benefits that had come as a result of having led a tumultuous life…

…and lived to tell about it.

EPILOGUE

I was released for good in March of 2007. I had a job that was better than I had any right to have. I had a home waiting for me with the sister I had wronged so many times. I had brothers willing to accept me back despite my careless self-centeredness. I got to sing with a choir and had learned music that helped to create a way of expression that I could use in church or in a singing group. I had my health, both mental and physical, and I was free of the overpowering urge to use.

To this very day, the same has remained true. I have gone on to greater heights than I could hope for. Not in material wealth, but in the strength of my family and friendship ties. I have accepted the finality that I had to be completely drug free, no nicotine, no alcohol, no nothing, in order to stay drug free. This was the piece that eluded me for so long, but was in my face the whole time.

Life can seem so strange and unpredictable. My attitude toward this strangeness has been one of aloof detachment, in an observational kind of way, and I have come away with a greater understanding of how all of this appears to work. Here's what that looks like to me:

- Life is not about what happens to you— because shit will happen—but it is completely about how you *respond* to what happens to you
- Good will never conquer evil, they mutually co-exist

- You keep what you have by giving it away, i.e.,
  if you want peace, give some to somebody else,
  if you want happiness, give some to somebody
  else; conversely, if you want anger, give some to
  somebody else, if you want pain, give some to
  somebody else; this is the true meaning of you
  reap what you sow
- Regardless of how things turn out or our role in
  it, all life is on Divine Time

All my years of religious and social education never told me these things in this way and I went through years of pain and suffering to learn these simple truths. Nothing in this world is without a cost, even the knowledge, wisdom and understanding we might gain from living this life however we choose to live it, but it is a cost we must bear if our living is to have any meaning at all.

I once was lost
But now, I'm found;
Was blind, but now I see.

ABOUT THE AUTHOR

Fred Moore was born and raised in Winston-Salem, NC, where he attended public schools, graduating from Parkland Senior High in 1975. He went on to obtain his bachelor's degree in Biology Education from Hampton University and matriculated to the College of William and Mary, North Carolina State University and the University of North Carolina-Chapel Hill, where he was accepted into medical school.

When he became involved with cocaine during medical school, the author went on to be incarcerated seven times, the last one in October, 1998.

He began to rebuild his life during this time (1998-2007), beginning with his first job in 15 years, at Parks Chevrolet in Kernersville NC. He stayed with Parks until the recession hit in the fall of 2008. This caused him to re-think his employment possibilities so, he went back to school at Forsyth Technical Community College, where he graduated in December of 2011 with an Associate's in Applied Science/Biotechnology and a 3.92 GPA.

He is currently employed at the Winston-Salem Urban League since February, 2012, and has been the music director at Greater Hope of Glory Missionary Baptist Church since December, 2010.

He is unmarried, has no children and lives with his sister in Kernersville NC.

This is his first book.

ABOUT THE ILLUSTRATOR

Doug Brown is the owner of a small design company, Newlife Graphics, located in the Washington, DC, metropolitan area. He has worked in design for more than 30 years. In addition, Doug is an artist and a Helen Hayes Award nominated actor.

Made in the USA
Charleston, SC
04 November 2013